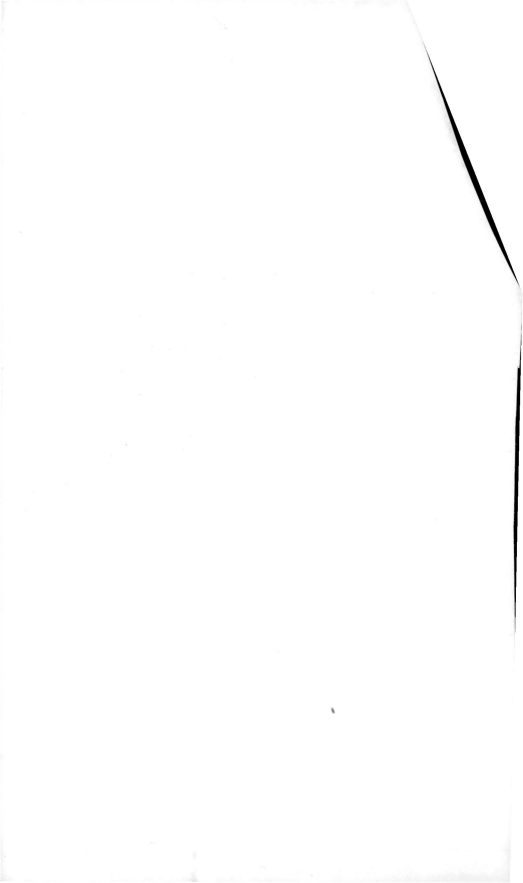

THE PRODIGY

THE PRODIGY

AMY WALLACE

E. P. DUTTON | NEW YORK

Grateful acknowledgment is made for permission to reprint
excerpts from the following works:
The Hesperia Constitution by William J. Sidis. Reprinted by
permission of the Harvard University Archives.
The Come As You Are Masquerade Party by Samuel Rosenberg,
© 1970 by Samuel Rosenberg.
Reprinted by permission of Prentice-Hall, Inc.

Published in the United States by
E. P. Dutton, a division of New American Library,
2 Park Avenue, New York, N.Y. 10016.

Library of Congress Cataloging-in-Publication Data
Wallace, Amy.
The prodigy.
Includes index.
1. Sidis, William James, 1898–1944. 2. Gifted children—United States—
Biography. 3. Genius—United States—Biography. I. Title.
BF723.G5S538   1986   155.4'55 [B]   85-31547

ISBN: 0-525-24404-2

Published simultaneously in Canada by
Fitzhenry & Whiteside Ltd., Toronto

COBE

DESIGNED BY MARK O'CONNOR

10 9 8 7 6 5 4 3 2 1

First Edition

FOR JOSEF MARC

Acknowledgments

I am especially grateful to the following people, whose unremitting encouragement and support made this book possible: Irving and Sylvia Wallace, Helena Sidis, Dan Mahony, Jannika Hurwitt, Joseph Kanon, and Ed Victor.

For their work researching, editing, typing, and photographing, I would like to thank: Helen Ginsburg, Elizabethe Kempthorne, Mark Malkas, Liz Vaughan, and Paul Duffy.

For granting me their time, memories and materials, thanks go to the following people and institutions (in alphabetical order): Muriel Burbank, Julius Eichel, Clifton Fadiman, William Fadiman, Ann Rab Feinzig, George Gloss, Dr. and Mrs. Jack Goldwyn, Harvard University, Margaret McGill, Mr. and Mrs. Joe Mandell, Bill Rab, Isaac

Rabinowitz, Rice University, B. C. Robison, David Sachs, Dr. and Mrs. Elliot Sagall, Dr. Paul Saunders, Shirley Smith, Dr. Abraham Sperling, Grace Spinelli, and the Swarthmore College Peace Collection.

Contents

Contents

TEN PAGES OF ILLUSTRATIONS FOLLOW PAGE 146.

You know the old saying—"As the twig is bent the tree's inclined." Parents cannot too soon begin the work of bending the minds of their children in the right direction, of training them so that they shall grow up complete, efficient, really rational men and women.

—BORIS SIDIS, 1909

The newspapers never missed a chance to try and prove that he was insane, or psychotic, or simply a freak. In truth, Billy was a completely normal child in every respect.

—SARAH SIDIS, 1952

It is possible to construct figures of the Fourth Dimension with a hundred and twenty sides called hecatonicosihedrigons, or figures with six hundred sides called hexacosihedrigons. I attach great value in the working out of my theories to the help given by polyhedral angles of the dodesecahedron which enter into many of the problems. Some of the things that I have found out about the Fourth Dimension will aid in the solution of many of the problems of elliptical geometry.

—WILLIAM JAMES SIDIS, age 11, 1909

I often tried to talk to him about the fourth dimension, mathematics. I was interested in mathematics myself at the time. I was about seventeen, he must have been about twenty-three. And he would turn upon me furiously, he *scared* me, saying, "I don't want to talk about that, I don't ever want to talk about that kind of thing!"

—CLIFTON FADIMAN, 1983

The Little Father

Boris Sidis was born in 1867 in Berdichev, a town near Kiev in the Russian Ukraine. His lineage could be traced back eight hundred years, and it was the family legend that each generation produced one brilliant man. Boris Sidis, his kin said, was that man.

Boris was one of five children born to Moses and Mary Sidis. Moses was a well-off merchant, and an intellectual who read Darwin and Huxley. The boy showed intellectual promise early. At eight, he knew several languages, was well read in history, and composed poetry that was put to music by the townspeople of Berdichev. Boris's early years were pleasant, or as pleasant as life could be for any Jew growing

up in the terrible climate of anti-Semitism that pervaded the Ukraine
of the 1800s.

At the time of Boris's birth, Russia was under the severe, autocra-
tic rule of Tsar Nicolas II. The Ukraine, a portion of southwestern
Russia with a population of nearly twenty million, was part of the
Jewish Pale of Settlement, established by Catherine the Great in 1791.
Nearly two million Jews inhabited this area, and few were allowed to
move "beyond the Pale."

By the mid-1800s the prevailing attitude of Russians toward their
large Jewish population was intensely hostile. A long history of persecution made the Jews easy prey for mass hysteria whipped up by the
government; Jewish economic success and land ownership was a threat
to many Russians, who claimed that the Christian population was
being exploited. Rumors circulated that Jews used the blood of Christian babies in their religious ceremonies.

In 1881, under the rule of the reactionary Tsar Alexander III, the
wave of hatred broke. The first of a vicious series of pogroms occurred
in southern Russia. Jews were assaulted in the streets, robbed, raped,
and murdered.

The pogroms spread, and in 1882 the Tsar ordered anti-Jewish
tribunals, ultimately passing the notorious "temporary" May Laws.
These forbade Jews within the Pale to leave their villages, and forced
multitudes of other Jews into the dense, overcrowded cities. Existence
for the average Jewish family was at best a struggle. The situation grew
increasingly grim, with little hope of improvement. The Russian
authorities were pressing Jews to emigrate, and Jews were anxious to
leave. America was now the promised land.

It was in the midst of this tumult that Boris Sidis grew up, though
his own town, Berdichev, had not suffered a pogrom. As a handsome,
healthy, intense teenager, Boris had already developed the values that
would guide his life—a hatred of ignorance and tyranny, a passion for
learning and teaching. His friends nicknamed him "The Little Father."

Although it was strictly against the law, at sixteen Boris organized a small group of friends and embarked on his first mission—teaching peasants to read. Compared to the Russian population as a whole, the Jewish literacy rate was high, but not high enough for these idealistic boys, who were willing to assume a great risk in the service of their ideals. When Boris was seventeen he and his friends enrolled in a preparatory school—the equivalent of junior college—in Keshnev, south of their hometown. There they continued teaching peasants, trekking to the countryside every Sunday afternoon.

After only three weeks in school, their rooms were raided by Tsarist police. Their landlady, sympathetic to their work, heard of the raid in advance and burned all the books she could find in Boris's room, destroying anything else that might implicate him. To no avail. The twelve boys were arrested. Two were hanged as an example to the others. Nine were marched barefoot in the snow to Siberia. Boris, who was discovered to be the leader, was clapped in a dungeon.

The governor of Keshnev released Boris for one night, and wined and dined the fiery-eyed dissident in his own home. Offered freedom if he would confess the details of his "plot," Boris insisted that there was no plot to confess. He was returned to his shackles, to solitary confinement and torture.

His cell was body-sized, and he was unable to recline except with his knees pressed against the wall. He spent the next two years in this cell. He was allowed neither books nor paper and pencil—he lived in a total vacuum. This utter emptiness, which would have driven an ordinary man insane, had an extraordinary effect on Boris. These vile years gave him something precious. He owed to them, he said, his courage and his ability to reason. By concentrating on ideas, he left his bodily anguish behind. He later regarded it as one of his greatest creative periods. He could not be broken, because in his stinking, wretched cell he had learned to think.

For two years, Moses Sidis had fought desperately to get his son paroled. He finally struck a deal with the authorities: If Boris agreed never again to leave his hometown, to report regularly to parole officers, and to renounce all education as teacher or student, he would be freed. On these conditions, Boris was released from solitary confinement and returned to Berdichev.

The conditions of his release, primarily the edict against learning, were agony to Boris. He prevailed upon his father to help him escape from Russia. The arrangements were made, and two other boys who had been paroled and placed under house arrest made plans to leave with him. Many Russians believed the rumors that the streets of America were paved with gold. Young Boris was probably not so gullible. He believed, more likely, in other rumors: that in America, jobs were abundant; that all immigrants were welcomed with open arms; and that if one worked honestly and hard, a life of plenty was there for the taking.

In 1886, Boris and two friends took the usual immigrant route out of the Ukraine. They crossed the Austro-Hungarian border illegally, traveled by train to Vienna and from there to Hamburg. There they boarded a ship that would take them to New York City. Few immigrants had a clue to the horror of the voyage ahead. The sheer misery of the trip, with people herded together in filthy steerage compartments, could last anywhere from three to fourteen weeks.

Awaiting the frayed and weary immigrants was Castle Garden. A huge, circular fort on the lower tip of Manhattan, it had been built in 1811 and used as a theater in the 1850s—such greats as Jenny Lind and Lola Montez performed there. Now, in 1886, it served as the main port of entry for throngs of immigrants.

After passing the interrogations of customs officials, Boris and his friends were released into the maw of New York City. At that time, the Lower East Side had an estimated 522 inhabitants per acre. Some areas were more crowded than the worst parts of Bombay. Its tenements were infamous. The most profound shock to greet the immigrants was the noise, the chaos, the pushing and shoving, the hurry and intensity of the Lower East Side, where four thousand people lived in a single block. For a peasant who had never been in a busier spot than the market square of his village, it was a far cry from the America of his dreams.

Like most Jews, Boris found his way to the Lower East Side, where he rented a room for less than five dollars a week. In one respect at least, Boris was far more fortunate than the average immigrant: He and his two friends had several hundred dollars between them. Only a small percentage of immigrants entered with over twenty dollars—the average was eight dollars—and many had nothing at all. With no money, and not a word of English at their command, New York was a terrifying shock. The harshness of life on the Lower East Side was combined for most immigrants with a feeling of profound dismay that life in the land of the free was, in many ways, as difficult as life in Russia had been. Boris, at least, was able to get his bearings, free of the necessity to find work immediately.

His first job was with the Singer Sewing Machine Company at five dollars a week. The average working day in a sweatshop or factory was thirteen hours; for many it was more. Conditions were grim. Boris Sidis was poor at manual labor, and he kept his factory job for only a week. He stretched the money for two weeks, subsisting on a diet of herring (a herring could be bought for a penny or two) and stale black bread (two cents a pound). Boris escaped misery and despair by feeding his mind. He spent his every free moment in the public library. His wife later wrote, "This was Boris's idea of a good life." After a mere four months in America, he learned to speak and write English.

His next job was in a New Jersey hat-pressing factory. By now he had formulated a plan: Work one week, study for two weeks. After a few months of living by this plan, Boris made a crucial decision. He moved to Boston. The slums were nearly as bad, the jobs paid no better, but for Boris it had a kind of glamour. He had heard that Boston was the American city where the mind was most revered, the city where intellect thrived.

Boris Sidis arrived in winter and rented a room for one dollar a week, a room so frigid that a glass of water left out overnight turned to ice. But Boris was happy. "When I first set foot in the Boston Public Library," he said, "I felt as though the gates of heaven had opened to me."

Boris Sidis was enthralled with his life centered around the library. At first, he followed his "Work one week, study for two weeks" program, and found time to write, publishing his first article in the *Boston Transcript*. Then, once he had mastered English, Boris's landlord suggested he tutor young Russian immigrants. His students paid him for an hour in the evening, but usually they all talked late into the night, until the last streetcar had run, and then walked happily home with their brimming minds.

During that first freezing winter, Boris had only the light coat he'd brought from Russia. In desperate need of winter clothes, he entered a shop near his home run by a Russian tailor. The cheapest coat was too expensive for Boris, but the men fell to chatting. The tailor revealed his single burning ambition, which he thought impossible to achieve. He wanted to learn to read in order to study Spinoza. A bargain was struck: Boris taught the illiterate tailor to read Spinoza, and that winter he kept warm in a heavy coat.

Sarah Mandelbaum was born on October 2, 1874, in Stara Constantine, a small but prosperous village in the southern Ukraine. Her mother, Fannie Rich, had been the village beauty, and at fourteen she married a sixteen-year-old student, Bernard Mandelbaum. In keeping with Russian custom, Fannie and Bernard lived with their parents until Bernard finished school and started a business as a grain merchant. Bernard's business was moderately successful. Fannie had fifteen children and three miscarriages.

Sarah was the fifth child, and at the age of five was already helping her older sister, Ida, with household tasks. Her father built a footstool for Sarah to stand on while she made the beds and dusted. Worn down by childbearing, Fannie did no housework. She was, in Sarah's words, "a pet." And thus, by the age of eight, Sarah was doing all the housecleaning while Ida did the cooking. The two girls tended their younger siblings full-time, calling them "our babies." Then, as a present, Sarah's father gave her a sewing machine, and soon she was making all the family clothes. So she could help him with his accounts, he taught her to add, subtract, and multiply.

Sarah didn't seem to resent all the burdens placed upon her. Her parents never spoke a harsh word, nor did they punish their large brood in any way. And Sarah noticed that if she treated "her babies" gently and kindly, they obeyed her properly. The first seeds of a philosophy of child rearing were thus taking root.

Suddenly, when Sarah was thirteen, her orderly, busy life was turned topsy-turvy. Until then, her family had been spared the assaults of the vicious pogroms. But one ugly day in 1887, a band of thugs attacked the household.

Bernard Mandelbaum stood in his doorway wielding a pitchfork and shouting to his children, "Run! Escape! Fly!"

The robbers overpowered him, caving in his front teeth. Fannie was knocked unconscious, and the baby she held in her arms was picked up and dashed to the floor. It was killed instantly.

Sarah, Ida, and their brother Harry ran out the back door and into snow-covered fields. They found a nearby brickyard, crawled into the warm oven where bricks had been baking, and fell asleep.

The robbers stole everything, and partially razed the house. All that Bernard Mandelbaum had struggled so hard for had been destroyed. He drew his family around him and announced, "We must leave a country where such things can happen."

He could raise only enough money for two to go to America. According to Sarah's unpublished memoirs, Bernard said, "I will take Sarah with me, she is the brightest." It was left to Ida and her grandparents to take over the rest of the housekeeping chores and the care of her mother and six brothers and sisters.

Bernard and Sarah traveled to Germany, where they planned to board a ship for New York, but as they were about to embark, they discovered they had only enough money for a fare and a half. Sarah was too old to travel half fare.

Bernard saw no solution. "We must go back to Russia and wait until we can raise more money."

Sarah, not to be daunted, pleaded with the captain of an English ship, who finally let her board for half fare. Once on board, she was overcome with anticipation. "We are going to America, where I can learn *everything!*"

Had she remained in Russia, she reflected, her fate would have been to marry the jeweler's son who had courted her, and by the time she was twenty, "there would have been nothing for me for the rest of my life except an endless grind of chores, childbearing, housework, living in ignorance, and eventually a premature death. This was the lot of all Russian women." Certainly, she would escape her mother's lot in life.

It was on the boat that she made her momentous decision: "In America I will become a doctor. . . . The most outrageously improbable thing for me to become, the goal furthest from my reach in Russia."

When the boat landed at Castle Garden, Bernard had fifty cents in his pocket and two tickets for the Fall River Line to Boston. But to disembark, he would have to show sufficient money to prove that he and his daughter would not be destitute. Bernard borrowed the money from other immigrants on the vessel, returning it after he and Sarah had safely passed customs.

Armed with a letter of introduction to a friend of a friend, they took the overnight steamship to Boston. Their host took the weary travelers in, put them up for three weeks, and would not accept payment. This same benefactress bought Sarah a corset, made her throw away her peasant scarf, and replaced it with a hat. After this immigrant rite of passage was completed, Sarah got her first job, sewing buttons on jackets twelve hours a day, for three dollars a week. Working conditions in the sweatshops of Boston's North and West ends were somewhat less severe than in New York; nonetheless, Sarah was crammed into a small, filthy room without sunlight or fresh air with ten other laborers.

Sarah recalled her first year in America as the worst year of her life. Her father got a job as a garment presser. Eventually, their combined salaries grew to fifteen dollars a week. Saving every penny, they were able to bring Ida over in a year. The next year they struggled to bring the rest of the Mandelbaums to America.

Sarah next got a job with the Singer Sewing Machine Company, glad of her previous experience with her sewing machine. She worked a ten-hour day, going to customers' houses and teaching them to use their new machines. As a money-saving scheme, she made this rule for herself: If the distance between customers was under two miles, she would walk and save the three cents carfare, an economy measure employed by many immigrants.

Two years after her arrival in America, Sarah's whole family was reunited in Boston. Bernard opened a homemade candy and ice cream store, and everyone in the family (except, of course, Fanny) worked. Sarah now had a job as a seamstress in an expensive dress shop.

Sarah and Ida still did all the cooking and cleaning. But even with all this activity, their thirst for knowledge was unassuaged. For a small fee, they persuaded two Russian immigrant college students to tutor them in reading and math. Both tutors fell in love with Sarah. She did not reciprocate the boys' feelings, and dissolved the class. She was suspicious of marriage, and had had enough of raising children and cleaning house.

In 1891, when she was seventeen, she heard of a young man reputed to be a genius who made his living teaching English at one dollar for three lessons. "I cannot afford three lessons a week," thought Sarah, "but perhaps he will give me two for sixty-five cents."

And so Sarah began to study with Boris Sidis. She was awestruck by him. He seemed to her infinitely wise, learned, and kind. Two evenings a week they met and studied; afternoons they met on the Boston Commons and talked for hours about their plans and aspirations.

Under Boris's tutelage, Sarah nurtured her dream of becoming a doctor. Medical school was the favorite ambition of European immigrants, and the schools' tuition fees were payable in installments, bringing the dream within reach of a dedicated few. Still, in 1891, only a few dozen European immigrants had become doctors in New York, and none of them were women.

When Boris suggested Sarah go to college, it was all the impetus she needed to formulate a plan. She would take night classes for two years, get her high school diploma, and enter the Boston University School of Medicine. But when the perky, pigtailed seventeen-year-old approached the admissions director of a Boston high school she was met with an unexpected and stern rebuff. She was told, "You are being absurd. You have never been to primary school or high school, and you expect to graduate in two years! It is ridiculous, and we cannot admit you. Nobody has ever done it."

Cowed, Sarah told Boris of her humiliation. Boris replied, "Maybe it is better this way. You can take the New York state board examinations for high school students in three weeks. Pass them, and you won't have to go to high school."

Sarah, who knew little math, despaired of learning algebra and geometry in three weeks. But Boris remained confident. He asked her for twenty-five cents, and purchased a secondhand Euclid. He explained the first five theorems in geometry, then said, "Use your good mind to work out the rest of them just as Euclid did. Don't try to memorize. Just try to understand, and then you can't help remembering."

She propped Euclid up above the sink, and studied while she washed the dishes. Sarah was severely ridiculed by her family, with the exception of her sister Ida. They told her that if she took the exams she would look foolish and embarrass them. "Nobody," they said, "does such things. Who do you think you are?"

Sarah bore the insults, secure in the knowledge that Boris was her ally. She quit her job at Singer and went to New York on the same Fall River Line that had originally brought her to Boston. For one dollar a friend let her sleep on a cot in her room during the week of the tests.

When Sarah returned home, she was ridiculed further. But soon she received her test results—and she had passed with honors. Now more confident, she began to study Latin and physics for her Boston University School of Medicine exams.

Meanwhile, Sarah urged Boris to attend Harvard University. Boris refused, saying, "What can they teach me? They will enmesh me in scholastic red tape." "What good is being the most brilliant man in the world," Sarah replied, "if you meet only the four walls?"

Sarah persisted. And soon Boris was enrolled in Harvard as a special student, taking physics, Latin, economics, and philosophy. While Boris never got over his hatred of "bureaucratic red tape," he fell in love with the rich intellectual life of Harvard, and in 1892, Harvard was a glorious place to be. It was the heyday of the long reign of President Charles William Eliot, a vigorous and controversial man of legendary accomplishments, including the appointment of a stellar group of intellectuals to his faculty—a group who would become Boris's teachers.

Foremost among these was the philosopher / psychologist / scientist William James, who was to figure heavily in the Sidises' lives. James, then fifty years old, was intense and energetic. He had overcome youthful years of severe depression and was in his prime as full professor of philosophy. His work was being read, and hotly debated, throughout America and Europe.

In addition to his philosophy course he offered a course in psychology. The birth of the American movement in psychology was taking place at Harvard in the eleven rooms of the Psychological Laboratory founded by James in 1891. It was the first of its kind in America. There was no psychology department as such—students drawn to this novel and experimental field came largely from the science and philosophy departments. Not all of James's students appreciated their mentor's psychological leanings. Morris Raphael Cohen, who went on to become a Harvard philosophy professor, wrote, "I could not . . . share James' psychologic approach to philosophy. His psychologic explanations of necessary truth did not seem to me to bear on their logical nature. . . . Our intellectual disagreements were often violent." Yet, like so many of James's students, Cohen found him "a never-failing source of warm inspiration" and "a trusted counselor in all my difficulties of health and finance."

The California-born philosopher Josiah Royce, recruited for Harvard by James, fit perfectly the stereotype of the philosopher. Pudgy, quiet, learned, and diligent, his disorderly appearance caused students to mistake him for the janitor of Sever Hall. Royce and James remained intimate associates for years, though their views were quite different and they argued frequently. Together these two formed the cornerstone of the Harvard psychology "department," drawing recognition of American philosophy from Europe.

While Boris took his first courses at Harvard, Sarah worked as a waitress in a resort hotel in the White Mountains. To her surprise, Boris appeared one day on her doorstep. He confessed that he had fallen in love with her at first sight, and had always suffered taking her money. "But," he said, "I thought that if I did not take it, you wouldn't come back, and I would never see you again. Please come home. I can't sleep. I can't go home without you." Sarah returned to Boston with Boris, and they decided to marry, but not immediately. Sarah's family disapproved of Boris, a poor student with no money and no interest in making any.

And when it came to money, Boris was adamant. He told his bride-to-be, "Making money and living the life I want to live don't go together. No man can read and study and think and write deeply and honestly, and think about making money. I promise you this, we won't have any." "Don't ever worry about it," Sarah insisted. "I can live on very little. I can make you silk shirts out of cheap remnants. I can take care of myself. A lack of money will never bother us."

According to Sarah, her irate mother secretly approached Boris, saying, "Look, why don't you leave Sarah alone? Why do you bother her? What can you offer her, a penniless student like yourself? Leave her alone, for there are young men who want her in marriage who can bring her a nice, easy life." Without visible rancor, Boris replied, "Let's let Sarah decide that." To Sarah he said only, "Your mother does what she thinks is best for you."

Sarah entered Boston University School of Medicine in 1892. A skinny girl in pigtails (her friends nicknamed her "The Toothpick"), she barely looked eighteen—her parents had to go to the school and swear she was of age. Her first semester's tuition was forty dollars, which she had to borrow from a rabbi friend of Boris's; she couldn't raise the money for the second semester, so she went to the dean and requested a leave of absence until she had earned the necessary funds. The dean had heard of her industry and gave her a scholarship on the spot. She never paid tuition again.

But even without that expense, it still cost Sarah no small effort to support herself. She worked as a waitress in the school cafeteria in trade for her lunches, and as a nurse two nights a week. Her nursing shift was twelve hours straight, and after staying up all night she still managed to drag herself to classes the next day. In addition to her work and studies, she cleaned her parents' house every Sunday.

Never timid, Sarah pluckily approached Boris's philosophy professor, the revered Josiah Royce. She asked him to use his influence to get Boris to enroll in Harvard for a degree. Though Boris was enjoying life as a special student, and had received superb grades, he was reluctant to enter school officially—as Sarah put it, "attaching degrees to learning annoyed him."

But in the end he did enroll, and that pivotal year he studied psychology, ethics, and philosophy with a pantheon of stimulating minds. If Boris was pleasantly surprised by Harvard, Harvard's professors were astounded by the fiery young Russian.

Once again, Sarah pressured Boris, urging him to speak to his teachers to see if he could graduate Harvard in two years instead of the normal four. The faculty did her suggestion one better—Boris was graduated in one year, magna cum laude. As usual, he had received all A's.

That Christmas vacation Boris and Sarah slipped off quietly to Providence, Rhode Island, where they were married by a judge. After a week's honeymoon in Providence, they returned to Boston and to their life of learning.

The following year, Boris received a fellowship through the J. P. Morgan Fund. He was given $750, and this, combined with his teaching and Sarah's earnings, was just enough to support the young couple. They rented two cheap attic rooms. They bought day-old bread and drank black coffee, joked about whether they would ever be able to afford cream. And every Sunday afternoon the impoverished young couple entertained. They hosted scores of students and revered teachers who came to discuss philosophy and psychology. The most renowned of them all, William James, frequently climbed the many stairs to their attic.

"Pray tell me," James would gently ask Sarah, "how can two people who are so poor be so happy?"

At the turn of the century, the field of psychology was still in a primitive state. In Europe, Sigmund Freud was gaining a small reputation among scientists, but lay Americans had never heard of him. The French psychologist Pierre Janet then dominated the field. Janet, taking the banner from his own teacher, Jean-Martin Charcot, was making inroads in "mental medicine" that were read of and admired intensely by the Boston group. (In years to come, Boris Sidis would be dubbed "the Janet of America" for his pioneering studies in hypnosis and mental illness.) None of the eager Bostonians gathered in the Sidises' attic could have guessed that a bitter feud would soon split the budding American psychoanalytic community into angry factions.

Those Sunday afternoons in the Sidises' attic were more than stimulating to the participants—they were to lay the cornerstones of American psychology. The guests experimented on each other with cards, numbers, squares, and patterns to study the effects of suggestion.

And they hypnotized each other. One afternoon James and Boris hypnotized one of the students, and James gave the boy this command: "Behave as Mr. Sidis does." Immediately the hypnotized student jumped up, went to the tiny closet that was Sarah's kitchen, lit the kerosene stove, and put the kettle on. "You will have tea, won't you? Everybody wants tea, don't they?" he asked. The guests roared with laughter—the boy was Boris to perfection.

The aim of these studies and experiments was to understand the previously unexplored subconscious, or what Sidis and James called "the subwaking mind." Under what conditions is the mind most suggestible? Could long-lost memories be recovered? Did suggestions given to a patient in a hypnotic trance last? And could this hypnotic state—which Sidis called "the hypnoidal state"—be used in healing mental and physical ills?

Boris had gained sufficient reputation at this point for a representative of the Tsar who was visiting Boston and being entertained by James to offer the expatriate full permission to return to Russia with a college position, laboratories, and research facilities placed at his disposal. Boris refused angrily, preferring to be poor and free in America over returning to Russia under even the best of conditions.

He had lost the overcoat made by the tailor who loved Spinoza, and James and Harvard's philosophy professor Herbert Palmer were disturbed to see their prize student coming to classes without a proper coat in the freezing Boston winter. James told Boris, "Look, you know I have a little money of my own, and I don't spend all they pay me at Harvard, so that I have a small fund to help students. Let me loan you two hundred dollars and you can repay me without interest when you begin to make money. Get yourself an overcoat." Boris replied hotly, "I don't need any money, and there are students here who do. Also, there are other students who want to come to Harvard who don't because they can't pay the tuition. Loan your money to them. They need it. I don't."

James reported his lack of success to Palmer. Palmer, a master of discreet benevolence who had helped countless poor students through Harvard, replied, "Ha, you tried to loan him too much. I'll make it a smaller amount, and he'll take it." To Palmer's dismay, Boris refused his money too. Palmer later told Sarah he had never met a man so proudly independent and so little concerned by the lack of material things that most people consider necessities.

* * *

The years 1896 and 1897 were important years for the Sidises. Boris taught Aristotelian logic for Royce at Harvard and published his second article, "A Study of the Mob," in the *Atlantic Monthly*. His third, "The Study of Mental Epidemics," was published in *Century Magazine,* for which Boris was paid one hundred dollars, a good deal of money at the time.

As if this were not enough for a man who only a few years before had arrived as a political exile, something still more exciting occurred. Sarah recalled the incident fifty years later:

"Boris came up the stairs into the apartment. He seemed all excited. 'James called me into his office today,' he said. I knew that Boris and James were great friends and saw each other constantly, so this bit of news didn't impress me very much.

" 'Well, go on,' I said. 'What did he say?'

" 'He wants me to see Teddy Roosevelt. I walked into James's office. He made me sit down. He said he and Palmer and Royce had had a long talk about me. First, James asked me what my plans were after I got my degree. I told him that I had applied for several teaching positions in the West and the South. He said, "You don't want to teach. You'll get in a rut. Look at me—I'm in a rut. I have too little time to study, I'm not contributing anything to the world. We can't have this happen to you. I'm going to give you a letter to Teddy Roosevelt. He'll only be in New York for a short time before he goes to the White House." ' "

Roosevelt was then governor of New York, and neither Boris nor Sarah knew what to expect of the meeting, or what the possibilities were. Nevertheless, Boris soon left for Albany, and, presenting a letter from James, requested a fifteen-minute interview with the governor. The men talked for two hours, and Roosevelt, delighted with Boris, urged him to stay on in New York where he, Roosevelt, would find a position for him. Despite Boris's protests that he had work to attend to in Boston, Roosevelt persuaded him to remain.

The New York State legislature had just formed a novel department, a Pathological Institute that was intended as an annex to the state hospital system, providing "instruction in brain pathology and other subjects for the medical officers of the state hospitals." The institute experimented with patients from state hospitals for the insane, and later on treated private patients. An innovative, brilliant physician, Dr. Ira van Gieson, was appointed director. He selected Boris as one of his staff of specialists, and, in 1896, work at the institute began in earnest. An appropriation of fifty thousand dollars was made by the state, and a laboratory was set up on the top floor of New York's new Metropolitan Building—a far cry from the New York of slums and sweatshops Boris had known only a few years before.

Boris's appointment was greeted with some disdain by New York professionals, who thought that at twenty-nine he was too young. Furthermore, he had neither an M.D. nor a Ph.D. Boris had received his B.A. when he was twenty-three, a year after entering Harvard, and his M.A. when he was twenty-four, scoffing at both—he regarded them as meaningless, these pieces of paper so universally coveted and struggled for. To Boris Sidis, degrees were never the proper symbols of a man's accomplishments.

Then, while Boris was in New York, Harvard requested that he submit a thesis for his Ph.D. His professors suggested The Psychology of Suggestion, the brainchild over which he had been slaving. He refused vehemently—no school, not even Harvard, was going to get credit for his work. When they realized he was refusing to submit this or any other thesis, the university officials relented, asking him to come to Boston for an oral examination. Boris again declined. "Red tape! Red tape!" he ranted. "Letters! What do they mean!"

Again, Sarah appealed to Professor Royce. "I'll meet with the faculty and discuss it," Royce replied.

Harvard mailed Boris his Ph.D. in June, waiving all ordinary formalities. James told Sarah, "They wouldn't do this much for me. . . . If they call me a genius, what superlative have they saved for this husband of yours?"

Meanwhile, Sarah too had taken a degree: She was one of a

handful of women to graduate from medical school before the turn of the century. As soon as she had graduated she joined Boris in New York. Though they missed their circle of friends in Boston, Boris kept in touch with James, and besides, his work at the institute was absorbing. He was perfecting his hypnosis for hysterical patients, putting the finishing touches on his first book, and evolving new theories of treatment. And Sarah was pregnant.

Certainly, it seemed, Boris was destined to be famous, to have a name that would make headlines. But it was their baby boy, born on April Fool's Day, 1898, who would completely eclipse his father both in fame and notoriety.

2

April Fool

Billy Sidis's birth, on April 1, 1898, was a perfectly normal one. He weighed seven pounds, six ounces, and according to his mother was "fat and happy and full of the devil." He was named after William James, who presented the baby with a silver cup bearing the inscription "To William James Sidis, from William James his godfather." Sarah Sidis, in her unpublished book *How to Make Your Child a Genius,* wrote in the third person about the restrictions her son's arrival placed on her:

"It was Sarah who first became a doctor and she encouraged her husband to get his degree. Her plan was to go along with him on cases to aid him in his studies. One of the incidents which restrained her somewhat in this capacity was the birth of their son, Billy."

Despite the sour note of disappointment in her remark, she insisted that Billy was a carefully planned baby, his arrival a welcome event. Of Boris's reaction, she wrote: "In all his brilliant life, you would have thought the most brilliant and marvelous thing he ever did was to have a son."

The couple was living on Central Park West, and when their first New York summer came, the oppressive heat would send them out of their apartment. At three in the morning they took Billy strolling in his carriage in Central Park, enjoying the cool hours until dawn. In the quiet morning they discussed their ideas for bringing up their boy. Sarah wrote, "The most important thing we agreed on was that we should always agree. We decided that we would always stand together in our decisions, and not pull and haul this infant between us in conflict. We agreed on discipline—the only discipline worth a thrip in building a worthwhile and upright person was the desire to please. If we brought Billy up to love us, by our love and gentleness, then he would want to please us. And if we were always pleased by good conduct, he would be a good boy.

"We decided from the start that we would treat Billy just like a grown-up. Children all want to be treated on equal footing with their elders. So many parents I've seen have been completely contradictory in their approach to their children. They treat them like babies, and then spank them for not behaving like grandfathers."

Boris told his wife, "Before a baby can talk, his mind is there, it is a tool that may be sharpened if his parents are always reasonable and truthful and logical with him. Minds are built with use. Muscles are not built by lying in bed. Encourage this baby of ours to think, to walk down every path his fancy dictates as long as he is interested. Answer all his questions as far as you can go and as long as he asks."

Besides their ideas about feeding Billy's mind and satisfying his intellectual curiosity at every turn, Sarah attempted to apply some of Boris's psychological principles to child rearing. Boris's studies of sleep indicated that the period just before falling asleep is a highly suggestible one, during which the mind is particularly receptive. This information bred in Sarah a concern about Billy's bedtime stories. "I always felt that it was very important not to tell him stories that were trite or commonplace or ugly. So much of the Grimm brothers' tales I found ugly, and Hans Christian Andersen seemed sad and melancholy, so I turned to the Greek myths for Billy's first bedtime stories."

In her early writings, Sarah claimed that in the beginning, she goo-goo'ed and ga-ga'ed as much as any mother, although both parents later declared that they disapproved of baby talk and always spoke to Billy as though he were an adult. Be that as it may, Boris showed an unexpected playful side. Sarah recalled coming home one day and hearing noise coming from the kitchen: the crash of a broken cup, "an extraordinarily happy laugh from Billy," and the crash of another cup. Sarah hurried in just in time to see Boris handing the baby a third cup.

"What do you do?!" demanded Sarah.

"But he laughs so marvelously when he breaks the cups," Boris replied shamefacedly.

When Billy was six months old his parents bought him a high chair. Boris insisted, "I don't care if the King of England comes to dinner. Billy will sit with us." Sarah wrote: "He had all his meals with us from the time he was six months old. He couldn't creep, and he couldn't walk and he couldn't talk, but he could observe." They gave him a spoon, and "for two months he hit his ear and his eye with the spoon, and sometimes his food landed on his head. And I would guide the spoon to his mouth. But after two months, lo, he hit his mouth. Such a crowing, such triumph! He crowed so that I thought at first he had burnt his mouth, but his face was radiant with success. After that he fed himself.

" 'See,' said Boris, 'he has learned to coordinate those muscles. In the same way he can learn to think, by using his mind. Keep on feeding him like some mothers do, he will still be eating from your hand when he is three years old. A baby is never too young to start learning anything.' "

Sarah claimed she was happy to stay home and take care of Billy, saying, "At the time of Billy's birth the current fad was to practically desert your child, to refuse him any affection or love. We thought this whole idea was monstrous."

As the Sidises' second winter in New York approached, Boris insisted that Sarah buy herself a new winter coat with twenty dollars she had saved (winter coats were a consistent problem for the Sidises). Sarah, however, was longing to buy things for Billy to play with, and that twenty dollars was all the extra cash they had. Secretly, she went to a remnant shop in downtown New York and for sixty cents bought three pounds of cotton batting and a few dollars' worth of material and, using her old spring coat as the lining, sewed a winter coat for herself. She did it all on the sly, and the ruse worked—Boris didn't find out until years later. Sarah at last had money to spend on Billy. She bought blocks, books, maps, and a little globe. Boris couldn't figure out where she'd gotten the money, but she just said mysteriously, "I saved."

Education began. Boris took two alphabet blocks—"A" and "B" —first holding them up in turn over Billy's crib, then forming a syllable until the baby said his first "ba-ba." Then Boris reversed the order of the blocks, so his son learned to say "ab." Soon Boris was making words with the blocks and pointing to the objects they represented. Sarah and Billy too would play in this way by the hour, cluttering the floor with words.

At six months, he spoke his first word, "door."

A few months later, when he had increased his vocabulary enough to explain, Sarah asked, "Why do you like the door so much?"

"Door moves. People come," was Billy's answer.

Billy was seven months old when he pointed to the moon and called it by name. That, Sarah later told a relative, was when she realized her son was a genius. She wrote, "The first thing my April Fool's boy wanted from the great outside world was the moon. We stood at the window of the apartment together in the evening, with Billy in Boris's arms, and admired the moon over Central Park. Billy chuckled and reached for it. The next night when he found that the moon was not in the same place, he seemed disturbed. Trips to the window became a nightly ritual, and he was always pleased when he could see the 'moo-n.'

"This led to Billy's mastering higher mathematics and planetary revolutions by the time he was eleven, and if that seems to be a ridiculous statement I can only say, 'Well, it did.' "

Billy played constantly with his maps and globe. He was not even a year old, but was learning to spell at a remarkable rate. Boris and Sarah named the letters to him for hours on end, and he grew proficient at combining and arranging them. He would toddle around carrying a red tin bucket filled with blocks, then plop himself down on his stomach to spell out "physiological psychology" or "effects of anesthesia" (titles on the lower shelf of his father's bookcase). At eighteen months he was reading *The New York Times,* and he could pluck from the bookshelf any book a visitor requested. At the same time that he was spelling, reading, and talking, Billy learned to count, also using blocks. He greeted visitors by telling them how many buttons they had on their dress or suit. When his parents pushed his carriage through Central Park, a crowd of children gathered round, asking him to count to one hundred, a feat he easily performed; the children were all older, but could not yet count.

Sarah bought Billy a child's encyclopedia, and when he encountered something he didn't know, they looked it up together. One day, after they had done this a few times, he asked Sarah a question, then told her, "But you will say, 'Let's look it up!' and I can look it up myself!" "That," wrote Sarah, "is the last lesson I gave Billy. During the day he would go occasionally to his room and close the door and read. He never studied."

By the time Billy turned three, his voracity for learning was in full swing, and it became apparent that he was not even an ordinarily precocious little boy. One day, as Sarah sat in her kitchen, she heard "the slow, purposeful thumping of the typewriter" from her husband's study. She recalled, "I didn't interrupt, and Billy brought me out a letter he had written. It was to Macy's, ordering toys. He addressed the envelope correctly and sealed the letter.

" 'Now I am very old, like Daddy, because I can typewrite. Maybe I am a hundred or two hundred years old.'

"He was delighted by my surprise, and proud to show me how he had pulled his high chair up to the typewriter when he found he couldn't reach it from his daddy's chair. 'Won't Daddy be surprised!' he crowed. His father's surprise was his greatest incentive."

Billy was always in the company of Boris and Sarah and their friends. Mr. and Mrs. Isidor Straus (they owned Macy's) were especially fond of little Billy, and Mrs. Straus often asked Sarah if she could "borrow" the boy, whom she took home to tea or for walks and drives around New York.

Mrs. Straus invited the Sidises and Billy to a costume ball. Billy, dressed in a little Russian costume Sarah had made, crawled under the magnificent dining room table and tickled the guests' toes during dinner. The amused adults picked him up and set him in the middle of the table. Mrs. Straus explained to the assemblage who Billy was and described his remarkable abilities. Billy held court, playing guessing games with the company, answering questions, and astonishing them by reciting railroad and bus timetables as if they were children's rhymes. It was the beginning of two decades of being onstage. From then on Billy was a regular at the Straus parties, holding the floor and entertaining the guests. One can only assume that, at the age of three, the blue-eyed, apple-cheeked boy reveled in the appreciative attention of so many enraptured adults.

Billy's proficiency in spelling was at that time his most extraordinary talent. Sarah and Boris stressed the roles of reason and logic to Billy—they never made him do any memorizing. He was a quick study when it came to learning prefixes and suffixes. There seemed to be no stopping him.

Once, as a test of Billy's powers, a friend of the family spelled out "Prince Maurocordatos, a friend of Byron," with alphabet blocks. Two weeks later she asked him, "What was the name of Byron's friend I spelled for you?" Billy immediately produced the phrase.

Billy's next coup occurred one evening when Boris had returned from a business trip to Chicago to celebrate his birthday, and the Sidises were entertaining company. Billy slipped into the room with a book hidden behind his back, waiting for a break in the conversation.

"Does anyone here happen to know Latin?" he asked innocently.

"Yes, I know a little," someone replied.

"Here," said Billy, thrusting a copy of Caesar's Gallic Wars into the visitor's hands. "I can read it, let me show you!"

Billy read the first page, then said, "Oh, Daddy, aren't you surprised?"

Billy had taught himself Latin as a birthday present for his father by studying his mother's old Latin primer and matching the English words with the Latin ones. A few months later, poking around in his father's books, he peeked into Plato and asked, "Daddy, why are these letters different from regular letters?" Following his philosophy of answering all Billy's questions, Boris taught his three-year-old the Greek alphabet. Then, with the aid of a Greek primer, Billy taught himself to read Homer. Boris, who was not a Greek scholar himself, was truly awestruck.

At four, Billy was typing proficiently and chattering away on difficult subjects. The following year, his abilities had so expanded that no one who encountered the child could fail to be astounded. Over the next few years, assisted by his father's own considerable knowledge of languages, Billy inhaled Russian, French, German, and Hebrew, and he soon added Turkish and Armenian to his repertoire.

When Billy was six, Boris gave his boy several calendars and explained them in detail. His affection for calendars and dates was so great that he quickly devised a game for himself, a game no adult was bright enough to match him in: He could calculate on what day of the week any given date would fall. Now at Mrs. Straus's dinner parties, he was able to amaze the guests by telling them what day of the week they had been born on, simply by being told the date and the year.

Sarah continued to insist on the normalcy of Billy's activities.

"The real secret was that at first when he learned he wanted to please and surprise the daddy he worshiped. And like all normal little fellows, he wanted often to be the center of attention. He found that learning new things made him the center, and this was his stimulant. Afterward he needed no stimulant, learning was in itself a pleasure."

Although Sarah later claimed that Billy played with other children, there is no evidence that this was so, and it is hard to imagine with whom he could have played. How many other toddlers like to discuss Caesar's Gallic Wars in the original Latin? With a possible rare exception, he was always in the company of adults.

The family spent the summers on Mount Hurricane in the Adirondacks. William James introduced them to the Davidson colony, a small, inexpensive summer resort. Intellectuals gathered there to go mountain climbing and to deliver informal lectures over tea. Boris's visits were brief, but Sarah and Billy stayed entire summers, relaxing with the James family and a variety of artists, professors, and scholars.

Prominent members of the colony were John Dewey (then head of the Department of Education at the University of Chicago) and his family. Sarah was fascinated and appalled by Mrs. Dewey's approach to child rearing. Mrs. Dewey was a believer in "self-expression and complete freedom for her children," who were, Sarah decided, "nice honest children with no formal manners, but pleasant." Sarah was horrified to see them running barefoot near perilous ravines and getting scratched by briars. Certainly, little Billy never ran barefoot. Despite Dewey's vast influence in the field of child education, none of it rubbed off on the Sidises. Said Sarah, "I could not see how falling off a cliff could be educational, and since there are many cliffs in this world I did not go along with Mrs. Dewey's ideas." In any case, the five-year-old Billy had other amusements besides physical play. He was made mail clerk and allowed to distribute the letters each day.

One summer evening at the colony, Billy complained of a toothache, but there was no dentist within miles. To distract Billy from the pain, Boris took him for an after-dinner walk in the lush New England countryside and explained Aristotelian logic, since the boy had been expressing interest in his father's Harvard lectures on the subject.

After an hour, father and son returned. Radiant, Billy announced to his mother, "Now I know all about logic!" A few years later he told a friend, "I'm sorry I put off logic so long. If I had studied it sooner it would have helped me a great deal."

It was at Mount Hurricane that Billy had his first encounter with a journalist—the first of hundreds. This astute reporter jotted down his observations in a diary, publishing them two years later in the *North American Review*. It was the first reporter's-eye view of Billy, and it casts him in a slightly different light from his mother's reportage:

"At a hotel in the mountains, it was the custom of the infant prodigy to read the menu with infinite care, looking about the room to see if all the dishes mentioned were represented on the tables and to inquire anxiously for those he did not see. Once he chanced to be brought in early to breakfast, namely, at 7:45, when upon consulting the menu he found that breakfast was served from 8 to 9. He was seized by perfect panic when the waiter brought in the breakfast ahead of time; he required that it be taken back at once, and finally was borne shrieking from the room, calling out like an irate Hebrew prophet: 'It is from 8 to 9. It has been written.' "

The *Review* is the first publication to give testament to Billy's amazing memory:

A lady coming in with an armful of joe-pye, gathered along the road, proffered some slight data concerning the flower, only to rouse the eager little listener to a sudden contradiction. "It is not so; consult Mrs. Dana, page 252." It was quite true that he not only remembered all he read, but the numbers of the pages upon which he read given information.

It was his pleasing custom to speak of all the guests in the house, in which he spent his summers, by the numbers of the rooms they occupied. A lady and a little girl passing him, he would absentmindedly comment, "Two No. 33's," or a gentleman and a dog going by, he would comment, "No. 57, the dog from kennel 4."

His most notable trait was that he could not be turned aside from any purpose or diverted as other children are. He had very little interest in humanity, and the only way to see an exhibition of his unusual knowledge was to feign ignorance. He already, at five years old, knew something of English, Russian, French and German. If one asked him to count in German, one would be met by a stony gaze of abstraction, so detached, so distant, that it was truly humiliating. If however, one came to him in the spirit of thirst for knowledge, saying, "I suppose the Germans count just as we do," he was lavish with instruction.

Unfortunately, Billy had virtually no physical activity to complement his intellectual gymnastics. His parents disdained sports; "football player" was one of Boris's favorite terms of disparagement. William James had tried to influence Boris, writing to him in the fall of 1902, "I congratulate you on W.J.S.—what you tell of him is wonderful. Exercise his motor activities exclusively for many years now. His intellect takes care of itself." This advice was promptly ignored, and Billy never had the slightest exposure to any childish outdoor games.

Billy's next interest was anatomy. Boris, who was studying for his M.D., despised memorizing and grumbled over his *Gray's Anatomy*. Billy kindly offered to help him, and occasionally drilled his father and the other medical students who dropped over to study. Sarah wrote, "I can hear his small, clear voice crowing triumphantly, 'Aha, you forgot the fifth cranial nerve!'"

For years, the Sidises literally kept a skeleton in their closet, which they used for their anatomy studies. Billy found it and, not the least bit frightened, studied it for hours. One day, a friend of Sarah's approached her in a tizzy, with this story: "You and Boris were both out, and Billy invited me in to wait for you. He had out that skeleton and was sitting on the floor poring over a big book. I saw that it was a textbook on obstetrics. 'What are you doing, Billy?' I asked. And he told me, 'I'm trying to find out how the baby comes out.'" With the skeleton and a *Gray's Anatomy,* Billy learned so much about physiology that, as Boris later told a reporter, "He could pass a medical student's examination at six years of age."

Billy also became preoccupied with the constant bus and streetcar rides his parents took him on to museums, libraries, parks, and zoos. He began avidly to collect streetcar transfers, with which he amused himself for hours at a time. He also took up stargazing, and began to make maps—the beginning of one of his greatest lifelong passions.

Only once, during his early childhood, did Billy leave Sarah at a loss for words. One evening, Billy walked Mr. and Mrs. Addington Bruce, close friends of the Sidises, to their car. Mr. Bruce handed the boy a quarter and instructed him to buy himself a treat with it.

Billy returned to the house upset, and asked his mother, "Why did he do that?"

"Ah, Mr. Bruce thought it would please you," she replied. "What did you do?"

"I didn't want to take it, but I didn't want him to feel bad. So I took it, and after he drove off, I threw it in the gutter."

Sarah wrote in her memoirs, "He's Boris all over again, with his savage contempt for largesse, for the padrone. What could I say to this son of mine who threw quarters in the gutter, without seeming to criticize his father, whose bone-deep scorn of money Billy had already absorbed? It was a problem for me, so I said nothing. . . . He was his father at six. Perhaps it was because he was so much like me in undiscriminating devotion to his father that he absorbed every shade and variation of Boris's attitude toward the world."

Boris did not like to accept payment for his services. Bewildered patients sought out Sarah because Boris had refused to take their money. He had an ever growing list of people who were not to be charged for his services: professors, students, and, especially, ministers, priests, and rabbis. This latter group was curious, because Boris was an atheist.

Sarah saw his view of organized religion as a mixture of contradictions. He numbered among his friends many men of the cloth who knew of his atheism. And yet he was a student of the Bible, the Talmud, and Hindu religious books. He read religious tomes in Arabic, Armenian, Persian, Greek, Hebrew, and Sanskrit, and whole shelves of his library were given over to these texts, which he discussed by the hour with priests and rabbis. But though these books fascinated him, he despised established religion.

When he published his most controversial book a number of years later he wrote, "A rabbi came to ask my advice about the education of his little boy. My advice was: 'Teach him not to be a Jew.' The man of God departed and never came again. The rabbi did not care for education, but for faith. He did not wish his boy to become a man, but to be a Jew." By the age of six, Billy was a confirmed atheist.

Showpiece that he was, Billy was hardly all that occupied the Sidises in the years between 1898 and 1904. Though both parents spent a great deal of time with their boy, they also managed to lead remarkably active lives outside of their home.

In 1898, the year of Billy's birth, Boris too gave birth to a beloved child. It was his first book, the one he had refused to submit as a thesis, *The Psychology of Suggestion*, with an introduction by William James. James wrote to Boris, "The whole thing is bold, original and radical like yourself and I like it." His second book, *The Nature of Hallucinations*, was published two years later. Two years after that he published his third. Like most writers, Boris found the process of writing arduous: After the completion of each book he grumbled that he never wanted to write another. He was to write seventeen books and fifty-two articles.

While Sarah entertained and took the greater part in raising Billy day to day, she prided herself on maintaining the Sidis household and managing the family's financial affairs single-handedly. This arrangement suited Boris, who simply gave her any money he made and let her oversee the budgeting.

"That none of my family except myself was ever practical one iota about the mechanics of living is perhaps due to vanity on my part," wrote Sarah. "Boris couldn't drive a nail, and the only time I ever saw [William] James try to drive a nail, he hit his thumb. So, naturally, Billy couldn't drive a nail. Since every creature must have a forte, it was my vanity to drive the nails for my two brilliant men."

In 1901 James Gordon Bennett, publisher of the *Herald Tribune,* helped to endow Boris with a hospital, which Boris dubbed the Psychopathological Hospital and Psychopathic Laboratory. Boris continued his work at the Pathological Institute, curing difficult cases—and saving them from brutal asylums—with his method of "hypnoidization," a form of hypnotism. He traveled extensively around New York State, initiating reforms and lecturing to heads of hospitals about the barbaric conditions of New York's insane asylums. His work was so impressive that in 1910 *American Magazine* could justly rank Boris Sidis with three other "masters of the mind": Pierre Janet of Paris, Morton Prince of Boston, and Sigmund Freud of Vienna.

This same article propounded Boris's theory of "reserve energy" and its role in the creation of the boy genius: "According to this doctrine, each of us possesses a stored-up fund of energy, of which we ordinarily do not make any use, but which we could be trained to use habitually to our great advantage. Dr. Sidis contends that it is by arousing this potential energy that the patients whom he treats are cured; and he further insists that, by the remarkable results he has obtained in educating his boy, he has demonstrated the possibility of

training people to draw readily and helpfully on their hidden energies."

William James claimed to have discovered this energy concur-
rently with Boris; in ten years, Billy would produce a startling expansion of his father's theory.

Though Boris's research was progressing well, he was running into
difficulties at the Pathological Institute, and, after only three years, it
was shut down by state authorities who were opposed to its emphasis
on experimental research. With this disappointment, the Sidises decided to leave New York. Despite the friends they had made, they
longed to return to Boston. They could now afford to live in Brookline, a suburb that was attracting an influx of up-and-coming professionals. And Boris, surprisingly, had decided to acquire his M.D. at
Harvard—perhaps as the result of Sarah's constant pressure, perhaps
because he regarded the M.D. as one degree with real practical value.
Sarah contended that "he wanted to study medicine so that he might
distinguish with more assurance between those cases which he wished
to treat and those which should be turned over to medicine, for by
now he wished only to practice psychiatry."

Harvard had been keeping up with New York in the field of
psychology. The philosophy department now had its own building,
Emerson Hall, built in 1903, complete with a laboratory specially
equipped for experimental psychology.

In 1904 the Sidis family moved to Brookline. Boris studied at
Harvard Medical School, maintained a private practice, and worked
closely with other scientists. Most importantly, he published *Multiple
Personalities,* a book that enhanced his reputation enormously.

In the ponderous style that had come to characterize Boris's
writing, *Multiple Personalities* recounts the cure of an amnesia victim,
Reverend Thomas Hanna. In the spring of 1897, Hanna, a twenty-five-
year-old Baptist minister, fell out of a carriage and landed on his head.
He was knocked unconscious, and awoke with total amnesia, reduced
to the mental state of a newborn infant. Boris and a colleague, Dr.

Simon Goodhart, taught him to speak, to eat, to go to the bathroom, as if he were a child. He learned quickly, and in a few weeks he could talk; but he had no memory of his former life.

Soon, Hanna began to have vivid dreams. They were scenes from his past, but he didn't recognize them. Boris and Goodhart alternated between hypnotizing Hanna and "stimulating" him, using such scientific methods as pinching, shouting, and throwing cold water in his face; they also tried a substantial dose of cannabis indica, which induced in the patient—not so surprisingly—a state of "euphoria, inner joyousness and mental buoyancy." They took Hanna to the theater, to the zoo, and to dinner with his family, attempting to "jog his memory" by re-creating scenes from his preaccident life. For two months his pre- and postaccident personalities alternated within him, fought for dominance. Finally, Hanna experienced a moment of crisis: He was aware of both past and present simultaneously. He recovered completely.

Despite its style, *Multiple Personalities* was widely read and widely reviewed. Critics were of several minds. One writer actually suggested that the book should "be carried along by tourists to note the dual personalities with which they may come in contact."

Boris Sidis had become famous, and the family that had left New York for a fine Boston suburb appeared to be on its way to a magnificent future.

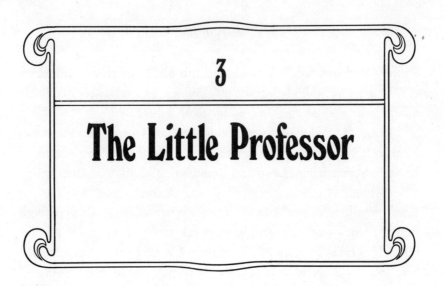

3

The Little Professor

Billy liked Brookline. He liked best climbing the hill behind the Sidises' big house at night, lying on his back, and gazing at the stars. He loved the night, and he loved the constellations. "I used to go with him to his hilltop," wrote Sarah, "but he soon told me he could see better and think more clearly when he was alone."

Billy had reached legal school age. Despite the fact that he could now speak and read at least eight languages, he would have to attend classes with other six-year-olds who did not yet read English or know how to print their names. His parents chose the Runkle School, a public school on Fisher Hill near their home. Sarah took Billy for a pre-enrollment test to determine whether the boy knew his letters.

When asked if he knew how to read, Billy suggested a spot of Shakespeare; he carried a volume of the bard with him wherever he went. To the teacher's bewilderment Billy delivered, with full expression, the first scene of the first act of *Julius Caesar*.

Having satisfied the entrance requirements, Billy began grammar school. Popular myth has it that he arrived at school the first day at 9:00 A.M., and when his mother came to pick him up at lunchtime he was in the third grade. This is a slight exaggeration—it actually took him three days to go from first grade to third. When his mother did pick him up that first day, however, he was instructing his teacher in a new way to do fractions.

An excellent account of his grammar-school days appeared in the *Boston Transcript*:

Naturally the teachers of the primary school felt weighed down with the responsibility for so rare a child—and were not a little embarrassed in managing him in class. While others were reaching a given point he had always soared miles beyond them and was fidgeting, wearily waiting for them to catch up. It seemed as if he could not bear to hear a second time what he had been taught or told. It was evident torture for him to sit by and listen to the plodding routine of the day's work in the school, and when a physically healthy boy of six or seven is in torture the teacher is likely to be so likewise. Even the repetition of the morning hymns and school songs seemed to cause the child intense exasperation and he would put his fingers into his ears, as he did when the conjugations in grammar were being drilled into the rest of the class—also at prayers, against which he had certain conscientious scruples of his own.

But if he was difficult to provide for in the class work he was still more of a problem at recess, on the playground. He took no part or interest in any of the games; never wrestled, ran or played tag with either girls or boys. His chief desire when out among the children, if he had anything at all to do with his schoolmates, seemed to be to instruct them in natural sciences. His teachers overheard him once expounding the nebular hypothesis to his school fellows on the playground. Naturally the boys being forbidden to haze him gave him a wide berth with his lectures.

The poor little genius was forlornly isolated and lonely. Then the teachers enlisted some of the bigger girls to take the phenomenon in hand and dutifully they rose to the emergency, as their sex always does. But before long they too struck against the prodigy. They came to the teacher and complained that William would not walk, or run, or play at any game. The seven-year-old wanted only to stand about and talk with them; he seemed to be absorbed and beset with the purpose of making them understand about the revolutions of the planets, the phases of the moon, and the probable elements of the incandescent atmosphere of the sun and such things.

William's year in primary school was interrupted by an attack of typhoid fever, yet the record from the school register of his advance runs:

FIRST GRADE—Only a day or two.
SECOND GRADE—A few days.
THIRD GRADE—Three months.
FOURTH GRADE—One week.
FIFTH GRADE—Fifteen weeks.
SIXTH AND SEVENTH GRADES—Five and a half weeks.

The *Boston Transcript* continued:

Equal in all to about one-half year of schooling.

Himself a grammarian in a way, William James Sidis could not abide the grammar-school grammar. At seven years of age he had his original ideas of a grammar of three languages running abreast, already in part typewritten (he writes in no other way, and this bothers, again, in school, of course), and the grammar taught in the schools was full of those exasperating sounds against which he covers up his ears. He despised it, and also the history which he had learned all about years before.

On the other hand, whenever he was at all interested, the teacher's problem was to suppress him; he wanted to take her task out of her hands and talk all the time. Started on any such question or allusion coming up in the class, he was full and ready to speak, and if allowed to have his way, would keep the children busy and entertained to the exclusion of all else set down in the school curriculum.

In the shop-room he was intensely curious, busy and eager, and the greatest care had to be taken lest he cut himself with rash handling of edged tools. His nervous rapidity in accomplishing whatever he was set to do made him a much greater care for the instructors than the slowest dullards. Care had to be taken, too, not to feed his vanity with the wonder and admiration which the stupefied teachers often could not conceal at his performances. They seemed to have been wholly conscientious and even tender with the wonder child.

They had one boy trained to look specially after him to see that he did not injure himself by his obliviousness to sublunary things—as for instance to follow him up at the end of school and see that he did not get out and start for home, as he was liable to do, without putting on either hat or overcoat.

As one might imagine, Billy's classroom antics were aggravating his teachers, who were already intimidated by the fact that he knew more than they did. Billy graduated after a mere seven months. In the words of the *Boston Herald*:

"He told his teachers he'd just as soon leave school. He knew all they could teach him anyway. He said this without self-pride, as one states a simple truth—and it was the truth. He added that it was very inconvenient for his mother to bring him to school each day, and take him home again, but that she had to do it, because he was horribly afraid of dogs."

(Perhaps Billy's fear of dogs was inherited from his mother. So strong was her phobia that in her seventies she wrote, "In my childhood I got two ideas that shaped my life: I thought I could do anything, and I was afraid of nothing but dogs." Billy did have a pet cat, which he adored.)

In spite of Billy's advancement in nearly every academic field, there was one curious omission: mathematics. According to H. Addington Bruce, the writer who was a close friend of the Sidises, Billy had developed an aversion to mathematics during his stint in grammar school. Bruce wrote that "no subject could possibly have been more distasteful to him," that he seemed "unable . . . or unwilling" to grasp it. This contradicts later newspaper accounts that have Billy showing mathematical brilliance at six. However, since Bruce was very close to the Sidises, he is probably an accurate source on this important point.

Boris and Sarah did not react to Billy's aversion by overtly pushing him to study arithmetic. Instead they bought toys—dominoes and marbles—and invented games requiring a knowledge of addition, subtraction, multiplication, and division. For a few hours every night, Boris and Sarah played with their son, according to Bruce, "deftly managing matters so that his interest in time shifted from the toys to the principles underlying their use." Boris also "in the boy's presence . . . continually discussed with Mrs. Sidis questions involving the practical application of arithmetic, and 'suggesting' its importance in the affairs of everyday life."

This technique must have worked well. Billy's plunge into the realm of numbers began at the age of seven and a half and followed a meteoric course for the next decade.

Although Boris and Sarah did not technically "push" Billy to study math, for the first time they had exerted pressure. Previously— if we are to believe their reports—they had nurtured, nudged, and guided Billy's explorations and passions, but had never before steered him toward something he hated. Despite their success in interesting him in math, this "steering" may have been responsible for disastrous consequences that would not manifest for years to come.

In a short time, Billy surpassed his father in mathematical ability. At the age of eight, he accomplished the spectacular feat of devising a new table of logarithms using a base of twelve instead of the normal ten—a favorite anecdote of the press in future years.

One evening when the Sidises were entertaining a Harvard mathematics professor, Dr. E. V. Huntington, Billy whiled away the time by reading the galleys of the professor's latest book. The boy noted several errors in the text and pointed them out to Dr. Huntington, who duly revised his work.

Math, astronomy, languages, anatomy, map- and calendar-making, and grammar were not the only subjects occupying Billy's eight-year-old mind. He had developed an avid interest in politics—an unusual interest for a mathematical and linguistic prodigy. He frequently wandered into Brookline stores to discuss politics with the shopkeepers; every day he retreated into his room with the morning newspapers, paying particular attention to political events. (He had developed his own speed-reading system, and had total recall of all that he read.)

Between the ages of six and eight, Billy wrote at least four books. Two of these, textbooks on anatomy and astronomy, are lost. The remaining two represent his feats in the fields of grammar, linguistics, and mathematics. They are written in textbook style, with all the childish charm of imitation schoolbooks. The first, a grammar, begins with this announcement of authorship:

MR. PROF. (DR.) WILLIAM JAMES SIDIS

Prof. (Professor in calendars and talker of English, Latin and Greek grammar) born, 1898, and began his books on Nov. 24

(better July 1), 1905, when he was less than 7 and 1/2 years, and wrote books on Astronomy, Calendars, English Grammar, and compends on it.

This is followed by the pun:

INTRODUCTION

My book, the reader—the reader, my book.

But the rest is no-nonsense—a reduction of the principles and forms of grammar to a succinct forty-one pages. The book differs from other grammars primarily in its brevity and minimum of repetition. While Billy invented nothing in this book, it is still a remarkable achievement. How many intelligent adults have mastered the rules of English? Curiously, though, while the abstract principles of grammar are clear and accurate, Billy occasionally slips and makes a grammatical error himself. For example: "The SUBJECT part is what is the sentence about."

His selection of examples range from the cute:

Conjunctions join the words together
as rain AND sunshine, wind OR weather.
Conjunctions sentences unite
as kittens scratch AND puppies bite.

to the unexpected as in this example of the third person:
"POPE GREGORY THIRTEENTH was the greatest man."
While most children would choose George Washington or Buffalo Bill, Billy's interests already lay elsewhere.

His examples of interjections are particularly charming:

An interjection shows surprise
as OH, how pretty, AH, how wise!

PRINCIPAL ONES.—the principal interjections are: aha, ah, alas, alack, hey, hurrah, huzza, hah, ho, hallo, hist, hush, lo, fe, mum, O(oh), pshaw, tush, woe, &c.

The following is the only reference to fathers, used to illustrate pronouns:

(I) am sorry that papa left (I) am sorry that (HE) left.

The only reference to mothers is strikingly different:

THE PERSONS ARE NAMED: first, second, third. The first person is the speaker, as, I PAUL have written it. The second person is the hearer, as, MOTHER, what is the trouble with YOUR brain.

Billy's most ambitious product in this period was the invention of a new language, Vendergood.

Again written in the manner of a school text, the forty-page *Book of Vendergood* outlines the basic rules, structure, and pronunciation of a language that is Latin-based but draws on German, French (of which Billy was particularly fond), and several other Romance languages. Reading it creates the same strange effect of Billy's other books: This marvelous, sophisticated achievement is tinged throughout with a childish fascination with form and pomposity; the adult reader feels constantly bounced between the work of a genius and that of a little boy.

Billy's fascination with order went to such extremes that he actually made up new elements of grammar, as if the topic weren't difficult enough. For example: "There are 8 Modes, the indicative, potential, imperative absolute, *strongeable,* subjunctive, *optative,* imperative & infinitive [emphasis added]." Chapters bear such intimidating titles as "Imperfect and Future Indicative Active"—hardly layman's lingo. One painfully difficult page contains a breakdown of the word "the" into an off-putting array of gender and inflection variations. He has made a simple article more complex than a Japanese verb, in the interest of exactitude of expression.

Other parts of Vendergood are refreshingly clear and simple, such as the explanation of the origin of Roman numerals. This, along with several pages of hard mathematics, is injected into the *Book of Vendergood* in the interest of promoting a mass move to base twelve, instead of base ten. Billy offers this explanation for the change:

Roman numerals are not all founded on the same principal [*sic*]. The first 3 are founded on the fingers. I, one, is the shape of one finger, V, five, is nearly the shape of a hand, which has five fingers; X, ten, is the shape of two hands crossing each other at the elbow, in which the hands together [*sic*] ten fingers, C, a hundred, is from Latin centum; M, a thousand, from Latin mille. The use of the Denary scale is easily seen for we have ten fingers. The reason of introducing the Duodenary Scale in Vendergood is seen as follows: The unit in selling things is 12 of those things and 12 is the smallest number that has four factors!

The numbers in Vendergood are then given in base 12:

eis	one
duet	two
tre	three
quar	four
quin	five
sex	six
sep	seven
oo (oe?)	eight
non	nine
ecem	ten
elevenos	eleven
dec	twelve
eidec (eis, dec)	thirteen

Most examples are presented in the form of tests:

TRANSLATE INTO VENDERGOOD: 1. Do I love the young man? 2. The bowman obscures. 3. I am learning Vendergood. 4. What do you learn? (sing.) 5. I obscure ten farmers.

The answers to this quiz, placed at the back of the book, are as follows:

1. Amevo (-)ne the neania? 2. The toxoteis obscurit. 3. (Euni) disceuo Vendergood. 4. Quen diseois-nar? 5. Obscureuo ecem agrieolai.

Vendergood is simpler than Esperanto, the only comparable language. Its limitations are that it is difficult to pronounce and is too streamlined to allow for many contractions. Vendergood would be an impressive achievement coming from an adult. It came from a seven-year-old.

When he was five, Billy had devised his method for instantly calculating the day of the week on which any given date, past or future, would fall. When he was seven and a half he wrote a two-part book on calendars. Only the first part, describing how to make a normal calendar, has survived. The title page reads:

FIRST BOOK ON CALENDARS
by
WILLIAM JAMES (SD) (SIDIS)? THE
CALENDARMAKER?
YES!

NOTE—This book is for people to know what their own calendars are, and how to make one themselves.

This is an excellently written little book, lucid, concise, and amusing. With only a smidgeon of editing, it would make an excellent primer for schoolchildren. Billy first clearly describes time zones, lunar phases, seasons ("Without the sun there would be no such thing as season,"), leap years, months, etc. He stresses the underlying principles involved, leaving little to rote memorization. In the same way that his father taught his mother Euclid (study the first three theorems, and figure out the rest), Billy teaches his readers.

Midway through the book is a list of "the principal holidays" comprising Washington's Birthday, St. Patrick's Day, etc. Displaying his growing taste for unusual bits of trivia, Billy also lists the Battle of Lexington, Decoration Day, the Yorktown Surrender, and the day the Pilgrims landed. The most charming of all the special days is "A holiday discovered in 1905—On Oct. 3rd, 1905, the first Tuesday in October, William James Sidis had a calendar on his bookcase, and put it on his bureau, &c. and since then it was called Calendar Moving day."

Billy racked up two more precocious feats in his seventh and eighth years: He passed the Harvard Medical School anatomy exam and the entrance examination for the Massachusetts Institute of Technology. Clearly, he was ready for high school.

But was the Brookline public school ready to have on its hands a little boy whose intellectual abilities would surpass those of its best teachers? The school superintendent, Professor Aldrich, met with Boris Sidis, William James, and several other prominent professors to discuss the matter. James pronounced his godson the most remarkable prodigy he had ever known of. This greatly impressed Aldrich, who decided to overlook his anxieties and accept Billy as a pupil, if he first passed an entrance exam. Asked to multiply 12 by 12 by 12, he gave the answer instantly. Having passed this and other tests, he was admitted to Brookline High.

Now that Billy was the world's youngest high school freshman, the press descended on him in earnest. To the boy's horror, reporters lay in wait for him near his house; if they succeeded in finding him alone, one would pounce and hold him while another took his picture. Since Billy loathed journalists, Headmaster Hitchcock arranged for a reporter from the *Boston Transcript* to spy on Billy at school, rather than interview him.

The reporter hovered with Hitchcock just inside a doorway and watched a troop of students parade from one class to the next. Dressed in Russian peasant clothes, Billy couldn't have been hard to spot. The reporter observed the passage of

> tall young fellows and girls twice the age of the wonder-child we were looking for: then, characteristically enough, the Sidis boy went all by himself. Presently we followed him up stairs to his assigned place between his algebra lesson and the coming hour in Latin and found him in the physics laboratory. At the end of the long room . . . we saw the lonely infant bending over his table. He had been putting together, according to printed instructions, the parts of a Dutch clock, one of the regular exercises of this department. He was just finishing as we came up, and when the clock was triumphantly hung ticking on the wall, we left him skipping and dancing about the many-windowed room like a child in his nursery. His high-pitched voice, "in childish treble," is the most infantile thing about him. His body seems strong, his color good; and altogether he looks the ordinary boy in normal health. His head is large, especially in the rear at the top, and his ears are of generous size. There is something weird and "intense" in his gray eye and the way he looks out from under his eyebrows. His mouth is well-shaped, with a large and firm upper lip —altogether a face that, if one caught the knit brows and sharp glance of the eye, one would look at twice.

Boris and Sarah arranged for Billy to attend school for a maximum of two hours a day—Sarah didn't want "to waste his brain capacities with too much cramming." She claimed that Billy "was somewhat disappointed at what he considered his 'slow' progress in high school." This "slow progress" consisted of completing the four-year curriculum in six weeks, and serving as a teachers' aide for another six, helping correct the seniors' papers. Billy was always eager to help his fellow students with their academic problems, and they nicknamed him "Professor." In fact, he taught seniors how to tackle physics problems before he had officially studied their branch of that science.

For all this, he was still a little boy. Though jaws dropped when he demonstrated an equation at the blackboard (for which he had to stand on a stool), his feet didn't touch the floor when he returned to his seat. In fact, he was bubbling over with energy and so full of antics and pranks that he seriously disrupted the classroom. Commented H. Addington Bruce, "In some respects he is more childlike than the average youngster." His uncurbed enthusiasm was not the only problem. The atheism that had so disturbed his grammar-school teachers was no less horrifying to the faculty of Brookline High. On one occasion, Headmaster Hitchcock began reading the Bible at a school assembly. Billy leaped out of his seat in front of a thousand students, pressed his hands over his ears, and exclaimed, "I don't believe in that. I don't want to hear that."

When his teachers began to complain that he didn't do his lessons, John C. Packard, the submaster and teacher of physics, investigated.

"William, is it true that you did only nine out of the twelve algebra problems?"

"That's all," replied Billy with a grin.

"Didn't you know how to do the others?"

"Of course!" the boy answered. "That's why I didn't do them." Mr. Packard looked puzzled. "Why should I spend my time on things I know," asked Billy, "when there are things I don't know?"

To his credit, Packard saw the point, and took Billy on as his special pupil. They invented problems in algebra and physics, trying to outwit each other. After three months Packard gave Billy the MIT entrance examination. Once again he passed with flying colors, scoring 100 in physics and mathematics.

At the end of three months Billy's parents withdrew him from high school. Despite Packard's appreciation of the boy, the rest of his teachers were relieved to see him go.

An orgy of inaccurate newsprint had followed Billy through his abbreviated high school career. The *Washington Herald* quoted Boris as bemoaning, "Where is my boy going to stop? . . . At first his mother and I were alarmed at his precocity. . . . At the outset, we did all we could to discourage him from studying. . . . We wanted him to go out and play like other children. . . . He exercises regularly." *Harper's Weekly* announced that "already the precocious boy's eyes are failing, and he has to wear double-lens glasses. In other respects his physical health is causing his father some anxiety." The *Harper's* piece was followed by rebuttals in the papers, chastising *Harper's* sloppiness, pointing out that Billy did not wear glasses and was in fine health. After all, both his parents were doctors. Other papers jubilantly proclaimed Billy "the most remarkable boy in the United States," and the *North American Review* uttered this stern injunction: "It is to be hoped that the premature development will not stop short, but that the boy's disinterested love of knowledge and of law may solve some of this world's scientific problems." It was the first public request that William James Sidis live up to his potential.

For the next two years, Billy received little press. He stayed at home, mastering trigonometry, geometry, and differential calculus. He was reading Einstein and checking for possible errors, and his sister believes that he and the great scientist corresponded. Billy's interest in politics continued to grow as he read the paper religiously. And he began to draw sophisticated maps, first of Brookline and then of Boston. His early years of bus riding and walking had crystallized in him a passion for the details of transportation and city layouts.

Despite his active schedule, Billy always had time to give a little helpful advice to a fellow intellectual in need. Boris was fond of telling this story: One evening in 1908, Harvard's venerable logic professor Josiah Royce stopped in for a visit with the Sidises. He was on his way to Europe and carried with him the manuscript of his latest, soon-to-be-published book. After reading it, Boris gave it to Billy, who perused it and declared to Professor Royce, "There are a few passages here I think you ought to delete. They're wrong." Not surprisingly, Royce, one of Harvard's most revered scholars, chose to ignore the advice of a nine-year-old. In a few weeks, Boris received a cable from Europe: "I took Billy's advice."

The *Boston Herald* ran this amusing anecdote about the nine-year-old prodigy:

One afternoon he met a friend who was in the second year at Technology. Under his arm the friend carried a standard mathematical work over which Tech sophomores groan.

"Let's see it," said Sidis. He turned the pages rapidly for a few minutes, muttering to himself.

"Any good?" said his friend ironically.

"Extremely comprehensive," answered the nine-year-old, graduating from monosyllables to polysyllables, as he always does with a transition from childish to erudite subjects. "I am not familiar with the author, but it is a comprehensive work. I think, though, that if the author had employed my theory of logarithms he would have been wiser. You know, I have a theory—" and into the astounded ears of the college man he poured his demonstrable system based on twelve instead of ten.

"They ought not to let you cram like that!" exclaimed the man in sheer self-defence.

"I am never compelled to study," replied William with dignity, "my parents allow me to stop studying whenever I desire. It is foolish to cram. The mind of youth can retain only so much, and when you crowd more in, you crowd out what was there before. And so you are back where you started."

Boris decided to enroll his nine-year-old son at Harvard. Despite the boy's obvious intellectual qualifications, the faculty balked at admitting a child not yet in puberty. A second try met with similar results. Finally, when Billy was eleven, one faculty member argued that it would be an honor to Harvard to accept the lad the newspapers were calling "the most wonderful boy in the world"—he was certain one day to reflect glory on his alma mater. Billy was accepted as a "special student."

The last few years had been momentous for the Sidis family. On February 26, 1910, Boris had received his M.D. Two weeks earlier, on February 12, their daughter, Helena, was born.

Helena had been a carefully planned baby. Because of Boris's intensive work schedule, he and Sarah had decided to wait over a decade after Billy's birth, until Sarah was thirty-five, to have a second child. Effie Perkins, Sarah's best friend from her school days, came to Brookline to see Sarah through the delivery.

Sarah had a difficult labor. In her pain, she strode up and down, exclaiming stridently, "I will not have this baby! I refuse to have this baby!" Boris shouted back at her, "You have to have it!"

The adult Helena, who heard the story from Effie, did not find it at all extraordinary. "It was very much in the order of what my mother would do. She would go along with something or other, some plan, and then she'd just throw it all up. Decide it was no good. Well, of course, you can't do that with a baby."

Helena was premature, and the delivery was a difficult one. In her memoirs, Sarah wrote only briefly of her daughter's birth and babyhood, claiming that, "Billy was always my boy in physique and temperament. But my tiny titian-haired Helena, from the moment she was born, was a Sidis. She grew up with that artistry and elegance of thought that was her father's." Sarah added, "The relationship between Billy and Boris in those years when Helena was a baby was one of dear companionship. By then, it was Billy who sat on the foot of the bed and talked his father to sleep."

Naturally, Boris had not been idle since his return to the Boston area. Between 1904 and 1910 he published eight books and a steady stream of articles. And he continued to study at Harvard Medical School, where he received unusual privileges. He was exempted completely from attending lectures and was required to take only anatomy, dissection, and obstetrics. He had already begun a private practice as a psychologist, with an office on Beacon Hill.

Boris continued his experimental research, working with several prominent figures in the academic community—most importantly, the energetic and likable Morton Prince, professor of neurology at Tufts College Medical School. Prince and Boris grew close, researching and writing articles together. They shared a profound interest in the study of hypnosis, multiple personalities, and the subconscious. When Boris suggested to Prince the need for a publication devoted solely to abnormal psychology, they began to brainstorm, and in February 1906, the influential *Journal of Abnormal Psychology* was born. It was the first English-language journal devoted solely to psychotherapy: The premiere issue introduced the word *psychoanalysis* to America. Prince was the editor, and Boris one of the associate editors.

In the *Journal*'s second issue, Boris reviewed Freud's *Psychopathology of Everyday Life*—it was one of Freud's first reviews in America. Sidis had recently recommended the book to William James, although he had reservations about Freud's theories.

By 1910 Freud and Sidis were at odds. Freud wrote to G. Stanley Hall, "I cannot suppress a certain unholy joy that you and Dr. Putnam have rejected Boris Sidis, who is neither very honest nor very intelligent. I mean he deserved nothing else." A few years later, Boris wrote, "Psychoanalysis is a conscious and more often a subconscious or unconscious debauching of the patient. Nothing is so diabolically calculated to suggest sexual perversion as psychoanalysis. Psychoanalysis . . . is a menace to the community. . . . Better Christian Science than psychoanalysis!"

To what extent little William kept abreast of his father's psychoanalytic battles we do not know. He did not appear to be developing any interest whatsoever in the subject. But then, he may have had other things on his mind—the year was 1909, William was eleven, and he was about to become the youngest student ever to enroll at Harvard University.

4

Sidis an Avatar?

On October 11, 1909, Billy made the front page of *The New York Times*—the first of many such occasions. The article, "Harvard's Child Prodigy," was riddled with inaccuracies (giving his age as thirteen and noting that he had spent two years at Tufts College), but it launched national attention.

Six days later *The New York Times Magazine* ran a four-column splash entitled "A Savant at Thirteen, Young Sidis on Entering Harvard Knows More Than Many on Leaving. A Scholar at Three." The same errors were made again.

In the article, the normal requirements for entrance to Harvard were dramatically contrasted with Billy's achievements. An entering freshman was required to know algebra and plane geometry; Billy had mastered integral calculus and was preparing to study quaternions, "a pinnacle few ever attain." A freshman needed to know his Xenophon and a smattering of Homer; Billy's Greek was flawless. He spoke twice as many languages as were required. The *Times* speculated that after graduating, Billy would "go abroad for his degree in Philosophy, and specialize in something profound and then—Well, then what? What will become of the wonder child? Will he go the way commonly supposed to be that of most boy prodigies, or will he make a name for himself? It will be interesting to watch."

The article was peppered with quotes from Billy, ostensibly obtained through a "friend." Reported the *Times*, "He did not see why people should have to pay bills. He proclaimed the use of money ridiculous. 'It all amounts to this,' he said, 'that a man might need something badly and not be able to get it merely because he had not money. You can't persuade me that's not ridiculous.'

"On Lincoln's birthday some years ago he said to a friend, 'I wonder if some day there will be a holiday for school children and they will be told that it is a holiday, because years ago on that date I began to experiment in my laboratory.' " (Boris had built him a small lab where he made thermometers and recorded daily meteorological observations.)

The *Times* proclaimed him to be free of conceit, saying, "He escaped, somehow, being a prig"; he was a "normal boy." He wasn't athletically inclined, they admitted, but he would surely cheer on the Harvard athletes like any other all-American lad.

After explaining Boris and James's theory of reserve energy and its place in Billy's training, the *Times* wrote, "Dr. Sidis is, in fact, rather impatient of the theory that the boy's heredity accounts for his development, and will have it that this system of education has more to do with the matter. Keep your child from slip-shod thinking, he says, and develop his 'hidden energy,' and the result will be startling. All the same, one may be pardoned for doubting if with any amount of education there would be a William Sidis." The *Times* proposed that much of Billy's ability could be attributed to his Russian Jewish heritage.

The very next day, October 18, the *Times* published two more articles on Billy. The first, "Sidis of Harvard," was a dull, speculative rehash of why President Lowell (he had just succeeded President Eliot) might want to enroll younger students. On the other hand, the second piece, "Sidis Could Read at Two Years Old," was a stimulating chronology of his childhood achievements.

Declaring Billy to be the most learned undergraduate ever to enter Harvard, the *Times* was the first paper to give voice to what was to become the press party line: "Sidis is a wonderfully successful result of a scientific forcing experiment, and as such furnishes one of the most interesting mental phenomena in history." Boris insisted that no "forcing" took place; that, rather, his son had learned to master his reserve energy as any child could with equally dramatic results. The debate raged.

The most expansive article yet, taking up a full two pages—six columns of newsprint and a picture—ran in the *Boston Sunday Herald* magazine section on November 7, 1909. It was the biggest, splashiest spread on Billy to date, its very size bespeaking the boy's growing fame and controversial status. The accompanying photograph spoke those famous thousand words. The guileless, gap-toothed boy of previous photos was gone. In his place was a lad of wary, riveting gaze; that "something weird and 'intense' in his gray eye," observed by one writer a few years before was plainly evident. The face radiated a searing intelligence, a fall from innocence, suspicion. He seemed to be looking beyond both photographer and reader with chilling gaze, surrounded by rows and rows of newsprint chronicling his relentless achievements.

The *Herald* article opened with an accounting of Billy's mathematical feats—his logarithmic tables, his theory of a "straight" curve, his proposition that there can be no perfect parabola, his studies in vector analysis (in which he was about to surpass his professor). Dr.

Daniel F. Comstock, professor of physics at MIT, had high words of praise for the prodigy: "His method of thinking is real intellect. It is not automatic. He does not cram his head with facts. He reasons. Karl Friedrich Gauss is the only example in history, of all prodigies, whom Sidis resembles. I predict that young Sidis will be a great astronomical mathematician. He will evolve new theories and invent new ways of calculating astronomical phenomena. I believe he will be a great mathematician, the leader in that science in the future."

The *Herald* pointed out that Billy was no mere mathematical whiz. He now composed original verse in Greek and Latin, and "is an astute historian and compiles lists of the 10 or 12 vital events in a nation's history. . . . In modern politics he takes a great interest. . . . But the boy is neither a Democrat nor a Republican. And he can, with great force and clearness, tell you why he is neither, and why you don't know why you are either. But Sidis is no pale, bespectacled abnormality. His cheeks are a healthy pink, his gray eyes are clear and bright, and his frequent squinting is a racial characteristic—his parents are Russian Jews—not a sign of weakness. His knicker-bockered legs carry him with most boyish and unacademic friskiness across the yard at Harvard and two steps at a time up into Sever Hall."

Sarah still accompanied him to school on the streetcar, taking him as far as the Harvard gate and meeting him there after school. The *Herald* noted the incongruity of this—why couldn't such a savant find his own way? And Billy protested, "But I don't like to have her come with me. She is afraid I'll get lost. I wouldn't. It really isn't necessary for her to come." Billy was anxious to be by himself on the streetcar —his only precious time alone was that which he spent in the evenings lying on the hill in back of the Brookline house.

Billy wanted to be alone to think, but he had learned how to do so even when forced to share a streetcar with his ever present mother. The *Herald* observed, "It is one of his peculiar characteristics that when his fingers are occupied with trivialities, his mind is treading profundities. It was while he was building castles with his blocks when he was a little boy that he evolved a theory of building arches and bridges.

All his apparently idle moments, while riding to and fro in cars, or walking from the end of the street to his home, he spends in thinking." Thinking—analyzing, pondering abstractions—was his refuge, his place of privacy and play. The more he hungered for privacy, the more famous he became, and the more reporters hounded him. His father seemed insensitive to his boy's plight as he busily flaunted his theories and named Billy as an example of what could be done with any child. His mother, equally indifferent to her boy's discomfort, did nothing to shield him from reporters. Billy's only refuge was in learning.

For all the pressure (and more was to come), Billy never entirely lost his good humor. The *Herald* reported, "In a conversation with him the other day mention was made of his extraordinary career, and the yet more extraordinary career that lies before him. Young Sidis seemed not unduly elated—it was rather a matter of course. But in the midst of the conversation he chuckled so heartily that he almost dropped his fat green bag filled with books.

"Utterly without self-conceit, but still with a broad grin for the humor of the situation—'It's very strange,' he remarked in his high, clear voice, 'but you know, I was born on April Fool's day!' "

All this press coverage disturbed the Harvard faculty. George W. Evans, a retired professor and close friend of the Sidises, tried to set the record straight in the *Harvard Graduate Magazine*. He wrote a letter to the editor intended to clear up all the "mistaken and sensational comment" Billy's arrival at Harvard had caused. He pointed out that Billy was a special student who did not live on campus and took only two math courses. His parents, explained Evans, were not trying to parade their creation before the public, but had sent Billy to Harvard that he might find intellectual companionship. The letter was a veiled plea for Harvard men and women to accept the boy wonder into their fold, or at least to stop treating him like a freak. Evans insisted that Billy was the product of a new system of education, not a genetic oddity. Though the boy was "happy, cheerful, and full of fun," contact with Harvard men would mature him intellectually and emotionally. "Harvard University is the one place where such a mind should find its home. Harvard should possess a mind of his calibre among its claims to distinction . . . [along with] a Sir Isaac Newton, a Blaise Pascal, a Sir William Hamilton. . . ." If Billy was the child of the future, it was Harvard's duty to "do its best for the preservation and protection of that new type."

Billy was not the only child prodigy at Harvard, but since he was the most amazing and the youngest, he got nearly all the press. The others were Cedric Wing Houghton, who died before his graduation; Roger Sessions, a fifteen-year-old musical prodigy and already a Ph.D. candidate; the fourteen-year-old Adolf A. Berle, whose brother and sisters were also prodigies; and Norbert Wiener, the future father of cybernetics.

The Berles' parents, like the Sidises, had trained their children to reason rather than memorize, and to think of learning as play. Like the Sidises they believed that training, not heredity, was responsible for their children's precocity. However, Adolf differed from Billy in that he was somewhat interested in athletics (having a little brother to box with helped) and was considerably more outgoing. Furthermore, his parents had emphasized the importance of the social graces: Adolf was courteous and poised. His father was raising him to be a statesman: He did become Assistant Secretary of State under Franklin Roosevelt.

It was Norbert Wiener, born in 1894, who was most often compared to Billy in the papers—and the similarities were striking. Norbert's father, Leo, was also a Russian Jew and a disciplined, self-made man, a professor of Slavic languages and literature at Harvard. Formidable and dominating, Leo Wiener undertook to raise his son on principles very like those of Boris Sidis. By the time he was three Norbert was reading and writing, and at six he was familiar with the works of Darwin. William James had written to Boris in 1902: "He [William] can apparently pair off with Wiener's infant prodigy, who at the age of seven, has done all the common school work, and of course can't get into high school, so that his father is perplexed what to do with him, since they make difficulties about admitting him to the manual training school at Cambridge."

Leo Wiener's approach to his son's education was far more severe in method than Boris and Sarah's. When Norbert made an error reciting his lessons, his father rained invective on his head, shouting "Fool! Donkey! Ass!" and reducing his son to tears. (In interviews, he said his method called for "a certain amount of tactful compulsion by the parent" administered "in a kindly manner.") Leo Wiener was not all harshness, however—when Norbert was accused of cheating on his Harvard exams, his father rushed to defend him. Despite generally oppressive treatment, Norbert continued to crave his father's praise and approval well into adulthood. At eleven, Norbert graduated from public high school at the head of his class, then enrolled in Tufts College, majoring in mathematics and classics and receiving his B.A. at fourteen. He moved on to Harvard for graduate work in 1909, the same year Billy Sidis entered as a special student.

Like Boris Sidis, Leo Wiener attributed 100 percent of his son's successes to his training, labeling all talk of heredity "nonsense." Thus, in some important ways, the two fathers were similar. But while Boris decried "meaningless games and silly, objectless sports," Leo Wiener often took his son hiking in the Adirondacks and on long nature walks where they identified flora and fauna. Norbert developed an enduring passion for nature, and discovered a means of getting exercise (he couldn't play basketball with the other boys because his thick glasses were often crushed).

Despite his father's efforts, by the time little Norbert reached Harvard he was painfully maladjusted socially. Short and dumpy, clumsy and bespectacled, he wrote in *Ex-Prodigy,* his memoirs, "I had no proper idea of personal cleanliness and personal neatness, and I myself never knew when I was to blurt out some unpardonable rudeness." He was shocked to see "poise and sense of social protocol" in the fourteen-year-old Adolf Berle, who carried kid gloves and presented Norbert with a formal visiting card. More distressing still, Norbert's parents had concealed from him that he was a Jew, leaving him completely unprepared for the anti-Semitism he encountered at Harvard.

[57]

But if poor, tubby, myopic Norbert felt himself an outcast, even he had someone to look askance at: Billy Sidis. "Sidis," he wrote in his memoirs, "was too young to be a companion for me, and much too eccentric, although we were in one class together in postulate theory and I respected the work he did. . . . He was considerably behind the majority of children of his age in social development and social adaptability. I was certainly no model of the social graces; but it was clear to me that no other child of his age would have gone down Brattle Street wildly swinging a pigskin bag, without either order or cleanliness. He was an infant with a full share of the infractuosities of a grown-up Dr. Johnson."

The New York Times had its own, fictional version of the relationship between the two prodigies: "While at Tufts he [William] met and became acquainted with Norbert Wiener. . . . They became fast friends and continue their acquaintance at Harvard, visiting each other occasionally at their homes."

Wiener did not dislike Billy—he liked him well enough. But contrary to the popular opinion of the time, high IQs were not a basis for friendship. Norbert did try to form a "prodigy club" for the five Harvard boys, but had to admit that "the attempt was ridiculous . . . we were not cut from the same piece of cloth." The fact that they were all precocious "was no more a basis for social unity than the wearing of glasses or the possession of false teeth."

Norbert Wiener and Adolf Berle had little more to talk about than Norbert and Sidis did, though they did plot a literary hoax together (planning to "find" a Shakespearean manuscript) and went bowling a few times. It is surprising that Berle and Sidis didn't spend time together, since they had similar bizarre hobbies. "Sidis," Wiener wrote, "had his collection of streetcar transfers to amuse him, and Berle had a fad almost as individual. He was interested in the various underground passages of Boston, such as the subways and the sewers and various forgotten bolt-holes."

Yet Norbert, himself a mathematical prodigy, had not failed to be impressed by Billy's genius. Billy was continuing his special courses in the most advanced mathematics Harvard had to offer, subjects reserved for a handful of seniors. His professor in vector analysis was the only person at Harvard who knew more about the subject than Billy.

At 8:15 P.M. on January 5, 1910, in Conant Hall at Harvard, William James Sidis delivered his celebrated two-hour lecture to the Harvard Mathematical Club. The talk was sponsored by Griffith Evans, one of Harvard's eminent mathematics professors and the son of the Sidis family friend George Evans. Billy arrived accompanied by his father, stepped to the front, and with a childish laugh began to speak. The paper was titled "Four-Dimensional Bodies." As *The New York Times* reported the next day,

> Sidis opened his lecture by saying that he had not expected to be asked to lecture so early in his life, and then easily dropped into the regular arts and methods of the college professor, gestures and all. The easy manner in which, in his discussions, he approached and passed over the word "paralleloppedon" made the professors gasp, and when he began to coin a few words and between breaths slipped out such words as "hecatonicosihedrigon" the president of the society had to open the windows to give the audience more air.
>
> After drawing figures and proving theories until everyone in the room was amazed, young Sidis suddenly glanced at his watch in true platform style and brought his lecture to a close.
>
> Then the professors asked him questions for a half hour. At least some of the unwary ones did, and it was a shame what he did to them. One of his questioners who wore the bow of his dress tie under his ear, the true symbol that he was a professor of mathematics, started to ask some questions and young Sidis, after a rapid-fire explanation of the problem involved, stopped at its conclusion and calmly asked, "Is that any plainer now?"
>
> The undergraduates who attended were in deep water most

of the time and it is doubtful if any of them gained many new ideas. . . . But everyone of them enjoyed two or three hearty chuckles at the sight of his own beloved instructor asking questions and hearing the boy Sidis only joke them gently, but often listening to their supposed apropos questions with raised eyebrows and saying with a rising inflection, "Huh?"

Another writer cited Billy's "lack of respect for older persons. . . . A question was asked, and one of the older professors answered it by explaining in different terms than those the boy had used; whereupon young Sidis turned to him saying: 'I can not see that you have added anything to the discussion.' "

Norbert Wiener remembered the event well, writing forty-three years later, "The talk would have done credit to a first- or second-year graduate student of any age, although all the material it contained was known elsewhere and was available in literature. . . . I am convinced that Sidis had no access to existing sources, and the talk represented the triumph of the unaided efforts of a very brilliant child."

Altogether, ninety-three men were present, representing not only Harvard's finest but distinguished math professors from all over New England. One can only imagine how awestruck they must have been at the rosy-cheeked eleven-year-old in short pants and a red kerchief, the uniform of boys in grade school.

The Math Club lecture spawned a rash of articles and editorials in newspapers all around America; many magazine pieces appeared in publications such as *Harper's Weekly, The Independent,* and *Current Literature.* The *Boston Transcript* christened Billy the intellectual prodigy of the age. The day after the lecture *The New York Times* ran a front-page story, followed the next day by an editorial under the heading "Topics of the Times" that described Boris's educational theories. Letters poured in debating the wisdom of Boris's methods (Sarah was rarely mentioned) and predicting the prodigy's future.

Two days after the lecture, the *Times* ran this poem by one Luran W. Sheldon:

To Get the Fourth Dimension of Space

As understood after reading article headed, 'Boy of Ten Addresses
    Harvard Teachers.'
Take a hecatonicosihedrigon and multiply by four,
A sexicosihedrigon plus half as many more:
Put in some polyhedrigons where gaps suggest a minus
And you'll have a polyhedral-perpendodicahedrinus.

Wilmer C. Powick of New York had a letter published in the
Times under the heading "Sidis an Avatar?": "For some days past I
have been interested in the accounts of young Sidis, the boy prodigy;
also somewhat wearied by the attempts to ascribe his unusual development to some special system of education. The whole thing is fully
explained by the Oriental doctrine of reincarnation, which asserts that
present ability is the result of work done in past earth lives, and that
we are determining to-day our condition in earth lives to come."

Some of the Boston papers were able to get the first-person
reports of people who claimed to have met the child sensation.

Dr. Jessie T. Bogle, a severe, prune-faced woman, claimed to have
met the Sidises through her cousin. A Boston paper told her story with
these ominous headlines:

SHE PITIES PRODIGY WHO NEVER LEARNED TO PLAY
SHE DOUBTS ROSY CHEEKS OF THE LITTLE SIDIS BOY

Remembers Him at Age of Six, a Bespectacled, Thin-Legged
Child, Sprawled on the Floor Beside Fire, Studying Geometry.

Dour Dr. Bogle, who was herself studying the ailments of children, blamed adult mediocrity "in professions or business" on childhood "cramming." She predicted, at best, a nervous breakdown for
little Billy, adding ominously, "There has never been a record kept of
those children who have died of overstudy, but there are many."

Dr. Jessie Bogle admonished any parents who might be inspired by Billy's achievements: "No matter what most parents think about their own particular prodigies, the modern child is neither a John Stuart Mill nor a Macaulay, and its education should begin and end with that fact in mind."

William compared favorably with history's greatest child prodigies. He was in a class apart from the average mathematical prodigy, or "lightning calculators" as they were called. One of the most famous of these was Zerah Colburn, born in Vermont in 1804. When he was six, his surprised parents (who had thought their son a little backward), overheard him muttering multiplication tables though he had had virtually no schooling. The child could perform amazing mental calculations, and his father exhibited him in America and Europe, where the seven-year-old answered such questions as "Can you name the cube root of 413,993,348,677?" Zerah delivered the right answer—7,453—in five seconds. When asked, "Admitting the distance between Concord and Boston to be sixty-five miles, how many steps must I take in going this distance, allowing that I go three feet at a step?" He gave the correct answer—114,400—in ten seconds. The boy insisted that he didn't know how he arrived at his answers, and he was unable to perform even the simplest multiplication and division on paper. By the time he was ten, Zerah began to lose his calculating ability; by adulthood it was gone completely.

Other children performed equally amazing mathematical feats but were backward or even stupid in all other areas. Henri Mondeux, an illiterate sheeptender's son, taught himself arithmetic by playing with pebbles. When presented to the Paris Academy of Science at the age of fourteen, Henri was asked, "How many minutes are there in fifty-two years?" After a few moments' thought he correctly answered, "Fifty-two years of 365 days each are composed of 27,331,200 minutes and of 1,639,872,000 seconds."

Jacques Inaudi, the famous Italian wunderkind, was born in 1867. At seven, he could name the day of the week on which a given date fell (one of Billy Sidis's abilities). He exhibited this skill in Europe and

America along with his mathematical abilities, which included multiplying five figures by five figures in his head.

Like Sidis, many prodigies had photographic memories. Antonio da Marco Magliabechi, born in Italy in 1633, read with extraordinary speed and recall. Once, after reading a manuscript, the boy wrote it out in its entirety without missing a comma. When he was asked for a certain rare volume, Antonio replied, "There is but one copy in the world; and that is in the Grand Signor's library in Constantinople, where it is the seventh book on the second shelf on the right hand as you go in."

Though most prodigies are limited to a single talent, William Sidis ranked with the handful who are well rounded and acquainted with the principles underlying their studies. One of the most famous such prodigies died in childhood. Christian Friedrich Heinecken, born in 1721 in Germany, was known throughout Europe as the Infant of Lübeck. It was said that when he was a year old he knew basic mathematics and all of the main events in the Bible. At three he was conversant with world history and geography and knew Latin and French. Shortly after an audience with the King of Denmark, Christian fell ill. He died at the age of four, soon after predicting his own death.

Billy Sidis was often compared to one of the greatest mathematicians in history, Carl Friedrich Gauss—born in Germany in 1777—who ranked beside Archimedes and Newton. Gauss's circumstances could hardly have been more different from Billy's. His father was a poor, uncouth laborer who had no interest in raising a prodigy. It was with reluctance that he allowed his amazing son to be educated; he had wanted him to be a gardener or a bricklayer. Gauss's mother was proud of her son, but only his uncle encouraged the growth of the boy's mind. At three Gauss showed his precocity, correcting his father's payroll computations. He soon coaxed his parents into revealing the letters of the alphabet, then taught himself to read. In adulthood, he liked to joke that he knew how to reckon before he could talk. Possessed of a brilliant gift for swift calculation, and the photographic memory so common to prodigies, Gauss stunned his teachers and flew through school. He soon mastered classical languages, literature, and philosophy. Gauss's adulthood was a series of intellectual triumphs in both pure and applied mathematics and astronomy. What set him apart from so many prodigies (and caused Sidis-watchers to compare the two) was his spectacular ability to reason, to grasp principles, and to invent solutions to problems.

Of all the child prodigies in history, though, one bears the most interesting comparison with Billy Sidis: John Stuart Mill, the renowned philosopher and economist. Mill was born in London in 1806, the son of the historian-economist-philosopher James Mill, who, like Boris Sidis, set out to educate his son according to his own theories. Those theories were similar to the Sidises'; cramming a child's mind full of facts was anathema, stressing the value of reason and understanding was paramount. But the methods were vastly different. James Mill was a harsh, severe authoritarian who constantly criticized his wife and children.

John Mill's classical education began at three utilizing a method commonly used today but unknown in 1809—flash cards. His father wrote common Greek words with their English meanings on cards, and displayed them next to the actual things they represented. When John had mastered Greek vocabulary, he was given Aesop's fables to translate (like Sarah Sidis, James Mill did not approve of fairy tales). Little John was soon reading heady material in voluminous quantities. Occasionally he was allowed a break from Plato, and then he would devour *Robinson Crusoe*. By the time he was eight he was writing steadily, reading Latin, and teaching his younger siblings—a task he hated, for he was accountable to his father for their failures. Mathematics followed, along with strict instruction in rhetoric and elocution. James Mill kept his son to a tight schedule, spending fully four hours each day working with him apart from the seven hours a day John studied alone.

John was kept away from boys his own age, and he knew nothing of sports or games, prompting him to remark in later life, "I never was a boy." John would eventually attribute to this lack of contact with other boys his physical awkwardness, lack of manual dexterity, and general lameness in dealing with the practical aspects of daily life.

Surpassing even Leo Wiener in his sarcasm and relentless demands on his son, James Mill was the ultimate "creator parent." He ruled his brood through fear, demanding the impossible and losing his temper when John did not perform up to his standard. James Mill wrote to his friend Jeremy Bentham, "If I were to die any time before this poor boy is a man, one of the things that would pinch me most sorely, would be the being obliged to leave his mind unmade to the degree of excellence of which I hope to make it."

James Mill showed his son no tenderness or love, and John's mother was wrapped up in domestic chores. John wrote in his famous *Autobiography,* "I thus grew up in the absence of love and in the presence of fear." The constant criticism left John with the feeling that he was a backward child who failed repeatedly.

Small wonder then that when James Mill took his fourteen-year-old son for a walk in Hyde Park, the boy was shocked to be told that he was a prodigy. His father had carefully guarded him from all praise, and John never knew that he was in any way unusual. James Mill now enlightened the boy, at the same time telling him that he was to take no credit for his abilities. It had merely been John's good fortune to have such an unusual father, one willing to take so much time and trouble over him. In sum, James Mill said, John should feel no pride when he knew more than others, only shame when he did not.

Since John had no sense that he was special, he was surprised to find that people who had known him as a child had found him conceited. He wrote that this must have been because he was "disputatious," never hesitating to argue. In this he was much like William Sidis. Mill claimed no one had ever planted in him the "usual respect" for adults. "My father did not correct this ill-breeding and impertinence." Like Sidis, Mill could be dogmatic, a logical arguing machine with no sense of social graces. Like Sidis, he was unconcerned with his manners and appearance.

John Stuart Mill dutifully performed the tasks of a prodigy: He wrote voluminously and effectively, he spoke impressively in debating societies. But in 1826, at the age of twenty, he broke down. He fell into a state of intense depression, a gloom so grim that he intended to commit suicide if he could not conquer it in a year. Mill's nervous breakdown has been the subject of much speculation and analysis, with most biographers attributing it to the severe nervous strain he had been under since infancy and his suppressed feelings of rebellion toward his father. He told no one about his condition, and continued with the affairs of his daily life. Years later, he wrote this touching passage: "If I had loved anyone sufficiently to make confiding my griefs a necessity, I should not have been in the condition I was. I felt, too, that mine was not an interesting, or in any way respectable distress. Advice, if I had known where to seek it, would have been most precious. . . . My father, to whom it would have been natural to me to have recourse in any practical difficulties, was the last person to whom, in such a case as this, I looked for help. . . . My education, which was wholly his work, had been conducted without any regard to the possibility of its ending in this result; and I saw no use in giving him the pain of thinking that his plans had failed."

Mill's depression lasted for six months. He conquered it with the mighty resolve to reject his father's joyless, utilitarian outlook and to strive for the experience and expression of his emotions—long suppressed—as well as his intellect. He found his greatest inspiration and relief in the poetry of Wordsworth.

John Stuart Mill went on to lead an influential life as a thinker and reformer, having thrown off to some extent the yoke of his father's training. In his *Autobiography,* he is equivocal about the effects of his education. Though he did not love his father, he wrote, "I was always loyally devoted to him. As regards my own education, I hesitate to pronounce whether I was more a gainer or a loser by his severity." Elsewhere, he took a stronger stand, saying that he owed all he had accomplished to his early training, which gave him "an advantage of a quarter of a century over my contemporaries." Like his father, and like Boris and Sarah Sidis, he insisted that any normal child could duplicate his intellectual feats.

At first glance the similarities between Mill and William Sidis may seem few: Boris was never the cruel taskmaster that James Mill was. But William, like John Mill, was to experience a crisis, and at nearly the same age; and William's trauma, like Mill's, would be resolved by a separation from the bondage of parental expectations. Is this merely the crisis of any adolescent? Perhaps. But John Stuart Mill and William James Sidis were two of history's most extraordinary youths, their lives extreme, overblown versions of what millions of ordinary adolescents have experienced. They were both products of well-intentioned parents who saw their children's achievements as extensions of their own success, whose children were their achievements to an exceptional degree.

For William Sidis, it was Sarah rather than Boris who increasingly began to take on the oppressive role, who drove him further and further into the exercises of the mind and its manifold pleasures as an escape.

5
Utopian Dreams

Immediately after the Math Club lecture William came down with flu. He was so newsworthy that his runny nose merited two stories in a single edition of *The New York Times,* one of them on the front page:

SIDIS, BOY PRODIGY, ILL
Attacked with Grip After
His Lecture on "The Fourth Dimension"

. . . The boy caught cold, and as he is frail and of an extremely nervous temperament, he took to his bed. It is thought that he will recover in another week or two, though he is gaining more slowly than the average boy. He had been weakened recently by overstudy in connection with a Latin and Greek grammar, which he was writing in addition to carrying on his work at Harvard.

On page eight, a longer story of a more sinister cast:

YOUNG SIDIS SUFFERS A BREAKDOWN

From Boston comes the news—sure to excite a loud chorus of "I told you so!"—that young Sidis, the marvelous boy of Harvard, the astonishing product of a new and better system of education, has broken down from overwork and is now in a state of nervous prostration seriously alarming his family and friends. [If this report was not an exaggeration] the Sidis method . . . is fatally bad and the inventor stands condemned of something worse than failure.

But it is not yet time to reach a conclusion. Young Sidis's breakdown may be due less to the ardor of his studying or the extent of his precocious attainments than to the morbid excitements and excessive attention to which he has been subjected ever since he leaped into fame as a result of his lecture. . . .

It is not improbable that these people [Boris and Sarah] have pestered the child into a condition of psychasthenia that had nothing at all to do with his work, and that the mistake was not in teaching or letting him learn too much, but in not protecting him from the wearisome exclamations and admirations of injudicious observers.

Indeed, no one had shielded William from the enormous publicity that attended his lecture. Reporters dogged his every step, pried into his personal life, pressured him to behave wondrously and perform marvels on command. Had his parents been wiser, they would have begun long ago to guard him from the detestable reporters. Now it was almost too late: The juggernaut of his fame was careening too wildly to be stopped. Boris told Billy about a time-honored method for dealing with reporters. "I have developed the perfect technique for handling these young men of the press, and it is unfortunate that you are too young to use it. They come to interview me, and I start them talking about themselves. I interview them. They go away in a glow, look me up in a newspaper morgue or in *Who's Who,* and write a nice story about me."

Billy was too young to manage such a stunt. He may have been a genius, but he was not an adult emotionally. Furthermore, at least one of his character traits was already completely formed: He was an honest, straightforward boy, with not an iota of the ability to charm by manipulation. Public attention was wearing him down, and he had no notion of how to keep it at bay.

The day after the "nervous breakdown" article appeared, *The New York Times* incredibly ran a third:

FEAR IS FELT FOR SIDIS
Harvard's Boy Scientist May Never
Resume His University Work

William James Sidis . . . is still confined to the house. There are rumors in Cambridge that he will never return to his studies. His illness has been officially declared to be a severe attack of grip, but friends of the family have asserted that too great mental exertion has had a great deal to do with the boy's sudden collapse.

"My son is getting along all right," said his father, Dr. Boris Sidis . . . "but I am not prepared to say when he will be able to return to his studies." Dr. Sidis has been consistently non-commital [*sic*] regarding the boy's illness, and has refused indignantly to discuss his son's mental condition.

Indeed, William did not return to school for several months. And by the time he did, the damage was done. It was widely believed that he had had a nervous breakdown, and when he returned to Harvard he was more of an anomaly than ever. From then on, any vacation William took was suspected to be evidence of another breakdown. The students whispered behind his back. These rumors were impossible to correct—the newspapers fed them gleefully, since they provided them with delicious copy rife with righteous choruses of I-told-you-so's. Boris made a feeble, ineffectual attempt to clear up the matter when he addressed the Harvard Summer School Association and said, "Mental labor never results in nervous prostration; it is rather the lack of interest that causes a nervous breakdown." He did not speak directly about his son, and did nothing more to correct the rumor that was to dog William Sidis for the rest of his life.

William had taken only one course his first term at Harvard: advanced mathematics. Curiously, he received a mere B. He was having the same problem he'd had in grade school and high school—he was too smart. When lessons were slow for him, William just couldn't sit quietly while his fellow students, all twenty-year-olds, sweated and struggled. In the words of one journalist, "In a class at Harvard where a formula was being explained the boy became bored and began to entertain himself by balancing his hat upside down on his head. This so distracted the rest of the class that he was asked to refrain. When asked to remain after class he said he couldn't do it; so the class was excused ten minutes early and the professor made an effort to have the youth see that he had no right to do anything which interfered with the best conditions for the whole class. But the boy would not see it in that light, and would only say, 'My father never told me that.' To him, it was merely an infringement upon his rights."

Billy could not seem to understand that the "greatest intellect of the age" should not balance his hat upside down on his head in class. He believed he had a right to do as he pleased, provided he didn't hurt anyone else. The concept of individual liberty fascinated him, particularly in its application to politics. Some of William's early political thoughts appeared in newsprint. One Boston paper ran this story:

HARVARD'S BOY WONDER WOULD CURB TRUSTS
Eleven-Year-Old W. J. Sidis Discusses
Relation of Gold Output to High Cost of Living

Looking at it from a purely scientific and businesslike point of view, I agree with Professor Fisher of Yale, and Professor T. N. Carver, of Harvard, that the gold output had much to do with bringing on the present situation. But looking at it from the point of view of humanity this explanation offers but little solace to the man with an empty stomach and hungry family.

The present big combinations ... know no law or humanity in their attempt to line their pocketbooks at the expense of their less fortunate brothers.

A financial panic is bound to come and very shortly, too, unless the Government steps in and brings to an abrupt stop the depredations of these so-called trusts and adopts drastic measures to prevent them from future lawless feeding on the resources of the whole people.

While most eleven-year-olds were playing with train sets, William Sidis was theorizing about the economy and the fourth dimension. Over the next few years, the increasing breadth of his interests continued to set William apart from other prodigies—from politics to mathematics, languages to astronomy, streetcars to anatomy—it appeared that William was rapidly becoming a one-of-a-kind prodigy.

At age thirteen, he composed an ode to the opening of the Cambridge-to-Boston subway. While public transit is certainly an odd choice of topic for verse, it must be remembered that the opening of the Boston subway was a much more important event than the average person today can imagine. Around 1913, only one in a hundred Americans had a car—and only two Harvard students out of a student body of 700.

Buckminster Fuller, who entered Harvard that year, remembered the event sixty-nine years later as "the most fundamentally indicative of the technical changes occurring in the human environment. . . . It took only seven minutes to reach Park Street, Boston (then the end of that line). This was phenomenal . . . as compared to my grandfather's and father's all-day trips from Cambridge to Boston by horse and buggy or on foot. . . . I was tempted by and frequently sought entrance into the new age. I invented the HCKP Club, named for the Boston-bound subway's terminals and way stations—Harvard, Central, Kendall, and Park." Fuller and William Sidis crossed paths only briefly at Harvard. Had they known each other better they might have made fast friends, with their passionate shared interest in rapid transit. Certainly Fuller's HCKP Club was the only Harvard club that could possibly have interested—or accepted—an oddity like William.

Meanwhile, Billy was writing a serious political document, a constitution for a utopian society dubbed "Hesperia." Fifty densely typed pages, consisting of "eight articles, fifty-nine sections, and five hundred and eighty-four provisions," are written in a legalese so ponderous one would think only a certified lawyer could have produced it. Billy was becoming as fluent in the lingo of the law as he was in Greek, Russian, or Armenian.

Structurally, Billy's paper utopia is reminiscent of the United States Constitution. Philosophically, it is a complete departure from the vision of the founding fathers. Billy's best of all possible worlds emerges as rigidly totalitarian, though he never uses that term.

Nor did he explain why he named his utopia Hesperia. In both Latin and Greek, Hesperia refers to western lands—to the ancient Greeks, this meant Italy; and later, to the Romans, it meant Spain or regions beyond. The word was adopted into English, and came to be a poetic term for any idyllic, western locale. Its root word, *hesperos,* is Greek for "the evening star." Billy was evidently indulging in a little word play—*sidus* is Latin for "star," "constellation," and "heavenly body," as well as "fame," "glory," and "destiny."

Like any constitution worthy of the name, Hesperia's begins with a preamble:

We, the people of Hesperia, desiring that the law should allow full personal liberty to every person in all cases where the personal property rights of others are not violated, and wishing to organize a government to the end that this liberty may be better obtained, do hereby form the Community of Hesperia and establish this Constitution therefor.

After this rather ordinary start, the eccentricity developed in true Sidis style. The Constitution, we are told, was completed "on this twenty-ninth of November in this year of the solar calendar one thousand nine hundred and fifty-eight, at thirty minutes after twenty-two o'clock." Next is the legal definition of a day in Hesperia—it contains twenty-four hours, ends at midnight, and so on. Hesperian weeks are not so conventional. Instead of seven-day slices, Hesperia has five-day "quintads," its days being named Primo, Altro, Trito, Quarto, and Quinto. Considerable space is devoted to the laws governing the proper construction of calendars and to naming the legal holidays—two of Billy's childhood obsessions that persisted into adolescence.

After these basics are set forth, an Orwellian tone begins to tinge the laws. Each inhabitant of Hesperia is designated a "name-number," odd for men and even for women. Billy signed the Constitution, in his still-childish scrawl, "C Forty-One," for reasons that remain obscure—it is unlikely that he had recruited forty Hesperian pilgrims from among his Harvard classmates.

It was not easy to become a citizen of Billy's utopia—naturalization policies were severe. A visitor who violated even a single law was ineligible for citizenship. Nor was being law-abiding enough—an aspirant to Hesperian citizenship had to pass an intelligence test, proving his familiarity with the Constitution's laws and his ability to read and write English. Beyond these stipulations, the contents of this important test remain murky. Billy wrote: "The term 'intelligence test' shall denote any means whatever for finding out the amount of particular specified kinds of information or of reasoning ability, or both, possessed by a person."

In order to vote one took an expanded test, which required knowledge of still more laws. Any citizen who couldn't pass the voting intelligence test was called a minor. Along with minors, "idiots and insane persons" were barred from voting.

Elections in Hesperia are quirky. Anyone could nominate themselves for an office "and all voluntary candidates shall file a motto of not more than fifteen words expressing what they intend to do if elected, said motto being placed on the ballot below the name of the candidate who filed it."

Billy's totalitarian learnings showed themselves throughout the Constitution. When a citizen dies, his property becomes that of "the Government of the Community." Virtually everyone works in a Government Union—there are unions of every imaginable trade and occupation. All goods produced by an employee are therefore government property. Should a citizen start his own business, he risks losing it at a whim of the Government, which is empowered to "buy any business which profits the owner." In return, the Government must pay the former owner forty times the average yearly net profit the business had earned. The employees are then required to join the appropriate union, where they are paid on a sliding scale in Government-issued "labor certificates," the purpose of the sliding scale being to reward good work with higher pay.

Other attempts at free enterprise are doomed to failure in Hesperia: the Government of the Community receives 80 percent of the royalties on a patented invention. Authors fare better than scientists, since they are allowed to retain 70 percent of their own royalties. If the Government approves an instructional book of any kind, the author may apply to the Government for a job teaching his specialty. Presumably, authors of novels or books of subway poetry receive no such privileges.

Throughout the Constitution Billy vents his spleen at his favorite peeve, religion. Having long ago decided upon atheism, he remained as irascible as his father on the subject. "Religious beliefs," he asserted, "are defined as beliefs, opinions, or creeds, which are in any way dogmatic or otherwise authoritative or which are in any way to be taken on faith or otherwise without criticism." Billy does not discuss the separation of church and state in his constitution, since churches are simply not recognized. In the courtroom, religious beliefs provide no defense for a criminal.

Here and there, in the midst of the dense field of provisions, articles, and bylaws, the occasional peculiar Sidisism pops up:

The legislature is empowered to make laws "to prevent explosions of any unreasonable noise or disagreeable smell."

Out of the blue it is written: "No titles of nobility shall be granted by the Community of Hesperia."

Also, no law could regulate the choice of dress, except for prison uniforms and certain Union workers, who were required to wear "special Union badges, not to be more than thirty centimeters in height nor more than twenty centimeters in width."

And there is the irresistibly odd Article 3 of Section IV, which states simply, "No person shall be compelled by law to do impossibilities."

By far the strangest articles in the Constitution of Hesperia are those pertaining to sex, marriage, and the family. In William Sidis's utopia, marriage is forbidden. No legal contracts between couples are binding, there is no community property, polygamy is completely legal.

What is more, the Government has the right to prevent cohabitation provided "one of the parties is insane or criminal, or has not proper health conditions." Those with "improper conditions"— venereal diseases—are dealt with in the following extraordinary manner:

> for such cases the men and women shall be placed in separate portions of the reserved land, the persons quarantined shall be excluded from cohabitation, and the Physicians' Union shall be authorized to make such operations of any of such persons operated on incapable of producing a birth.

Billy's medieval solution to the problem of venereal disease was not motivated by sadism, but by naïveté. As he played happily at the vast game of creating rules for utopia, the citizens of utopia were only so many ants to be dealt with in whatever way best served the state. That enforced sterilization is inhumane probably never crossed Billy's mind as he fit together the pieces of his jigsaw puzzle.

This blindness is even more clearly illustrated in the Constitution's dictates about child rearing:

All minors shall, at some age less than eighteen months which may be specified by the Legislature, be given to the individual charge of some member of the Guardians' Union, assigned in such a manner as the Board of Trade may provide.

Male children shall be assigned to the charge of male guardians, and female children to the charge of female guardians.

To qualify for the Guardians' Union, one must have had experience caring for and training children, and "have a knowledge of subjects in general somewhat more than that required for the intelligence test for voting." The child's blood mother receives a "birth payment" for two years; guardians receive housing and salary for raising children, in addition to their regular Union wages. Minors also receive an allowance from the Government.

It is the guardian's job to take full charge of his minor and to prepare him to pass the intelligence test for voting. The teaching of religious beliefs to minors is strictly forbidden. Minors are not required to perform any services for their guardians, and the guardians are not allowed "to use authority in any way." Dissatisfied minors may apply for a change of guardian. When a minor has passed the voting test (apparently this can be done at any age—child prodigies are allowed in Hesperia) or when his guardian has vouched for his ability to pass it, the minor is entitled to eight years of free education and/or trade school.

Not surprisingly, Billy's laws concerning sex crimes are eccentric.

For example, "Any person who forces a man and a woman to cohabit . . . shall be punished by imprisonment for six years." If a man rapes a woman, the punishment is the same. On the other hand, "Any woman who cohabits or attempts to cohabit with a man without his consent shall be punished by imprisonment for three years, and, in the case of a birth resulting therefrom, shall be deprived of the right to draw the regular disability insurance or birth payment . . . the child shall not be deprived of any money or other privileges."

So strong are Billy's feelings on the subject of marriage that he cannot resist a parting salvo in his Constitution, an adamant, officious summing-up to protect future generations from the horrors of the nuclear family. From the height of his eleven-year-old soapbox, he pronounces:

> 7. No amendments shall be passed before the year of the solar calendar two thousand one hundred which shall in any way or manner make valid any agreements for cohabitation of a man with a woman, or which shall in any way or manner affect, change, or alter the fifth clause of Section VIII of the third Article of this Constitution, or which shall in any way regulate or restrict or authorize the regulation or restriction of cohabitation of a man with a woman except as mentioned in clauses 19, 20, and 21 of Section VII of the second Article and in clause 13 of Section VII of the third Article of this Constitution.

In Billy Sidis's utopia, there would be no binding agreements between the sexes, no shared property, no nuclear family. Boys like Billy would not be subjected to bothersome mothers, as long as there were male guardians to replace them. In utopia, there is no Harvard University, where proud parents could send their brilliant children. And presumably, in utopia, there are no reporters.

By 1911, William was teetering on the edge of his endurance to public exposure. The average thirteen-year-old is awkward enough. William, constantly in the spotlight against his will, was more so. During this crucial period, the time of Billy's delicate adolescence, Boris made a foolish move. He published a book that drew even more attention to his son. The controversial work, *Philistine and Genius,* was a scathing indictment of institutional education. Using his son as an illustration of his theories, Boris urged parents to teach their children themselves, rather than subject them to the dulling routines of the classroom. The message was strong, motivated by Boris's profound social conscience; but in his determination to present his theories to the world, he ignored any damage he might do to his son. Now Billy appeared even more a guinea pig.

The book caused a sensation. It was virulent and unrelenting in its criticism of every facet of grade school, high school, and university education. The present-day school system, railed Boris, should be abolished completely, America should be rid of "petty bureaucrats animated with a hatred towards talent and genius," "the goody-goody school ma'am," and "the educator with his pseudo-scientific pseudo-psychological pseudogogics. . . . Never in the history of mankind have teachers fallen to such a low level of mediocrity as in our times and in our country. . . . The time is at hand when we shall be justified in writing over the gates of our school-shops, 'Mediocrity made here!' " Even worse than the system's fostering of mediocrity was its suppression of genius. "We should remember that there is genius in every healthy, normal child. . . . Like savages, we are afraid of genius, especially when it is manifested as 'precocity in children.' " Boris charged that schools regarded genius as a disruptive element. Educators expelled brilliant pupils because their presence upset the status quo.

Quoting John Stuart Mill, Boris implored parents to "aim at something noble." Regarding exactly how children could be raised to fulfill their latent nobility, *Philistine and Genius* was less specific than readers might have wished. However, Boris did lay down some basic guidelines:

Children should be taught early the difference between good and evil. Reality should never be obfuscated: The child's critical judgment and the courage of his convictions are paramount values.

Fairy tales were a pet peeve of Boris and Sarah's, promoting, they felt, a belief in the unreal and the mystical and making of the child's soul "a dunghill full of superstitions and fear." There should be no "jingles and gibberish, memorization of Mother Goose wisdom, repetition of incomprehensible prayers and articles of creed, unintelligent aping of good manners, silly games, and fears of the supernatural."

The most controversial question to be answered, of course, was when to begin teaching the child. The crucial period, Boris claimed, was between the second and third years. "To delay is a mistake and a wrong to the child." The child who is badgering his parents with constant questions (no matter how embarrassing) should be indulged completely. "Nothing should be suppressed and tabooed as too sacred for examination."

"We claim we are afraid to force the child's mind. We claim we are afraid to strain his brain prematurely. This is an error. In directing the course of the use of the child's energies we do not force the child. If you do not direct the energies in the right course, the child will waste them in the wrong direction. . . .

"We do not care to develop a love of knowledge in their early life for fear of brain injury, and then when it is too late to acquire the interest, we force them to study, and we cram them and feed them like geese. What you often get is fatty degeneration of the mental liver."

"The wrong direction" was that of "meaningless games and objectless sports." If Boris hated fairy tales, he detested "silly games." If he detested games, he despised sports. "The brutalities of football and prize-fights" were his greatest bugaboo, lowering Americans to the level of bloodthirsty spectators at a Roman circus.

Finally, Boris stressed avoiding routines and habits, cultivating variety. In this way the child's reserve energy would be stimulated. Ultimately, proper training could produce "a great race of geniuses, with powers of rational control of their latent, potential reserve energy."

Without mentioning William by name, *Philistine and Genius* described a boy "brought up in the love and enjoyment of knowledge for its own sake." After listing many of the boy's accomplishments, Boris concluded:

At the age of twelve the boy has a fair understanding of comparative philology and mythology. He is well versed in logic, ancient history, American history and has a general insight into our politics and the groundwork of our Constitution. At the same time he is of extremely happy disposition, brimming over with humor and fun.

His physical condition is splendid, his cheeks glow with health. Many a girl would envy his complexion. Being above five feet four he towers above the average boy of his age. His physical constitution, weight, form and hardihood of organs far surpasses that of the ordinary schoolboy. He looks like a boy of sixteen. He is healthy, strong and sturdy.

In an angry tirade Boris refuted the accusations that the boy had had a nervous breakdown, ranting about those conditions he felt do cause children to "crack": "No doubt, the cramming, the routine, the mental and moral tyranny of the principal and school-superintendent do tend to nervous degeneracy and mental break-down. Poor old college owls, academic barn-yard-fowls and worn out sickly school-bats, you are panic-stricken by the power of sunlight, you are in agonizing, in mortal terror of critical, reflective thought, you dread and suppress the genius of the young."

In a veiled reference to William, Boris went so far as to admonish college professors who "expel promising students from the lecture-room for 'the good of the class as a whole,' because the students happen to handle their hats in the middle of a lecture."

Naturally, readers and reviewers recognized the son in the father's prose—Boris was by now more famous as William's father than he was for his own pioneering work. Sarah reflected forty years later: "Boris pulled down upon his stout head, and upon Billy who was so very young, the anger that comes from hurt pride. Educators, psychologists, editorial writers and newspaper readers were furious with him. And their fury was a factor in Billy's life upon which we had not counted."

The publication of *Philistine and Genius* was not the only thing to put Boris's name in the papers. Another remarkable event occurred in the Sidises' busy lives, bringing them into the public eye.

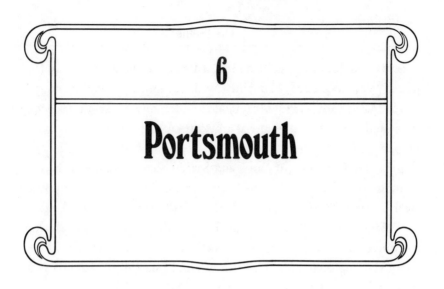

6

Portsmouth

With Boris's growing reputation and prosperity had come an office on Beacon Hill and a burgeoning clientele that included several prestigious, wealthy citizens come to shed their neuroses, among them Martha Jones, the widow of an ale baron. Frank Jones, a rags-to-riches multimillionaire, had owned most of Portsmouth, New Hampshire. In the manner of J. P. Morgan and Rockefeller, Jones had built a financial empire out of nothing. He owned booming businesses and hotels all over New England, but it was his brewery that was the foundation of his fortune. When he died in 1902, he left an estate valued at more than five million dollars.

According to Helena Sidis, her father had successfully treated the entire Jones family, who were all "very nervous." One of these grateful patients was Jones's granddaughter, Mrs. Buck Whittemore, a Bostonian who socialized frequently with the Sidises. One evening in 1909, Martha Jones and her granddaughter offered an unsuspecting Boris and Sarah a unique gift as an expression of their appreciation— Maplewood Farms, the fabulous late-Victorian family estate in New Hampshire. The estate, if Boris and Sarah accepted it, was to become a unique sanctuary for patients beset with nervous ills, run entirely on Boris's principles. Nothing of the kind had ever existed in America.

After making their offer, the hostesses left Boris and Sarah alone to confer. Boris was adamant: "I will not take it. What do I know about running such a place? When would I find time to read or work or study if I had this big elephant to think of? What a headache it would be!"

Sarah, who moments before had "felt like Cinderella when her fairy godmother turned the pumpkin into a coach," was crushed by her husband's obstinacy. Despondent, she gave the morose verdict to Mrs. Whittemore and Mrs. Jones. But the ladies would not take no for an answer. They gave Sarah a rousing pep talk, appealing to her boundless energy. "We know you, you can run it and never bother him. You can make a marvelous place for him to work and study, you can do it." Still cowed by Boris's reaction, Sarah wanted to know how many servants Frank Jones had required to run the estate. The task appeared to be financially beyond her. The Sidises had but six hundred dollars in the bank.

"Sixty-five," replied Mrs. Whittemore. "But I'll show you how to run it with five. Let your husband stay in Boston for a month, and I'll teach you everything."

Sarah returned to the dubious Boris and implored him to accept the estate, promising he need never give a moment's thought to running it. Finally, Boris relented on one condition. "You will really give me your solemn word that I will never be bothered by it for one second?"

Maplewood Farms was deeded to the Sidises for one dollar. They were to remain in Portsmouth for fifteen years.

The donation of the estate was a newsworthy event. The newspapers called it "a sanitarium to cure the blues," alternately describing Boris as "a psychological savant" and as "the father of the twelve-year-old prodigy"; and for one brief period, father and son were equally renowned.

The purpose of the sanatorium, Boris told the press, was to treat a few of the "thousands upon thousands of persons in New England who are neither sane nor insane, neither well nor sick in the strict interpretation of these terms. These are cases of people who are not actually insane, but who are on the verge of that condition. As things are now, such cases are often sent to an insane asylum of a hospital." The papers were intrigued by his plan "to treat persons who are suffering from obsessions and insistent ideas, in other words, persons who are hobby-ridden." Boris announced his intention to begin with a dozen patients, confident that more would follow since "slight mental troubles are probably the most frequent of all American afflictions."

The first advertisement for the sanatorium ran in a 1910 issue of the *Journal of Abnormal Psychology*:

DR. SIDIS' MAPLEWOOD FARMS
For the Treatment of Nervous Patients Only

Under the personal care of DR. BORIS SIDIS, applying his special psychopathological and clinical methods of examination, observation, and treatment.

Beautiful grounds, private parks, rare trees, greenhouses, sun parlors, palatial rooms, luxuriously furnished home-like surroundings, own milk supply and vegetables.

One hour and a half from North Station, Boston, Mass.

An attractive fifteen-page pamphlet was printed, featuring pictures of the estate's thirty acres of fabulous ponds, statuary, and ornate interiors, and "a large, beautiful solarium for nervous patients." It also promised crisp New Hampshire air, ocean views, and the magnificent White Mountains; a superb collection of flora and fauna, including trees imported from around the world; miles of walks spotted with ponds, fountains, and summer houses. What rich nervous patient could have resisted such a haven? Small wonder that Sarah, so recently a peasant in backwoods Russia, felt like Cinderella.

Explaining his form of treatment in the pamphlet, Boris was nebulous as usual, promising "the latest methods" and "hygienic and dietetic regulation, electrotherapy and hydrotherapy." A patient could go to Maplewood Farms to be cured of fears and anxieties, disturbances of memory, or psychosomatic maladies of the heart, stomach, intestines, or any other internal organ. The pamphlet concluded on a strikingly modern note: "The Sidis Psychopathic Institute has about it little of the atmosphere of the hospital. Full privacy is given to the patient, who can have the feeling of life in a country house, combined with the rest, care, and medical attendance afforded by a modern psychotherapeutic hospital and health resort."

The Institute readily attracted applicants, but Boris had decided to take on only eight or nine patients at a time. He wished to devote himself to each one, have time to enjoy their company and still leave himself leisure for research and writing. Boris chose carefully. Portsmouth was his home, and if a patient didn't fit in, he would be treated in Boston instead. Only rarely was a patient turned out once admitted. Recalled Helena, "My father was very selective. He had his choice— or no one. He took people of above-average intelligence—he did not like stupid people. I never really knew any nuts until I got out in the world."

Naturally, treatment at the Institute was costly, upward of fifty to one hundred dollars a week for a minimum of four weeks. But Boris's patients could easily afford it, and while he always had his pick of wealthy applicants, he often accepted a patient he liked free of charge. He was forever adding to the list of people who didn't have to pay and absentmindedly neglecting to charge those who could, much to his wife's dismay. His free-treatment list included professors, students, and again, numerous priests and rabbis.

The Institute sported a colorful collection of characters. Mixed in with the nervous rabbis and students was a dazzling array of the nervous rich. All of the Sidises' living relatives are reluctant to disclose the names of Boris's patients—but all say they were powerful, famous, influential, "leaders of the world." Sarah fondly remembered learning the stock market from patients who were nationally known brokers and bankers, and the dinner conversation with writers, historians, teachers, and philosophers was bracing. One nephew, Jack Goldwyn, remembered the visits of Dr. Herbert T. Kalmus, the man who invented the Technicolor process. Said Goldwyn, "He used to see Boris occasionally. He would always bring him a box of cigars and in it he'd put a couple of hundred dollar bills. And my aunt Sarah used to see that it was properly cared for. She was the brains. They had the leading minds of the country visiting them." Many of Boris's patients, once cured, remained devoted friends and returned to Portsmouth as guests.

In addition to patients and visiting friends, a steady stream of relatives rolled through. All of the members of Sarah's huge family had by then emigrated to the United States and had families of their own. Even in Brookline, Sarah had thrived on guests, and now she opened the gates of Portsmouth to her favorite siblings, nephews, nieces, and cousins.

One and all, they were awestruck by the splendor of Portsmouth. Waxing fondly about his visits, Jack Goldwyn remembered "carpets that were almost up to your knees. We used to have our own cows and would make buttermilk; all kinds of fruits. A solarium with thick glass, about fifty feet tall. If Aunt Sarah had had a hundred people, she couldn't have kept it up! Forty-four rooms and fourteen bathrooms! She usually had only one maid and one guy outside, and a cook." Another nephew, William Fadiman, said, "It had one of the most beautiful greenhouses I've ever seen. Enormous. It had a grass tennis court—elegant in those days. Five or ten acres of walks. Lovely

[87]

croquet grounds. The bedrooms had gold-leafed ceilings, they were not gilded. The beds were enormous. It was a palace of its kind."

The relatives' feelings about the Sidises were mixed. Certainly they had "made good" in an extraordinary way, and were a source of pride to the Mandelbaums. While most of Sarah's relatives were living typically impoverished immigrant lives, struggling to eat and to go to college, Boris and Sarah had achieved the highest academic honors, lived in a magical mansion, and hobnobbed with patients and friends who wore fur coats and drove steam-powered cars. Recalling his first visit, nephew Clifton Fadiman, later to become a well-known author and celebrity, said, "We were overwhelmed that three regular meals a day were served!" Naturally, Billy's fame and achievements were a source of family pride as well, although privately some of the relatives nurtured their doubts. They speculated that his upbringing had made him into a freak and no good would come of it. Others were jealous as they watched their own sons and daughters go through the normal paces of childhood. What misgivings they had about Billy they kept to themselves.

William and Clifton Fadiman, the sons of Sarah's sister Bessie, came up from Brookline to stay at Portsmouth on several occasions. Clifton Fadiman described his family's attitude toward his aunt and uncle: "Our relationship with the Sidises was a peculiar one for this reason—we stood in great awe of them. Because we understood that Boris was a good friend of William James. Our curiosity was largely the curiosity that poor people have about rich people. We were kind of proud of having such oddities in the family. They made good and he was a poor professor and they had this strange child. . . . And in a way we boasted about it. After all, we had nothing else to boast about. Having distinguished relatives of this sort awed us. There was a lot of family conversation about Billy—'What will this poor Billy do now?' and so forth.

"Sarah was disliked by the whole family, but maybe because she was rich and all the rest of us were poor. But I think they disliked her because she had no kindness in her. She was one of five sisters, and the others, like my mother, were simple, kindly people. Whereas Sarah was an imperialist. My mother and Sarah disliked each other, though my mother, who was a pacific person, would never get into a fury of rage about it. She just didn't like her. And she was afraid of her. So was I. So were we all. Because she seemed to have a hold on life that we didn't have. Domineering. Pushy. Ill-mannered. Push her way into the conversation and take it over."

William Fadiman, now a successful film producer and novelist, agreed: "She was not the gentlest of people. She was a nervous, tense, busy person. She was short. She was assiduous. She was harried, and harassed, in running this establishment. Because they were dealing with people who were off their rockers and it wasn't easy to know what the hell to do to please them at all times."

Another nephew, Joe Mandell, had similar memories of his aunt: "Her personality was absolutely . . . unbounded, if I may use the expression. She was autocratic, and very strong-willed. She was stronger than any other person I knew in my entire history. And I'm seventy-nine years old."

Especially offensive was Sarah's insistence that her sisters raise geniuses too. This was a tribulation for Sarah's nephew, Elliot Sagall, who first visited Portsmouth as a toddler. "I remember Sarah well," he said more than sixty years later, "because I disliked her for some time. My mother would help me read the comic strips and Sarah came down once, when I was four or five, and said to me, 'How ridiculous that she's reading you the newspaper! Why don't you read it yourself? Don't you know how to read?' "

Sarah launched a campaign to raise Elliot properly. She gave her sister a trunk full of toys that had belonged to Billy and Helena; they were early educational toys, building blocks with an architectural slant, very sophisticated for 1910.

Sarah railed against the slowness with which Elliot was learning to read, and finally persuaded her sister to raise him according to Boris's ideas. Her sister had scant defenses against Sarah. As Elliot put it, "She used to come over and my mother would quake. Mother would shiver with Sarah. She took command of the house. You couldn't talk to her." Sarah prevailed. "My mother, influenced by my aunt, taught me to read and write and do arithmetic before I was in the first grade. And I went into the first grade and I was bored. I've got memories of being in the back row of the first grade and doing crossword puzzles. I knew what was going on. And they would ask me to count on my fingers and I said no, I could count without my fingers. One of Sarah's hang-ups about a child was that he shouldn't learn how to count on his fingers, he should just go right into it."

When Dr. Sagall grew up and had his own children, he maintained contact with the Sidises. Sarah pressured him about the raising of his children, telling him not to waste time with baby talk. The subject became a source of intense conflict between them. "I was always frightened by the specter of William and his sister, Helena," Elliot said adamantly. "I think that their parents' theories ruined both of these children. My wife always said she hoped our children would be normal and not geniuses."

The same nieces and nephews who remember Sarah so vividly have but dim memories of Boris. According to William Fadiman, "The relationship between Boris and Sarah was remote and ambiguous. They were rarely seen together in what we called the public or living room. She was always busy doing something and so was he. Usually in his study. And she and he rarely appeared together as man and wife. . . . Boris had nothing whatsoever to do with anything which involved making the household run effectively, efficiently, or economically. He was an artist, scientist, practitioner at all times. She called him Dr. Science, and said, 'Dr. Science, what would you like for dinner?' God. He was a god figure. And of course, he was a god in the sense that he cured human beings. In those days particularly, long before good psychiatry and psychoanalysis, he was in there."

Jack Goldwyn had a unique relationship with Boris. Jack was two years younger than Billy, and Boris treated him as a second son, tutoring him and eventually putting him through medical school. During Jack's first idyllic vacations at Portsmouth, he rarely saw Billy, who was away at Harvard. He remembers a Boris that no one else spoke of, certainly not Billy or Helena. "My uncle was so affectionate. We used to greet each other with a hug. My aunt never could show affection. Some people are not too demonstrative. But my uncle was so tender with me. He was the kindest man I've ever known, and the most brilliant. . . . He always used to come up with little stories and jokes. He autographed a couple of books 'to my dearest boy.' We used to make up songs and sing them together. We had a hell of a lot of fun. . . . We used to go walking through the parks, with gorgeous statues from all over the world, made with the finest imported marble. We'd walk through these parks and discuss logic, and do problems in geometry. We discussed his total disagreement with Freud's ideas, and I got interested in psychiatry. And we'd sing little Russian songs. And then he'd say, 'Now, Jack, keep away from your aunt because if she sees you she'll put you to work. So we'll keep away from her. You let her alone. Let her do what she wants.' "

Jack, like the rest of his cousins, was expected to be a playmate to Billy when he was home from school. But most of them found him unapproachable. Recalled William Fadiman, "I never saw him playing games. He was always reading. He was a very serious kid. He was a genius, and to be a genius you have to do a lot of work too, you know."

As often as not, the cousins wound up as playmates to the patients of Maplewood Farms instead. They swam with them, took walks, and played croquet and tennis. Most of the patients were so pleasant, cultured, and witty that an outsider might easily mistake them for guests at an exclusive country club. Sarah was once taken aside by a judge who had been a patient for a week; he whispered to her, "I don't mean to be impertinent, but do you mind telling me where you keep your other patients?"

The patients were not without their eccentricities, however. William Fadiman recalled the portly Bostonian who suffered from an imaginary pregnancy. Each time Boris cured her of the symptoms, they recurred four months later. She was a puzzle to William: "She never ate any food, and she was quite fat. I was a little boy, and couldn't quite understand how she existed, until one day I got to her bedroom out of curiosity. There was a very famous candymaker called Page and Shaw in Boston, and this woman used to order by mail eight-, ten-, twelve-pound boxes of candy which she ate night and day. There were many odd people there but none of them were of a nature that would cause any fear. They weren't lunatics in our sense of the word. They weren't even psychotic, they were neurotics, and a lot of them were rich women who had nothing to do with their lives. It was kind of a weird place—even weird for Portsmouth, New Hampshire."

Presiding over this bizarre country club cum sanatorium was Sarah, who seemed always to be in ten places at once. "New England and I," she pronounced, "were made for each other."

The Whittemores and Joneses had been as good as their word, instructing Sarah in every detail of Portsmouth's upkeep. They gave the Sidises a pair of horses and a carriage, a little money, and a Ukrainian hired hand named Vasil. Vasil was as much a workaholic as Sarah, and the two of them combined forces to keep the vast estate afloat. Vasil taught Sarah to upholster sofas, prune trees, paint houses, and can fruit. In return, Boris taught Vasil to read and Billy taught him math. Sarah wrote in her memoirs, "There are times when I doubted that Billy Sidis had any claim to genius, and I have never doubted that Vasil was a genius."

Sarah managed all of Portsmouth's finances. She governed the estate with the same indomitable energy she had used to run her family's home in Russia. She was up at five every morning, working in the greenhouses, supervising the groundskeeping, the stables, the canning, the cleaning, the cooking, the patients' needs. In the opinion of Jack Goldwyn, "My aunt was an absolute genius. She harvested Boris' talents properly—she had him organized. I remember that they had one cook and a maid. And they both walked out while my aunt was entertaining fifteen people for dinner. And she got in that kitchen and dissected all those chickens. She prepared the whole thing for these very important people. And not a bit of dirt in the kitchen."

Jack Goldwyn's wife told similar tales: "Auntie came in one day when we were just married and visiting Portsmouth. I was dusting something and she said to me, 'Now Polly, I want to show you the quickest and best way to dust.' I said, 'Of course.' She said, 'Now don't go to the right of the room when you first start. Go to the left and go all the way around.' Now, I didn't know whether it was true— it didn't matter, I did it that way. And then I was cleaning some green beans that night for dinner, she took them from me and said, 'I'm going to show you how to clean those quickly.' She had short cuts to everything. You never saw a woman as quick. The cook would be thinking about making a pie, and Auntie had picked the fresh strawberries and rhubarb and had it in the oven. And you never in your life tasted a pie like that!"

Mrs. Whittemore taught Sarah to drive, and soon she was buzzing into town in her new Reo. Boris was rarely seen by the locals, who regarded him with a mixture of awe and resentment. They whispered that the Sidis Psychopathic Institute was "a nuthouse" run by a Jew, and they had heard rumors about his strange son. Unlike the estate's previous owner, Boris employed only a few of the townspeople, which led to some sour feeling. Sarah was oblivious to any such tensions. She socialized with members of Portsmouth's high society, and felt confident that her New England virtues made her popular: "They said that I could sweep five miles of walk before breakfast," she wrote. "They liked it when I pruned our trees. They liked it when I painted the City Club's big hall in which we staged plays." One of the Sidises' immediate neighbors remembered Sarah as "just an average middle-aged woman. She didn't dress up. She wasn't at all stylish. It was apparent she was a Jewish lady—her hair was dark. I'd often see her working, digging up the garden."

All of Sarah's efforts to the contrary, no one in Portsmouth could have failed to notice that the Sidises were an odd family. Boris Sidis hypnotized rich neurotics; his son discussed vector analysis and subway transfers; his wife had the disconcerting habit of sitting on coffee tables. "She never sat on chairs," groaned a nephew, "I was always afraid that the coffee table would collapse." They really were a most unusual family.

Boris was not greatly interested in Portsmouth's social life. He was very hard at work. He slept little. When not treating patients or writing, he studied Einstein's equations or advanced Euclidean geometry, which he and Billy discussed for hours, although Boris was not up to his son's level.

Boris's literary output continued unabated. In 1909, he published *An Experimental Study of Sleep,* a technical work that described his further inquiries into the nature of his pet "hypnoidal state," and in 1911, *Philistine and Genius* appeared. In 1913, he brought out one of his most popular and widely reviewed books, *The Psychology of Laughter.*

Boris's steady stream of scholarly works were read widely by his peers. As irascible as ever, he continued to inveigh against Freud. A review of his 1914 book, *Symptomatology, Psychognosis and Diagnosis of Psychopathic Diseases,* in the *Journal of Abnormal Psychology* concluded: "Sidis knows what he wants to say. He knows how to say it. He makes sure you understand him. There is no ambiguity. He strikes straight out from the shoulder. He deals hammer blows. He pounds his ideas into you. For fear that you may fail to grasp his meaning, he beats his more important conclusions into you in italics. The reader can almost imagine him delivering his propositions in true Rooseveltian style."

Despite his prodigious output, Boris was frustrated creatively. He longed to write philosophy; he still read Plato and Aristotle late into the night. But he could never have supported his family as a professional philosopher; and he was beginning to have trouble with Sarah because he devoted so much time to writing. There was a certain dichotomy in her thinking about Boris. On the one hand, she worshiped "Dr. Science"; on the other, as Helena put it, "She had no appreciation of writing—though she would never have said that. Her idea of work was physical labor. Mowing the grass tennis courts. If my father wrote a book, that wasn't work. She wanted him not only to write all those books, to treat the patients, and do all the work connected with it; she also wanted him to supervise the groundwork, the house, etc. She actually complained that he didn't work. But I think she was envious of the fact that he wrote—she never liked taking a backseat."

Sarah's promise to Boris—that he would never lift a finger to oversee the running of Portsmouth—was being observed, but with a certain bitterness. If she didn't dare ask her husband to do the yard-work, she had no qualms about asking others. Her sister Bessie Fadiman arrived with a group of relatives and friends one summer, and in no time Sarah had them weeding the driveway. When Boris hired a group of local Russians and Lithuanians to work on the house, he would chat with them during their break in Russian—until Sarah's appearance put the inevitable damper on the conversation. As Helena described it, "My mother was the one that bossed them around. That spoiled it—as soon as she got around anyone she'd start to give orders, make them do the dirty work. People didn't want to put up with it. She had difficulty getting along with the patients, too."

Sarah had painted herself into an unfortunate corner. She probably thought that nothing would get done without her overseeing, that this enormous estate would go to seed—and indeed, she was probably right. Boris was hardly the type to manage the money and the estate properly; the job did call for a human dynamo like Sarah. But her abrasive, nagging, complaining manner offended almost everyone.

Sarah had changed. The high-spirited, charming schoolgirl in pigtails was long vanished, reappearing only at dinner parties and social functions. Maplewood Farms was in many ways the fulfillment of Sarah's dreams, but the strain of running the estate had taken a toll. Increasingly, she lost her temper at anyone and everyone. Helena recalled, "I was afraid of her. She would fly off into these rages, about little things. It took so much out of me. It took a lot out of everybody. My brother would say that she just completely wore him out. And the next minute, she would be perfectly calm. She had wonderful blood pressure. And she never had ulcers. She would be able to go into these rages, tire everybody else out, and she would be perfectly calm at the end. Then she would sit down and play solitaire, or go out driving. A friend once told me my mother reminded her of William James' two classifications of people—one is strenuous and the other is everybody else. And she said, 'Your mother is a strenuous.' "

A lot of Sarah's steam blew off in Billy's direction. She nagged and criticized him over trivialities, increasing the strain between them. To observers they appeared remote, rarely speaking to each other. When she was old enough, Billy confided in Helena that it made him miserable to listen to Sarah's complaints about their father. As she scrubbed the floors of the estate, she complained that she hated the drudgery, that Boris didn't work. All Billy could think of as a reply was that Sarah Sidis, M.D., didn't have to scrub floors.

Considerable tension was created by Boris and Sarah's attitudes toward "woman's work." Although the couple had met over books, and although Boris had taught his wife, he took a dim view of women's education. Surprisingly, Sarah at times agreed with this point of view. "Time after time," said Helena, "I'd hear my mother talking with a woman friend, saying that if a woman stoops to professional work, it affects her husband. He doesn't work as hard." (Perhaps this is why, despite Sarah's extraordinary accomplishment—becoming a doctor at Boston University—she never chose to practice medicine. But Helena claimed that she never really cared for it. Furthermore, she was envious of Boris and Billy for having gone to Harvard, while she had gone to B.U.)

These factors led to a peculiar choice on Boris and Sarah's part. Although they had raised a genius and preached that all children should be reared as Billy had been, they did not educate Helena. She was not sent to school, had no tutors, and received meager education at home. While this was not uncharacteristic of typical parents in the first decades of the century, it was astonishing in the context of their freethinking, outspoken idealism. The parents of Billy's prodigy class-mate Norbert Wiener raised their two girls exactly the way they raised

Norbert, and with similar, if less spectacular, results. Adolf Berle, the third Harvard prodigy, had two sisters who were also raised to be prodigies. His sister Lina, for example, was educated in several languages by the age of three. Ironically, Adolf Berle, Sr., told the press, "Mind you, there was no 'forcing.' We simply acted on the principle that Dr. Sidis has set forth—namely, that the child is essentially a thinking animal." Why, then, was Helena so singularly ignored as an intellectual being?

Her parents offered little explanation. The usual rationalization they gave was her delicate health. As a premature baby, she began life precariously and led a sickly childhood plagued with operations, the first at the age of six. Indeed, Boris was advised by his friend Teddy Roosevelt to treat Helena as Roosevelt's own father had treated him —to encourage her to play outside and be as active as possible instead of studying. She could always make up the book work, Roosevelt had insisted. Sarah wrote: "The woods around Portsmouth, the snow on which she so gracefully skiied, and her father's library, were Helena's school. The school superintendent was a friend of ours, and he used to ask it as a favor that we send Helena to school, if only for a few hours a day. But we told him she had been a frail baby, and we thought that a life out-of-doors was best for her." So while Billy spent no time outdoors, Helena became a tomboy.

Boris told his daughter that if she had not been born a woman, she would have been very intelligent. And Helena was exceptionally bright. With Billy's help she taught herself to read, and Boris encouraged her to choose advanced books. Occasionally she read children's books, though Boris disapproved: "You want to read that? Well, it's up to you." Sarah gave her daughter a few lessons in geography and history, and made a slight attempt to teach her mathematics. But when Helena told her parents, "I hate arithmetic worse than prunes," they let it go at that.

Helena enjoyed her situation enormously—she did whatever she wanted. Aside from her frail health, her mother's nagging was her only source of woe. Boris was usually there to defend her against Sarah, and little Helena sometimes returned the favor. When Boris burned his hand and swore vehemently, Sarah reprimanded him. Helena rushed to his defense, saying, "You mustn't blame him for swearing, Mother. He is a man and can't cry!"

From a very early age, Helena and Billy formed an alliance that would last a lifetime. Billy taught his six-year-old sister to write, regaled her with tales of Harvard, and explained theories of physics to her that she could not possibly have understood. When Helena was six and Billy sixteen, he asked her for advice about something. She replied, "But, Billy, I'm a child. Why do you ask me?" He answered, "You have good common sense."

And so Helena's education advanced haphazardly. When she was eight, Boris asked her to write a composition for him. Then he asked her to write another and decreed, "That's very good. You don't have to study anymore, because you can write." He suggested a few books —Aristotle, Plato, and Rousseau's *Emile*—and seemed satisfied that she was garnering a suitable liberal education.

In spite of the fact that he didn't see fit to educate her, Boris and Helena had a close relationship. Helena remembers: "My father was very strict when I was sick in bed so many times, and he would be rather stern. He would say, 'You must learn to depend on yourself. I don't want you to be like your mother.' My mother came from an enormous family, and she had a lot of people around." Helena duly became an independent little girl.

Billy, Helena, and Boris would discuss politics, languages, mathematics, ideas. "My father and brother used to have a lot of talks together, and my mother was left out . . . she just didn't fit in. And I did even though I was much younger." The more her family regarded Sarah as a harridan, the more they clung to their solitary pursuits or their common intellectual amusements to avoid her nagging. Helena remembers a vicious cycle beginning when she was very young: The more they excluded Sarah, the more irritating she became; the more she irritated them, the more they excluded her. "We should have included my mother," said Helena. "We just didn't. We assumed that she didn't have a sense of humor. Years later I realized that in her own way, she did have one. . . . It wasn't quite the sense of humor that my father, my brother, and I had, but it was a sense of humor."

In her memoirs, Sarah wrote nothing of this. She made but one brief comment about family life at Portsmouth. "None of us were ever anything but happy in our life at the Institute. Those New Hampshire woods and gardens, snows and summers, are the background for memories that were for us unalloyed love. . . . The full summer of my life were those years at Portsmouth."

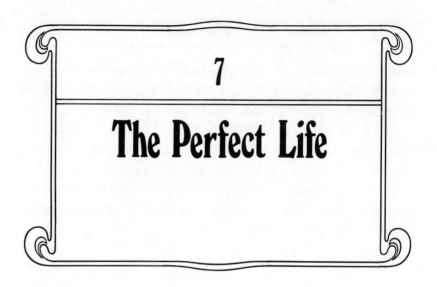

7

The Perfect Life

In his thirteenth year, Billy went to board at a Harvard dorm. It was probably a move based largely on practicality, aimed at saving Billy the long commute from New Hampshire to Boston. Very little is known about his experiences in the dorm, but they must have been hellish. He had never been on his own before, and everything was against him. A complete freak in the eyes of his fellow students, he had none of the social graces, no interest in sports or girls, and was several years younger.

Furthermore, Harvard itself oozed a special brand of snobbery. In the words of Norbert Wiener: "I had felt myself to be a misfit [at Harvard] from the first. Harvard impressed me as being overwhelmingly right-thinking. In such an atmosphere, a prodigy is likely to be regarded as an insolence toward the gods. My father's publicly announced attitude toward my education had aroused hostility among his colleagues which made my lot no easier.

"I had hoped to find a free intellectual life among my fellow students. . . . But in the Harvard order of things, a gentlemanly indifference, a studious coldness, an intellectual imperturbability joined with the graces of society made the ideal Harvard man."

How much the worse for Billy, in the brighter glare of publicity his father attracted—and how he differed from the ideal Harvard man. Disaster seemed certain.

To make matters worse, rumors of Billy's nervous breakdown had continued to dog him since his return to Harvard. Now that his permanent home was in a sanatorium, the confusion grew greater. When Billy went home to Portsmouth at vacation time, it was generally rumored that he was being committed to an asylum.

In response to all these pressures, Billy was growing increasingly eccentric. Thought to be subject to fits of insanity and recurrent nervous breakdowns, he was horribly ostracized. Not surprisingly, he became the butt of practical jokes. Radcliffe girls pretended to flirt with him, and the hapless genius would brag about it to his classmates. A few practical jokers even composed fake love letters proposing marriage; he never caught on to the gag.

One of Billy's roommates was the playwright S. N. Behrman. Forty years later, Behrman still remembered that a group of boys had ridiculed Billy because the young Einstein couldn't make change for a phone call. This incident so severely humiliated and angered Billy that Boris decided it was time to move his son out of the dormitory and into an apartment of his own near the college. Sarah would drive down to Boston on Fridays, pick Billy up, and bring him back to Portsmouth for the weekends.

He was out of the dorms, but his trials were hardly over. Some fifty years later another renowned classmate, Buckminster Fuller, recalled: "Most students considered him a freak. . . . His family put the young man at a considerable disadvantage by insisting on dressing him in very short kids' pants even though he was my height at eleven. Our class used to boast about him, because he regularly lectured to the Harvard Mathematics Department. Some of us thought he was being dangerously overloaded, and he showed some signs of distress, but no one imagined anything but the greatest success for him." During his sophomore year, Billy donned his first pair of long pants. The newspapers called it "a college event."

Derisive articles continued to appear in the press throughout Billy's stay at Harvard. One of the harshest appeared in 1912 in a prominent educational journal, the *Pedagogical Seminary*. Written by Katherine Dolbear, the article attacked Harvard's trio of prodigies, relying heavily on interviews with their peers. Dolbear attacked Billy for being disrespectful of his elders, egotistical, and high-strung:

> That he is egotistical is shown from the fact of his remarking: "I wonder whether the school children in future generations will celebrate this as a holiday because it was the day on which I began the study of the physical sciences." That he is of an imaginative and nervous temperament was shown in his early childhood. It is reported that a guest was sitting in the room near the boy, and she thoughtlessly started to tear up a piece of paper, when the child sprang upon her fiercely. His mother explained that to him all things were alive and that tearing paper was hurting something.
>
> The effect of his education seems to have been to produce a boy who can do wonderful, even brilliant reasoning in mathematics but has difficulty in transferring that reasoning power to everyday affairs.

Norbert Wiener, who received similar treatment in his segment, was completely humiliated. In adulthood he wrote,

> I had long been aware that my social development was far behind my intellectual progress, but I was mortified to find how much

of a bore, boor and nuisance Miss Dolbear's record made me out to be. I had thought that I was well on my way to the solution of my problems. Miss Dolbear's article made me feel like the player of parchesi whom an unfortunate cast of the dice has sent back to the beginning of the board.

I showed the article to my father, who was as furious as I had been humiliated. Father sent a letter of protest to be published in the next number of the *Pedagogical Seminary,* although this did not serve any particular end. Our family lawyer was unable to give us much satisfaction in the matter. An attempt to seek a legal remedy would have subjected me to publicity far more dangerous and vicious than anything to which I had yet been exposed.

Humiliation followed the boy geniuses everywhere, dogged the steps of their every intellectual triumph. Not the least of their problems was Harvard's anti-Semitism, which was considerable. Many undergraduates favored the quotas limiting the number of Jews. As one student put it, "In harmony with their policy of getting all they can for as little as possible, Jews incidentally take a majority of the scholarships. They deprive many worthy men of other races a chance." Jews were considered too intelligent—they kept the level of scholarship too high, did too well on exams, and made the best grades. Jews were barred from membership in many of the prestigious Harvard clubs, and were regarded with bitterness and envy. As caricatures of those despised Jewish traits—intellectual competence and academic achievement—the prodigies were doubly shunned.

As Norbert and Billy suffered toward graduation, they were never allowed to forget that there was to be no rest for the weary. As *The New York Times* pointed out, "Even after they complete their college careers the eyes of the world will be upon them, and the effect of the several theories involved in their education will be universally studied."

What Boris and Sarah thought of their son's life in this period, or how much they understood it, is not known. Billy never spoke of it for the rest of his life, nor did Boris. Sarah gave the Harvard years scant attention in her memoirs, writing only: "About a college education, Boris had very definite and violent theories, as he did about primary education. And Billy was a straight product of these theories. Boris's phobia was specializing. He said, 'We teach our doctors medicine and our lawyers law, and we set our poor little musical prodigies to practice six hours a day so they may delight roomfuls of people. We don't seem to care that we make them educated boobs.'

"Though the publicity embarrassed Billy he enjoyed his four years at Harvard. He took much mathematics under his and our friend Huntington, and he studied a good deal of Greek. But his favorite subject became American history, and he announced before he got his B.A. degree that he wanted to be a lawyer."

Billy's grades are the only continuous record of his years as a Harvard undergraduate.

In his first year, 1909–1910, he took only math, and received a B. The next year, when he was twelve, he got two A's—in astronomy and math—and four B's, in math, philology, and two astronomy courses. The following year, 1911–1912, he shifted the balance with three A's in physics, math, and French, and only two B's, in astronomy and math.

His junior year, when Billy was fourteen, he assumed a massive course load—seven subjects—and his grades took a strange turn. As usual, he picked up two A's in his best subjects, mathematics and French. But for the first time he received C's, four of them. He got a C in English; and it is difficult to guess why, unless he was trying to teach an unreceptive professor his method of revising English grammar. His C in Economics 1 may have had similar origins— perhaps he was trying to impress upon the class his unorthodox views of a utopian society, or maybe recruiting members for a Hesperian club. Especially bizarre were his mediocre philosophy grades, two C's and a B.

For a lad more learned in the Greek philosophers than any of his fellow students, it is hard to understand what Billy could have done to avoid racking up A's. Perhaps it was one of these classes in which, utterly bored, he balanced his hat on his head. But in his senior year he was back on familiar ground, taking A's in French, math, and physics, and a B in the History of Science. He completed his last year's coursework extraordinarily quickly, but had to wait for his class to catch up before he could graduate and receive his B.A.

Despite his heavy course load, Billy found time for constant reading and writing, which he still executed in his strangely childish scrawl. In 1914, at age sixteen, he published his first piece, and it did not disappoint the prodigy-followers. His eight-page essay, "Unconscious Intelligence," appeared as an appendix to his father's book, *Symptomatology, Psychognosis and Diagnosis of Psychopathic Diseases.* It was Billy's sole venture into his father's field.

The essay championed the then popular theory that the subconscious was an "unconscious intelligence." With staggering sophistication, Billy used brilliant semantics to prove that the subconscious is conscious. The perfection of his logical thinking is shown in the article's second paragraph, wherein he discusses the question of conscious versus unconscious intelligence:

> The first of these methods [for proving that the subconscious is an "unconscious intelligence"] is the method of isomorphism. This depends on the supposition that, if in two hypotheses the consequences are the same, the two hypotheses may be considered as identical for all purposes of further reasoning. In other words, there is no use in drawing arbitrary distinctions where none really exist. When we reason from a hypothesis, its consequences come into play at every step of the reasoning; and if those consequences are the same, all reasoning will be the same, and therefore no difference can really be drawn. Again, a question of decision between two theories whose consequences are and must be the same must necessarily be one where no evidence is obtainable, and is therefore a question which cannot be discussed at all. It is like

the old question of the man and the monkey: "If a monkey is on a pole, constantly facing a man who walks round the pole, has the man gone round the monkey?"

On June 24, 1914, William James Sidis graduated cum laude from Harvard University (rumor had it that his mother was furious it was not a magna cum laude). Though the papers now dubbed him "the most remarkable youth in the world," Billy had no intention of flaunting it. Acidly he told reporters, "I want to live the perfect life. The only way to live the perfect life is to live it in seclusion. I have always hated crowds."

Shortly after his graduation, Billy did something highly un-characteristic—he granted an in-depth interview to a reporter from the *Boston Herald.* Perhaps he wanted to set the record straight at last. The *Herald* story took up two full pages; it flourished an enormous repro-duction of his Harvard graduation photo showing a well-groomed, stocky, good-looking Billy with warm eyes and a Mona Lisa smile— the very picture of wholesome all-American youth. Gone was the skinny, suspicious boy of previous photographs. In his place was a sturdy, apparently self-confident young man. He was William now, not Billy (except to his family); and despite all his trials and humilia-tions, he seemed to have his mind made up about life. This fellow would not buckle. He would seek out his "perfect life" in seclusion, living by rules of his own making, a code that he revealed in all sincerity. The headlines read:

HARVARD'S BOY PRODIGY VOWS NEVER TO MARRY
Sidis Pledges Celibacy Beneath Sturdy Oak,
Has 154 Rules Which Govern His Life,
"Women Do Not Appeal To Me" He Says; He Is 16.

On either side of the photograph were large cartoons: William beneath a tree pledging never to marry; William riding a trolley;

William munching crackers and milk; William in his room hanging his ties on the Venus de Milo.

William hated the cartoons. He had finally been reduced literally to a comic character, a freak so bizarre he merited his own cartoon strip. Yet despite its sensational presentation, the article is enormously revealing—for once, something of the real William James Sidis peeks from the quotes.

William received the reporter in his third-floor apartment at 51 Brattle Street. "The newspapers," he explained, "have said a great many things about me, most of which have been untrue. I have never talked for publication. I am averse to it."

The piece is bursting with fascinating Sidis trivia. The child marvel relaxes by holding a pillow against his cheek; he eats crackers and milk for breakfast, crackers and cheese for lunch, and crackers and milk for dinner; he dislikes flowers and music; his favorite diversion is "trolling," riding around on a trolley car. (Just for the record, when asked on what day Christmas would fall in the year 2011, Billy put his hands to his head, paced a moment, and gave the correct answer.) He was, in the reporter's opinion, "an egoist."

But it was not tidbits like these that gave the article its sensational value and caused it to be much quoted. It was the boy wonder's sex life revealed. William told the reporter of a solemn vow of celibacy; of the medal he had struck to commemorate his decision, which he wore suspended from his coat. Once a year, he explained, he returned to the oak in Cambridge beneath which he had taken his vow. He displayed a photograph of the tree, which he carried in his pocket. His pockets must have been bulging, for he was never without the code of rules (154!) that he had written to guide his conduct. All this he explained in detail:

> "I resolved never to marry following a certain episode that took place in my life. A woman had something to do with it. My oath was taken beneath an oak tree, after I had reasoned the whole

thing out." The mathematical marvel drew from his pocket a silver medal bearing a large star in the centre with the words around the outer edge of the coin: AUGUST SIXTEENTH. That was the date in 1912 when the vow was made.

"In addition I have many other things to remind me of my pledge," he said. "For instance, see that automobile number plate," he pointed to an ordinary plate resting on the marble mantel with the blue enamel number conspicuous. "That number plate," he said, "is another reminder of my vow. These rules help me to keep this pledge, which is the most important of all. I was not too young to realize its importance when I made it. In fact, by making the pledge at an early age and safeguarding it with so many different rules and reminders, I have easily fixed it in my consciousness as a fundamental rule of life. Of course before I made it I became fully satisfied that it was the best thing for my happiness. Thus far it has proven so. I have no desire to marry and have children.

"Many of my rules are checks rather than hard and fast laws. They act as safety valves. They can be evaded without harm. Yet each one is valuable in helping maintain my individual theories.

"For instance, one rule declares that I shall never call upon a girl. On the other hand, I can call upon a girl's brother. No rule is so arbitrary as to be irksome.

"When I am in doubt about anything I draw out my rules and glance them over. The guidance is sure to be there."

Young Sidis admits that his rule code, though invaluable to his own conduct, may be of little or no value to others.

"Reason and inclination play synonymous parts in our lives," he declared. "The reason I decided upon celibacy was because I had made up my mind that sentiment would make too much of an upset in my life. I have tried to strengthen my resolve in many ways; I have not the least fear I shall break it."

In proof of his strength of mind, young Sidis declared that he has already declined six proposals of marriage since he made the vow and will heartlessly refuse all that are forthcoming in the future.

"Women do not appeal to me," he said. "You speak of a pretty woman and it seems to mean something to you, it means nothing to me. I cannot understand what a person has in mind when declaiming on what they term beauty.

"The word art means very little to me. Why will people waste so much energy on statuary, painting, drawing, etching and the like? I fail to comprehend the reason for art because I know absolutely nothing of the thing that is termed artistic in art."

When reminded that there are two statues in his apartments, one of a Venus de Milo, the other of a Psyche, the youth shrugged his shoulders in scorn. "This is my mother's apartment," he said. "At least she leases it and pays for it so she has the right to bring such things here. They have no interest to me—they mean nothing. I use that one (indicating the Venus) to hang my neckties on."

William went on to explain more of his philosophy and "rules":

"I do not believe in smoking or drinking; not because they are wrong, but because they have no particular interest to me. I have never read the Bible. I don't swear, but I can't see why others should not if they choose to do so. It doesn't mean anything, anyway. . . .

"I have a quick temper; ergo, I will not mingle a great deal with the fellows around me, then I shall not have occasion to lose my temper." He follows the rule. He is naturally shy of strangers; yet his convictions are so deep-rooted that it takes a great deal of convincing to make him change an opinion. "To make me believe a thing," he said, "you must show me."

Young Sidis is completely opposed to all forms of athletic play. It is what he terms unnecessary work. One of his rules is against all "unnecessary work."

On politics: "In a way I am a Socialist; that is on the same principle that a man belonging to a labor union is a Socialist. No one should be dependent upon the good-will of others for support when too young to support himself."

On education: "The superman can be produced, not so much by our plans for eugenics as by changing our system of education. The superman would develop himself automatically providing we start human beings right—that is stop forcing children in the early stages of their education."

On the family: "I am not at all a believer in home life. I think it subverts and detracts from our natural progress; there is too much restriction in the home, particularly for the child."

And finally, William let drop this puzzling remark: "I am not in the least interested in the Fourth Dimension, though there was no faking about it when I lectured before the scientific club that heard me talk."

Of his future, he said simply, "My only plan and purpose for the future is to live near Boston as much as possible and seek happiness in my own way."

8

Rice

The *New York Times* got hold of William's revealing interview in the *Boston Herald*. It was irresistible. With his sex life, or lack of it, now on parade, his remarks about marriage and women inspired gleeful jibes. In an editorial entitled "This Plan Is Full of Promise," the *Times* sarcastically remarked that the child prodigy was now "viewing life from the mature standpoint of seventeen." The *Times* quoted a writer from the *Chicago Journal* who "opined that young Sidis is 'an intolerable prig,' and advised the following course of treatment: What W. J. Sidis needs is not proposals of marriage, but incitements to propose. He ought to be introduced to some charming widow of about twenty-eight, some handsome, accomplished woman whose mourning has kept her out of the world

just long enough to make her hungry to test her powers of conquest
. . . she could teach him to sit up, roll over, fetch, carry and jump
through a hoop. . . . It wouldn't take more than three weeks, and any
woman can spare that much time in a good cause."

The *Times* went on, "The profoundest psychotherapist could not
prescribe a more promising treatment for anybody suffering as this
wonder youth is said to be. And if he isn't—and is half as wise as his
advertisers claim—he will just smile broadly with the rest of us at the
recipe suggested by the Chicago expert."

Most likely, William didn't smile broadly. He took his "Constitution" seriously. If he had had any hopes that speaking frankly to a
member of the press would make his public image more bearable, they
were dashed by this latest flurry of snide editorials reviling his most
personal thoughts. It was the last interview he ever gave freely.

One day after school—William had enrolled in the Harvard
Graduate School of Arts and Sciences—the inevitable finally occurred.
A gang of Harvard boys took William outside and threatened to beat
him up. Though his mother was fond of saying he was "built like a
truck driver," the boy was outnumbered; and besides, what did William James Sidis know about fistfighting? He confided his rage and
humiliation only to his five-year-old sister. However, Boris suspected
things were going badly for his son; he was irritable, had few friends,
and suffered the agonies of a hunted man. So Boris and Sarah decided
that William needed to leave the hostile environment of the Harvard
campus. To this end, they enlisted the help of Griffith Evans, the
Harvard professor who had sponsored William's Math Club lecture.
Evans was then head of the mathematics department at the new Rice
Institute, later Rice University, in faraway Houston. He secured a
position for William as professor of mathematics with a stipend of
$750 per annum. Officially, William was a Graduate Fellow working
toward his doctorate degree. He was to teach three courses: freshman
math, and Euclidean and non-Euclidean geometry. He wrote his own
textbook for the class in Euclidean geometry—in Greek. William

arrived at Rice in December 1915, a stocky lad of seventeen, socially awkward, and a stranger in a very strange land.

Houston in 1915 was undergoing a rapid transformation from a lazy Southern city to a center of industry. Its population had just passed 100,000; oil, cotton, and lumber had become lucrative exports; Houston was a town on the rise. But not literally—one of the most striking things about it, for a visitor from the East, was its implacable flatness. One suburb was known as Houston Heights because it was eight feet higher than the center of town.

Though Houston was on the move industrially, it must have seemed backward to a boy like William, a true son of Boston. Rice Institute, however, could boast considerable brain power. President Edgar Odell Lovett had filled his faculty with a superlative hand-picked collection of intellectuals.

Established in 1912 with a vast endowment from the late, eccentric philanthropist William Marsh Rice, the Institute had spared nothing in preparing for a tenure of splendor, and it was welcomed enthusiastically by the community as a proud symbol of modernization and culture. And what the grounds lost in topographical monotony, they made up in abundance, consisting as they did of three hundred acres. The students were few and scrupulously selected. In Rice's first year (three years before William's arrival), only fifty-nine freshmen were enrolled. The body count was only slightly higher in 1915, and William was facing a small, intimate coterie of Texans—surely a shock for a boy who had been accustomed to hiding himself among Harvard's throngs. Evans decided that it would be wise to have William lodge with him and two other professors in the Bachelor House—"the bach"—a residence nearly a mile from campus, set prettily among sugar pines.

At first glance, it seemed the Bachelor House was the ideal place for the boy prodigy. Obviously, he could not have survived another dormitory, especially with students older than himself who were his pupils. And his three companions at "the bach" were intelligent, fascinating men. Griffith Evans, of course, was a distinguished mathematician. Harvard was forever trying to lure him back to their fold. He was well read and musically inclined, attributes he shared with the second resident, A. L. Hughes, a Welsh physicist. The third in the house was the brilliant Julian Huxley, who headed up the biology department. Huxley, recruited from England, came from a pedigreed family that seemed unable to produce mediocre men. (Something of a child prodigy himself, he had at seven corrected his grandfather, the distinguished scientist T. H. Huxley, regarding the vagaries of parental behavior among fishes. His younger brother too had shown prodigious ability in mathematics, but was subject to fits of melancholia that eventually ended in suicide. Huxley himself was subject to extreme changes of mood. But certainly, he seemed well fitted out to understand a prodigy). And across the street from "the bach" was the home of the much-beloved Bulgarian philosophy professor, Radoslav Andrea Tsanoff. Griffith Evans felt certain that William, surrounded by men of substance, far from the persecutions of Boston and of Harvard and of family strife, would thrive.

His hopes were soon dashed. Any young man expected to instruct, and discipline, students older than himself might be sore pressed, even if his manner and bearing were impeccable. Billy's were anything but. The *Boston Herald* photo notwithstanding, he had become quite slovenly in the last year or two, and he was so weird socially that next to no one befriended him. To make matters worse, although William's arrival at Rice had not been overplayed in the press, his reputation naturally preceded him. Nor was the matter of culture shock to be taken lightly; William had never before left New England.

Classes proved impossible. In the words of Blakely Smith, a Rice alumnus: "I took freshman trig from Sidis, but we never studied math because at the beginning of every class two or three boys would tease him about girls and his hands would start to shake. He would put his hands over his face or hold his arms out in front of him and his hands and arms would tremble violently. I think he had a crush on Camille

Waggaman, a real blonde beauty, but didn't have the brains to do anything about it." (If William did have a crush on Camille Waggaman, he had chosen far beyond his reach. Camille was a glamorous and self-assured tennis star, so appealing that she sometimes escorted important visitors at the university. It was rumored that she once had asked the Archbishop of Canterbury, "May I call you Archie?")

Like the Radcliffe girls, Rice coeds took up the game of mad crushes on their ungainly math professor. One alumna admitted, "I was one of the girls who ran after him. It was a joke. We didn't really want to hurt him, we simply wanted him to come out of his shell." Reported another graduate, "People always played jokes on him. The girls pretended to be in love with him. And he kept his watch set on Eastern time, so people always asked him the time as a joke." According to another report, he carried two watches, one with Boston time and one with Houston time. Although this was probably a sentimental gesture, students gossiped that the genius couldn't calculate a two-hour time change.

Other grads commented on Sidis's reprehensible appearance: "He mostly stayed to himself, but occasionally tried to mingle with the rest of us. He only had one suit of clothes, the sort of heavy, rough woolens worn by Englishmen. Most of us felt sorry for him. He was absent-minded, not a man about town. Dr. Evans had to make him shave and bathe, and his hair needed cutting."

Misfit that he was, William found but a single social pursuit at Rice, one that would color the rest of his life. It was radical political organizing. Only one brief reference to this student activity survives. The December/January 1915–1916 issue of *The Intercollegiate Socialist* reported: "W. J. Sidis and H. W. Freeman are making efforts to organize a Chapter at Rice Institute. In all probability Rice will soon fall in line."

Where and when William joined the Socialist party is a mystery. He may have been introduced to it at Harvard, one of the first universities to have a chapter of the Intercollegiate Socialist Society, a group founded by Upton Sinclair for "intellectuals and professionals." Jack London was the society's first president; at Harvard, activist Walter Lippmann became the group's president in 1908, just before William's arrival. By the next academic year, that of William's Math Club lecture, the Harvard branch boasted fifty members out of two hundred undergraduates. The organization received the blessing of William James and other luminaries, and grew rapidly in the next few years, influencing both the college and the community. Chapters sprang up around the country, though Rice never did "fall in line."

In 1915, Woodrow Wilson was President and America teetered on the verge of war. Industrial Workers of the World ("Wobblies") organizer Joe Hill had recently been executed by firing squad, wiring "Big Bill" Haywood on the eve of his death, "Don't waste any time in mourning. Organize." A radical mood was rippling through America, particularly in intellectual centers such as New York and Boston. Labor organizing, the special province of the Wobblies, no longer satisfied a large segment of American leftists, who dreamed not merely of reforms, but of a complete proletarian revolution. The ranks of the American Socialist party, founded in 1901, had swelled mightily in the last decade, inspired in great part by the charismatic Eugene Debs, Socialist candidate for President.

The party was by no means composed of a unified membership. A hodgepodge of intellectuals, blue-collar workers, farmers, ethnic minorities, and all manner of radicals, it was neither wild nor anarchistic, but basically moderate, good-natured, and loosely organized. It possessed nothing of the rigidity that would later characterize the Communist party. Debs was symbolic of its temper—humble, beloved, the Dale Carnegie of radicalism. Socialists found the IWW too militant, and did not support it. Mired in a mess of mixed premises, the IWW dreamed of the collapse of American capitalism while never veering so far to the left as to be classed with the bomb-throwing anarchists. The division between moderates (who envisioned reform within the capitalist system), middle-of-the-roaders (who accepted the notion of reforms as a path to a fully Socialist government of the future), and radicals (who had no truck with reform and pacifism and dreamed of violent overthrow of the government) kept the party continuously split, and kept vast numbers of Socialists busier with intrafraternal squabbling than with furthering the cause.

Exactly where William stood in the fray in 1915 is unknown. His utopia on paper, Hesperia, was not a Socialist document. Perhaps, in the years since he wrote it, he had moved away from his totalitarian vision, or perhaps he simply interpreted socialism creatively. So fluid was the Socialist movement, and so varied and complex the beliefs of its leaders, that it is useless to speculate with whom and with what beliefs William had aligned himself, except to say that like the majority of American Socialists he was adamantly antiwar.

The antiwar sentiments that William had begun to vocalize so freely offended his roommates at the Bachelor House. And that was not all they found off-putting. Houston was a social town, and Rice's president, Dr. Lovett, encouraged mingling between his faculty and the local society. Albert Léon Guérard, the chairman of the department of Romance languages, was so fond of Houston's social whirl that he considered it a return to an eighteenth-century utopia, to "an age where sociability was the supreme art. . . . In such a world, shabbiness is a sin. . . . Within the charmed circle, the first rule is courtesy."

When the men of Bachelor House entertained, the presence of young Sidis was an excruciating embarrassment. It was bad enough that he aired his radical politics—worse still, he had no social instincts. A student who attended one of these awkward evenings recalled, "He behaved like a child—he ate his dinner and dessert quickly, then left. Evans talked to him like he was a little boy." For such was the dichotomy inherent in the task of managing his young ward: Evans could not help but patronize the boy whose genius in mathematics—Evans's own field—vastly surpassed his own best efforts.

One faculty wife who occasionally visited "the bach" declared, "Sidis's behavior was very much to be criticized, and he didn't make a great many friends. . . . He was very spoiled, a tragic person." At last the situation came to a head. Whenever there was company, William would leave.

One professor's daughter, Kathleen Wilson Henderson, was fascinated by his quirks: "Sidis lived by a constitution that regulated when he got up and when he went to bed, etc. When the faculty were invited to my parents' house, Sidis would sometimes take a knife and divide the cake on the tea table in half and eat the whole half. I don't know if that was in his constitution or not!"

William made a sufficient impression on Julian Huxley to appear in his memoirs many, many years later. "He was brilliant at mathematics, but in all other subjects he was childishly ignorant; he spent his time mooning about and prattling to the Tsanoffs' infant daughter. He was also untidy and rather dirty."

The Rice yearbook, *The Campanile,* summed up the state of affairs at the Bachelor House when it published this poem, undoubtedly mortifying to its subject:

HEARD AT THE BACHELOR'S HOME

William, put down that knife.
William, it is time to go to bed.
William, you really need a shave and clean collar
William, you haven't gone calling in a long time.

One of William's few sympathizers on the faculty was Dr. Guérard, chairman of the department of Romance languages. William had always excelled in French, and he joined the French Club because it offered the only chance to converse in that language in Houston. Perhaps this common passion engendered a kinship between Guérard and Sidis. In any case, one of the most benevolent and astute of all observations made about William James Sidis appeared in Guérard's memoirs: "The boy was healthy, sane, and, I believe, normal in every respect. He was the victim not of intensive education given him by his father, Dr. Boris Sidis, nor of the romantic curse called Genius, but of the thoughtless cruelty of the public. He was treated like a two-headed calf. His boyish singularities—and what lad of seventeen is a pattern of mellow wisdom—were mercilessly exposed and amplified. Because he blurted out that he had never kissed a girl, he was made the butt of endless practical jokes."

It was Dr. Guérard's son, novelist Albert Joseph Guérard, who recalled how his family took in the bereft genius:

> Sidis lived across the street from us. My mother felt maternal toward Sidis, who was very shy. He would not indulge in any entertainment, but was willing to have a good time in an academic ambience: he played charades with the French Club. Once he refused normal refreshments, but my mother felt he wanted something. She offered him porridge, which he welcomed. At one gathering he came out to the kitchen to play with me and my sisters, perhaps aged four and eight. The family legends: (1) He pumped us up in our swing, using a different language for each number; (2) He borrowed the book on international languages my father had written and the next day returned with a long essay in Esperanto, showing how American culture reached Europe or vice-versa via Atlantis. My parents' memories were indulgent and affectionate.

No amount of emotional trauma could dampen William's boundless intellectual curiosity—if anything, it enhanced it. The world of ideas was not a world that envied, that ridiculed, that lived by uncertain or foreign rules. The more human beings proved to be disappointing, the greater the pull of the mind.

He wrote constantly. According to the research of Ruth Reynolds, a *New York Sunday News* reporter, "[William] kept a diary which he wrote in three or four languages, and then, because he was suspicious, assigned new meanings to his alien words so that no one could possibly translate his entries." His essay on the lost continent of

Atlantis, which he had given Guérard (in Esperanto), would later become the subject of an entire book and the foundation of some of William's most important historical theories. He had recently developed an intense fascination with geographic and meteorologic conditions and their effects on populations; he was especially intrigued by the Galveston flood of 1900 (in which six thousand people were drowned under a million tons of waves), and during those hours when he left Bachelor House an outcast, he sought out survivors for conversation. In addition, William had begun to take notes on what in just a few years would become an outstanding contribution to science and cosmological theory. He apparently did not discuss this work often, but in 1916, from Portsmouth, he wrote to Julian Huxley: "How has everything been this summer with you? I myself have been writing out that theory of mine regarding the second law of thermodynamics."

After eight months at Rice, Billy returned to Boston. Griffith Evans wrote Huxley saying that he had found another Harvard man to "take WJS's place on the stem of the rose" as mathematics professor. For the rest of his life, William rarely spoke of Rice. His friends didn't like to bring up the subject. When one finally dared to ask him why he had left, he replied flatly, "I never knew why they gave me the job in the first place—I'm not much of a teacher. I didn't leave—I was asked to go."

9

Too Radical
for the Radicals

$\mathbf{I}$f William thought he could slip quietly back to Boston, leaving his memories of Rice Institute behind, he was sorely mistaken. His arrival was greeted with a flurry of news articles so embarrassing, so widely syndicated, that William could only watch in despair as he was mercilessly ridiculed yet again.

None of his escapades at Rice were lost on the rapacious reporters of Boston and New York. William's sexual blunders at Rice made exciting news. "Puritanical Boston," wrote the *New York Evening Telegram*, "was shocked a few days ago when William James Sidis returned to that centre of culture and codfish from Houston, Texas ... and told his friends he was practically forced to resign his professorship and flee from Texas because the girls of the Lone Star State were besieging him with proposals of marriage." He was quoted nationwide as saying, "It's terrible in Texas. They want to naturalize you, and the best way they can think of is to get you married to one of their girls. Gosh, it's fierce!"

" 'Do you mean,' asked a friend, 'that they were making matches for you?'

" 'Worse!' ejaculated Sidis. 'The girls even proposed to me in public. It was awful. The newspapers got hold of it and I had a dreadful time.'

" 'How do you like the Texas girls?' someone asked.

" 'I don't,' was the decisive reply. 'They flirt too much. It was very annoying. But I am happy to say that Article 22 of my constitution which prohibits kissing or familiarity with females is still unblemished.' "

A full-page broadside in a Boston paper was illustrated with the now de rigueur cartoons of William, this time fleeing a lariat-slinging Texas belle on horseback with preacher in tow; and repulsing the advances of other smooch-hungry young ladies. The headline read:

"WHY WON'T GIRLS LEAVE ME ALONE?"
HE'S A WOMAN HATER, THAT'S WHY!

How the Bold Young Women of Boston and Texas by Constantly Proposing Marriage to the Wary William James Sidis, Prove the Old Belief That the Feminine Heart Longs to Conquer Masculine Indifference.

The article painted William as a diehard misogynist, distorting the now infamous interview from the *Boston Herald*: "At fifteen he graduated from Harvard University and gave to the world his woman-hater's code. He prided himself upon scorn of femininity. No girl could approach him if he could avoid it. He hated to ride on street cars because he had to be jostled and be seated alongside them. He said it wasn't that he was afraid of them, merely that he didn't see anything attractive about them. They bored him, they were flippant and destructive to real accomplishment. He just simply didn't want anything to do with them."

The author concluded that the cause of William's unnatural condition was his mathematical genius. Surely brilliance and mental health could never go hand in hand.

The brouhaha did not end there. Not only was William "unnatural," he had another flaw—no sense of humor. He was upbraided for not being a sport, as if it came naturally to any adolescent to be made a national laughingstock. The *New York Morning Telegraph* wrote an editorial on this failing:

A "KID PHENOMENON" TAKES IT ALL TOO SERIOUSLY WHEN TEXAS GIRLS "KID" HIM

In this era of co-ordination we seem to have overlooked the necessity of a Defense League to defend infant prodigies against the machinations of designing females. There is not general understanding of the infant prodigy. The general run of just plain folk do not realize that although he is so richly endowed in other respects by some strange trick of fate he has been denied a sense of humor. . . . If he were natural he would know, probably, that the girls of Texas were merely having fun with him because of the fact that he has been heralded as a beardless Solomon. Regarding him as a "kid phenomenon" they "kidded" him. However, there seems to be a dent in his cranium where the bump of humor develops in normal persons, and he took their overtures seriously. . . . Our advice to this unblemished young person's friends is that they get him in a corner and put him wise to the comedy features of his complaint.

When the syndicated stories reached Texas, they caused a violent stink. One Rice student snapped at Julian Huxley, "The little toad, he isn't worth noticing, even the fact that one has to ignore him is too much!"

The *Houston Post* felt obliged to enter the fray. Well, maybe young Sidis had made those remarks, but the Boston papers had behaved irresponsibly in printing them. Infant prodigies, after all, were unbalanced and apt to say foolish things. Rice Institute's campus paper, *The Thresher,* responded with a gentle defense of their erstwhile professor. Why, it was all a hoot—wasn't Sidis already bragging of proposals from Boston females when he arrived in Texas?

If *The Thresher* was inclined to forgive, Della Rains, a twenty-year-old Dallas art student, was not. An interview with this important personage was syndicated throughout the country; the headline read "Unkissed High Brows a Joke to Texas Girls; No Harvard Types for Them," and the piece was illustrated with a picture of a vivacious brunette. "A meeting between these two people," opined the reporter, "would be the most interesting event of the day." Miss Rains, just returned from a horseback ride, cuddled into her couch, batted her long eyelashes, and delivered a salvo against the boy who had dared insult Texas womanhood:

"My candid opinion is that this professor will never recover from his infant prodigy days. I have lived in Texas all my life, and I never saw a girl chase a man to marry him. We marry when we are ready, and when we do take a husband we take one that has not been raised on dead languages and Harvard etiquette. Harvard is all right, I suppose, but if young Mr. Sidis is a typical example of its output it is educating in the wrong direction.

"Oh, if I could only catch that gentleman in Texas sometime, I'd put up a job on him. What would I do? I'd take him horseback riding. I'd tie him to the wildest horse I could find, and I'd make him see that Texas women could do more than flirt.

"I bet that he is a sissy, sports a wristwatch and wears his handkerchief in his sleeve. The truth is that Texas girls discovered he was a 'Nancy' who had never been kissed, and they kidded him and he took it seriously.

"If you should see William James Sidis," said Miss Rains in parting, "give him my regards and tell him not to forget to let his wristwatch run down. And tell him I hope to meet him —in Texas."

William enrolled in Harvard Law School in September 1916, somewhat to the consternation of his mother, who had hoped he would become a doctor. Most of his relatives doubted he had the social graces to become a successful attorney.

If he had ambitions to practice, he kept them to himself. Law was well suited to William's mind—orderly, precise, and at the same time complex and challenging. With his photographic memory, he found the work simple; simple enough to leave him time for a myriad of other activities.

To avoid incidents, William was permitted to live alone, visiting Portsmouth periodically. His parents found an apartment in Cambridge, so that his beloved libraries would be a mere stride away. Though he was now the same age as his fellow students, he was more isolated from them than ever. He lived completely outside the Harvard world of clubs, athletics, school magazines, and dorm life.

Despite its general tolerance and sympathy for the Harvard Socialist Club, Harvard was prowar, and by the time William entered law school in 1916, pacifists and antiwar radicals on campus were being ostracized. Even the Harvard Socialist Club's founder, Walter Lippmann, was now sympathetic to the Allies. By 1917, there was no antiwar movement left at Harvard, and William was one of a sprinkling of stray pacifists.

Mercifully, the press was beginning to die down. William was scrupulously careful not to make printable remarks to anyone who might betray him, and for once his life was one of relative peace and solitude.

He responded to the quiet and isolation by making ever greater intellectual leaps. He was preparing the foundation for his masterwork on physics, which would not emerge for several years. Simultaneously, he became deeply absorbed in the study of Boston history, having told acquaintances upon his return from Rice that he was a diehard "New England Yankee." He made maps of the city, pondered its streetcar routes, and lost himself in the tales of its founding fathers.

During his visits to Portsmouth, he and his father brainstormed about physics, plumbing Einstein's latest theories. Few people, including Boris, could discuss mathematics or physics at William's level.

His reputation as a math genius kept William in the constant service of his beleaguered cousins, who struggled with their homework. Jack Goldwyn, who was suffering the pains of geometry in high school, said, "I was a C student. I got hold of Billy and he taught me geometry and I went from a C to an A—my teacher couldn't understand what had happened."

Elliot Sagall recalled, "As fast as I could write my algebra problems, he could do them. And I remember the time I was interested in seeing how many words I could make out of the letters of Constantinople. And he sat down and—*brooomp!*—column after column. Whatever problem I had in school, he could handle it with no difficulty and no time out even to think. As fast as he could talk, or as fast as he could write . . . the problem would come into him, and the answer would come out of him."

William also amused himself by producing a few translations from his favorite languages. His incomparable grasp of linguistics had not lessened, and now he was explaining Chinese pictographs and Bantu dialects to his seven-year-old sister. William could learn a language in a day. According to Helena, "Billy knew all the languages in the world, while my father only knew twenty-seven. I wonder if there were any Billy didn't know."

William's favorite languages were English, Russian, and French. One of his most amusing exercises was a translation of Mark Twain's famous essay "The Jumping Frog of Calaveras County" into "proper"

French—that is, French without slang or colloquialisms of any kind —and back again, into "proper" English. If collecting streetcar transfers seems odd, at first glance this effort appears to be a waste of time bordering on the aberrant. In fact, besides being terrifically funny, it illustrates a point William was fond of making throughout his life: that slang and dialect give language its color and joie de vivre; and that when it is removed, after the stifling manner of traditional classroom translations, the lifeblood seeps from the writing. William wrote numerous dictionaries and "textbooks" of American slang and "lingo," as he called it.

Of William's Russian translations, few remain except two one-act plays by Anton Chekhov. Both concern the plight of henpecked husbands, a matter of apparent interest to William.

Busy as he was, William found time to pen yet another book, of an entirely frivolous nature and born of a most unusual source—the Ouija board.

Boris and Sarah frowned on anything "psychic" and refused to join Helena, William, and friends in their explorations of the age-old party game. Whereas Helena and other hopefuls never succeeded in rousing the spirits to anything more than a half-hearted "yes" or "no," William and the disembodied denizens of other worlds had an easy rapport. Under his touch, the heart-shaped pointer fairly flew across the board, spelling out words and sentences almost faster than they could be read. When the spirits of the Ouija board declared themselves to be citizens of the planet Venus, William and Helena took the news in stride and began to take careful notes, scrupulously avoiding telling their parents about this turn of events. (In 1917, it was widely believed that Venus was a sister planet to Earth, with the same atmospheric conditions and capable of supporting life.) William started to use a planchette, a pointer with a pencil attached to it, so he could take spiritual dictation at length.

Soon the Venusians were communicating with William in their own language, which he ably decoded. Helena recalls the language as a blend of the multitude of tongues William had mastered, akin to Esperanto or his own Vendergood. In his usual methodical manner, William concocted a full grammar in Venusian. He posed questions about Venusian civilization and recorded the answers (decoded) in a little book in tiny handwriting.

When his notebook was full, he spun the material into his first science-fiction novel, now lost. The plot, as Helena remembers it, was sketchy—a simple structure upon which to hang a study of Venusian culture. The tribulations of hero and heroine, thwarted in their efforts to get together but ultimately overcoming all obstacles, warranted a minimum of ink. William saved his loving detail for an accounting of their social customs, morals, and mores. On Venus (as in Hesperia) there was no such thing as an illegitimate child, no such thing as a nuclear family. If a couple chose to part, they were free to do so. The products of their union were legitimate in the eyes of society, and were raised communally, rather in the style of an Israeli kibbutz. The novel was nearly two hundred pages of typescript.

Curious about the appearance of the Venusians, William "channeled" drawings, this time without the help of the planchette or the Ouija board, simply sketching figures as they appeared to him and regarding them as psychic transmissions. According to Helena, the Venusians looked just like Earthlings, except that Venusians wore very little in the way of clothing.

William's interest in the Ouija board persisted for several years, puzzling the few acquaintances who observed it. They were unable to account for this attack of mysticism in a young man whose rational mind was his very calling card. But in time, William put away his board and planchette, and with them his interest in spirits and Venusians.

More compelling to William than any of his other pursuits was politics. In 1916, Woodrow Wilson was running for President promising to keep America out of the war. But as the conflict escalated, the tenor of popular opinion shifted, and the Socialist party became the single remaining organization that was antiwar. Even so, there was considerable dissension in its ranks over the war issue. When America entered the fray on April 6, 1917, the party held an emergency convention and publicly restated its pacifist stance; virtually all of the big-name intellectuals deserted en masse. Though it gained twelve thousand new members in the first two months of the war, the party had lost its intellectual backbone. Many of the new members were Democrats disappointed with Wilson who joined only to cast an antiwar vote, not because they believed in socialism.

On June 5, 1917, the federal government passed the Espionage Act, which made opposition to the draft or to enlistment punishable by a fine of up to ten thousand dollars and twenty years in prison, and gave the government the power to censor and ban radical literature from the mails. The act was soon broadened to include such crimes as "profane, scurrilous, and abusive language," and any activities that could be construed as anti-American.

A civilian from Tulsa, Oklahoma, stated the prevailing mood most graphically: "The first step in the whipping of Germany is to strangle the IWWs. Don't scotch 'em. . . . Kill 'em dead. It is not time to waste money on trials. . . . All that is necessary is the evidence and a firing squad."

In addition to the government crackdown, there was rampant mob violence. Anyone remotely "radical" was subject to being beaten or horsewhipped. Socialist meetings and offices were raided, Socialist journals were banned from the mails, professors were dismissed if they criticized government policy. Religious pacifists were jailed and tortured. Two thousand people were tried under the Espionage Act. Nearly every major Socialist party leader was indicted during the war; Socialists were rarely acquitted, and a case against a leftist was a sure notch in the Justice Department's belt. The antiradical hysteria culminated in the arrest of Eugene Debs after a two-hour speech in Canton, Ohio. He was sentenced to ten years in prison.

Conscientious objection began with many Americans refusing to register. Many didn't appear for their physicals or gave their draft boards false addresses, registering only to get draft cards. In New York City, so many draftees—70 percent—filed exemption claims that the government couldn't keep up with the demand for exemption forms. Other protesters stole draft lists, and a few protested violently by attacking soldiers.

When the Russian Revolution occurred in November 1917, its effect on American radicals was exhilarating. Matters were grim on the leftist home front, what with poor electoral showings for Socialists and persecution from mobs and the government. Socialism had begun to take on a difficult, plodding, compromising air to many of the party members, while all-out communism had a glamorous appeal. If revolution could happen in Russia, the most backward of countries, why couldn't it happen here? So reasoned American Socialists, bursting with wishful thinking. Since they received little information about what was actually going on in Russia, their romantic dreams seemed all the more feasible.

William spent a fair amount of time in Portsmouth during these years, and he and his father discussed politics at length. On certain major issues, they were in accord—the right of the individual to speak freely and to protest, for example. They frequently aired their mutual disgust with the poor reportage of political events in the news. But Boris was not a Socialist, and the two disagreed on numerous matters of principle.

In 1918, William published his second article, which appeared in the *Journal of Abnormal Psychology*. It dealt with the topic of revolts, revolutions, and wars. Boris wrote a brief introduction to his son's article, a generalized ramble about the grimness of the World War, now nearing its close, and the value of William's contribution to the understanding of the causes of revolts.

The article, "A Remark on the Occurrence of Revolutions," proposes that when a people are strained and oppressed by a myriad of conditions, a drastic change in environment such as severe cold or heat, with resultant crop failures and similar disasters, can be the straw that breaks the camel's back. The result is an uprising. "Revolutions," William wrote, "and revolts in general (a revolt being a revolution that has not quite succeeded) are connected in some way or other with direct, obvious, physical discomfort, especially hunger, and possible lack of clothing and fuel." Periodicity in the climate, he observed, seems to cause these changes in conditions, and that periodicity occurs in the number of spots on the sun.

> Sun-spots are rifts in the surface of the sun, exposing a lower layer. This lower layer gives less light and heat than the surface, and therefore, the more spots there are on the sun, the less heat the sun will give, and the cooler will be the climate.... The last sun-spot minimum was in 1911. Thus it appears that revolts and revolutions take place in warm countries near the minimum of sun-spots; in each case, when the weather is such as to tend to poor crops.
>
> However, I do not wish to be understood as saying that the sun-spots cause revolutions. An appearance of sun-spots could not, by itself, produce revolution unless other circumstances are already such as to cause the revolution. All such revolutions would occur anyway, even without the sun-spot variations; but these sun-spot variations superadd natural extremes of climate, causing not only physical discomfort but danger to life and health, thus hastening a revolt that might otherwise have waited for a very long time.
>
> A government not based on the will of the people must, in the nature of things, rule by fear, *by keeping the people in constant subjection; and the people will be kept in subjection as long as they can be made to fear.* The tendency of such oppression is to exasperate the people and excite them to desperate measures, especially if the oppression affects their means of livelihood. But if circumstances suddenly become such that many lives, or the health of many people, are seriously threatened as by extreme cold, famine, etc., this superadds the instinct of self-preservation, and the fear

is entirely counteracted. The power of the government to keep the people in subjection is weakened, and the rebellious tendencies come to the foreground, resulting in open revolt. This will happen especially if there is a poor crop; and this probably takes place every eleven years, in accordance with the sun-spot variations.

This rule would, therefore, apply only to the date of the beginning of a revolt; therefore all revolts included in my list were dated from the time of the outbreak, and not of the culmination.

The list, yet another example of William's awesome scholarship, traces thirty-three revolts and their respective minimum or maximum of sunspots, providing impressive evidence to support his case.

This essay was clearer than William's previous efforts, and as original as ever. In emphasizing the role of fear and the "fear instinct," he is echoing one of his father's pet theories—that the fear instinct is the cornerstone of all mass hysteria, neurosis, and human trouble, a subject on which Boris had written at great length. Father and son appeared to have been enjoying stimulating intellectual repartee, and a sharing of certain sophisticated ideas. But terrible trouble lurked around the corner, and Boris's and William's names side by side on the *Journal*'s contents page were no omen of things to come.

By 1918 William was of age—old enough to register for the draft. He claimed exemption as a conscientious objector, and it was only the armistice of 1918 that spared him a prison term. Boris and Sarah began to worry about their son's activities, afraid he would suffer the same harsh punishments Boris had undergone as a dissident in Russia.

And so they recruited William's cousin Jack Goldwyn, a great favorite of Boris's, to keep an eye on him. Jack was fond of William, and thought of him as "a terrific person, a little bit odd, but as honest as you make 'em. No subterfuge. No conniving. No dishonesty. But not too practical and he was very naïve." Jack, who was presumably less naïve, accompanied William to his radical haunts. Jack recalled, "There was a little rift in the family . . . so I was in touch with William as much as possible to keep him out of trouble. I joined the Party, and I went with him to Socialist Party meetings in Boston, and met a lot of people. Because he was honest, he thought everybody else was honest. So I pointed out flaws that I saw. I'd say 'This guy is good,' or 'That girl's a phony.' I didn't trust any of them. I wasn't a Socialist. But I joined the party to be with him. I was there to see that he didn't get hurt. Billy was such an idealist."

But for his part, Billy was growing disgusted with Socialists. He found the interparty bickering distasteful, and he had a reputation among the membership as being "too radical for the radicals." After the Russian Revolution, the Soviets lent their support only to the Socialist Party's left wing, disowning the rest. When the party underwent its Great Rift in 1919, William predictably veered to the left.

In many ways he was a typical member of that left—born of Russian parents, nearly twenty at the time of the revolution in Russia, and fiery in his beliefs. Most young leftists were in favor of an American uprising like the Russian, with a vanguard party, violence, and a dictatorship of the proletariat. The older, more conservative Socialists who had worked for years with the party—the right wing —resented these young upstarts, so recently joined, who told them fiercely what true socialism was.

The American public was indifferent to these altercations that held so much meaning for the radicals. When the war ended on November 11, 1918, antiradical hysteria in America did not abate— it intensified. An advertisement that ran in two Washington newspapers expressed the common point of view, however crudely: "We must smash every un-American and anti-American organization in the land. We must put to death the leaders of this gigantic conspiracy of murder, pillage and revolution. We must imprison for life all its aiders and abetters of native birth. We must deport all aliens."

Boris and Sarah had good reason to fear for their son.

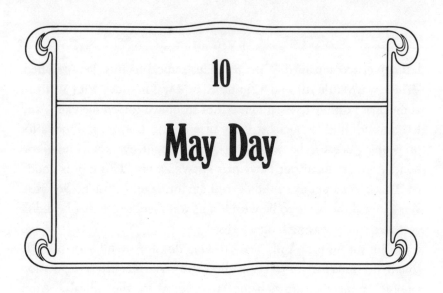

10

May Day

I t was 1918, the year of the great Spanish flu epidemic that killed more than twenty-one million people —over twice the number killed in World War I. As flu swept through New England in the fall, Boris fell ill. In those years before antibiotics, he failed to make a complete recovery.

According to Sarah's memoirs, her married life had been a perfect one up to this point. Then, she bemoaned, "The first frost touched this life. It was a bad time. My mother and father died in the flu epidemic. My baby brother, Jack, who lived with us as one of the family for many years, got pneumonia. Helena had flu twice. Billy and I never got sick."

Boris's doctors advised a move to a warmer climate. It was

decided that the Institute should be closed for the winter, and the family departed for California. Boris, Sarah, Helena, and Jack made plans to rent a home in San Diego. William stayed in Boston. He had been studying at Harvard Law School since 1916. Now, for some mysterious reason of his own, he quit in his last semester although in good standing academically, thus failing to earn a law degree.

Sarah was furious. Her son had disappointed her once by opting for law rather than medicine; now he was throwing away his chances for entering a solid, respectable profession. For the rest of her life—and in her memoirs—she said that the war closed down the law school, and that was the only reason William left. In fact, the Harvard Law School did not close down, although two-thirds of the student body went to war.

Out of school at last, William got his first job through a family friend, Professor Daniel Comstock of MIT, who needed an assistant in his laboratory, which was developing a submarine-detection program. Comstock explained to Sarah that he was hiring William for two reasons—he needed a brilliant mind, and he hoped to keep the boy out of jail for his refusal to go to war. Comstock gave the young radical some advanced theoretical problems without telling him of their military applications. William, blissfully at work in the higher reaches of theoretical physics, had no idea that he was contributing to the war effort. When he finally found out several months later, he was extremely indignant and resigned immediately.

Entirely free of his family, William began to expand his social life. He was meeting a great many radicals, and he threw himself deeply into political activities.

Meanwhile, Boris, Sarah, Helena, and Jack had arrived in San Diego. They were greeted by a welcoming committee comprised of the city's finest doctors and were escorted to a hotel. "It was strange and moving to me," Sarah wrote, "and I was remembering the money my father and I had borrowed when we arrived at Castle Gardens from Russia so many years before. To be thus unexpectedly welcomed to California pleased me as it would a child." Sarah was delighted with

San Diego. The Sidises rented a beautiful home, Helena happily played front-yard football with the local boys, and Sarah and Boris socialized with the crème of California's intellectuals and influential citizens.

Their comfortable stay was interrupted by shocking news from home. Wrote Sarah, "It was while we were in California that Billy began to grow up—the Sidis way. We received a long-distance call one day saying that he had spent some hours in a Boston jail. The charge was 'incitement to riot.' While we were enjoying California Republicans, Billy had become a Communist of purest ray serene!"

Technically speaking, William was not actually a Communist—yet. There was no American Communist party until June 1919, when the troubled Socialist party split. The bitterness, the backbiting, and the slandering that characterized the growing rift within the party were repugnant to William, though he was to be embroiled in similar disputes for the rest of his life.

William became involved with Boston's most dogmatic young Socialist radicals, who had been infected with a slavish devotion to anything Russian. These firebrands felt certain the American working-man's instincts would lead him away from the drudgery of electoral progress (which the old-time Socialists still believed in) and toward insurrection—violent, if necessary.

The Socialist party of 1919 was heavily dominated by groups that spoke a foreign language as their native tongue. The Eastern European groups—Ukrainians, Letts (Latvians), Poles, etc.—were strongly pro-Bolshevik, wanting above all else to see an American October Revolution. (William, with his superhuman abilities to speak and read any language perfectly, was in the unique position of being able to communicate with members of all of the foreign-language federations, and to translate propagandist tracts.) To the modern eye the Bolshevik leftists seem extraordinarily deluded and more than a trifle absurd in their grasp of American life, and in their failure to see that America was nothing like Russia in spirit and circumstance; or to see that they were a despised minority, and not a moving force in American politics; and that a proletarian revolution was virtually impossible in America in 1919.

One of the things that fed the radicals' confidence was the degree of terror Americans felt about them, a degree disproportionate to their actual power. Postwar America was in a confused condition, ripe for the mass hysteria that would come to be known as the "Red Scare." Americans were exhausted from wartime sacrifices, ready to enjoy a period of prosperity, and unprepared to meet extreme inflation. For the average family the cost of living in 1919 was 99 percent higher than in 1914. The world that had been made "Safe for Democracy" was not as fruitful as Americans had dreamed it would be.

America had depended on its industrialists and businessmen during the war—they had shouldered the burden of operating America's factories, producing the steel ore and the financial creativity that fueled the war effort. Now, as organized labor demanded higher wages and collective bargaining—and painted America's businessmen as robber barons—hostilities reached a boiling point. The result of these tensions was a period of massive strikes. In 1919, there were 3,600 strikes with more than four million participants.

By and large, the strikers were not Russian sympathizers, although leftists tried desperately to recruit them. In the confused mind of the public, abetted by hints from the press, strikers were equated with the hated Bolsheviks, and America itself seemed infected by the Red Menace.

The most feared and hated Reds in America were the aliens— and though they composed a large part of the radical movement (53 percent of the Socialist party in 1919), they were but a tiny part of the alien population. In their fear Americans saw a bomb-wielding, bushy-haired, fiery-eyed Jewish anarchist in every alien, and there to nurture this stereotype were certain branches of the government. Rallied by Attorney General Alexander Mitchell Palmer, the Department of Defense and the FBI devoted themselves passionately to crushing the Bolshevik menace.

Palmer was operating in a situation well suited to the development of his infamous anti-Red crackdowns, the "Palmer raids." The Espionage Act laid the groundwork for the suppression of leftists. In October 1918, another discriminatory law was passed, this one aimed at aliens: Any alien who was an anarchist was denied admission to the United States, and any alien who became an anarchist or radical of any stripe was to be deported. Palmer zealously engineered mass deportations, beginning in the fall of 1919.

Palmerized Americans, drenched in hysterical newspaper reports and struggling financially, succumbed to mass hysteria. When Boris Sidis labeled the American state of mind in these years a mental epidemic, a fear complex, he was quite correct. The true power of the radicals was insufficient to warrant the suppression they received. The American public honored the disorganized, strife-ridden group with a competence and influence it did not possess, and went on a rampage against its members.

An Indiana jury took two minutes to acquit a man who shot and killed an alien who had shouted, "To hell with the United States!" Aliens merely suspected of subversive activity were deported en masse. For all the fussing the radicals made about which group they belonged to, and whether it was the left or right faction of that group, the American public made no such distinctions. An anarchist was as evil as a pacifist, a Socialist was no better than a Communist.

It was in this electrically charged atmosphere that William Sidis found himself in the months preceding his Great Trouble. May Day was approaching, and Boston radicals, like their brethren across the country, were determined to make the most of it. Traditionally, May 1 had been a day of marches and protests throughout the world, with the exception of the United States. American radicals were determined to change all that. Inspired by the Russian Revolution, they planned rallies, parades, and meetings. Heightening the pre–May Day tension was a series of frightening bomb threats that were terrorizing the country.

As Americans read their morning papers with alarm, the May

Day melees had begun. Not surprisingly, the violence that blackened demonstrations throughout America was not, for the most part, instigated by radicals. American servicemen were so enraged by the pro-Bolshevik demonstrations that they lost all control. In New York, citizens, soldiers, and sailors went on a rampage attacking radicals and smashing their meeting halls. In Cleveland there was terrible violence. A large Red Flag parade was disrupted, and in the ensuing riot twenty Socialists were hurt. Two other major riots occurred at the same time, and one person was killed and more than forty injured. Only radicals were arrested.

Boston was the third city hit hard by May Day riots. It was at the same time one of America's most patriotic cities and one of its most radical. Its Socialist activity was dominated by the pro-Bolshevik Lettish Workmen's Association, an immigrant group that owned a meeting hall and a printing press in Roxbury, where William now lived.

The Roxbury Letts had applied to the city for a permit to hold a May Day parade. Their request was denied. In defiance of the permit refusal, more than five hundred Socialists held a meeting at the Dudley Street Opera House, then proceeded from there toward another meeting hall in Roxbury. Waving red flags and shouting "To hell with the permit!" they marched, with twenty-one-year-old William James Sidis at their helm, carrying a red flag and wearing a red necktie.

Civilians glared balefully at the women in red dresses and the men with red flowers in their buttonholes. The spectators' ranks were peppered with soldiers and sailors who began to jeer, hissing, "Bolshevik!" According to the police, a police officer who asked the marchers if they had a permit was attacked. A patrol car was speedily dispatched to the scene, which was fast dissolving into brutal chaos. The police descended on the marchers with drawn guns, ordering the rebels to disperse. Their commands were met with jeers, and the incensed police yanked the red flags from the protesters' hands.

In minutes Warren Street was a maelstrom of fists, sticks and stones, billy clubs, knives, and gunshots. Policemen from five stations poured onto the scene, and wild-eyed spectators joined the riot. A passerby was shot in the foot, as was a policeman; another lost a finger, and a police captain suffered a fatal heart attack. Clubs split heads and faces gushed blood. Fleeing protesters were pursued by civilians and police, and soon the neighborhood was a battlefield of mini-riots. Socialists were rounded up and dragged off to the Dudley Street and Roxbury Crossing police stations, where an armed mob of two thousand enraged, hysterical civilians and soldiers lay in wait. The police pulled their prisoners past a bloodthirsty gauntlet, to screams of "Down with the Bolsheviks!" and "Kill them! Kill them!"

The riots raged into the night, and any unlucky onlooker who expressed sympathy for the marchers was swarmed by the mob. Many were taken into police custody for safety. These unfortunates had to leave the station house by the rear exit to escape attack. The police machine-gun squad waited in abeyance, but the riot was finally quelled after midnight. Arrests totaled 114.

William was one of the first to be arrested. He had been badly beaten up, and he was not alone. At Roxbury Police Station #9, the walls and booking desk were already splashed with blood, and a doctor hurriedly attended to the steady stream of maimed rioters being brought in.

William was booked and installed in a cell. In a nearby cell was a fiery young Socialist named Martha Foley. A twenty-year-old Irish girl who had grown up in Boston, Martha had caught William's eye. Though she was hardly what anyone would call pretty—five feet tall, too skinny, and wearing spectacles on what she referred to as her "blob of a nose"—she possessed a radiant charisma that dazzled William. It was the first time feminine charms had touched him, and he fell hard. The following day, Martha would share headlines with William. She was already well known in the Socialist movement, in which there were relatively few prominent female activists, among them Helen Keller, Margaret Singer, and "Mother" Jones.

Martha and William had a number of things in common—her father was a Harvard graduate and a doctor who had made her earn her allowance by memorizing poetry—Shelley's "Ode to a Skylark" was fifty cents, Milton's "Il Penseroso" was seventy-five cents. She was a bright child, and as with William, books had been her dearest companions. She had attended Boston University for two years but never graduated; her passions lay elsewhere, in writing and politics. (She was later to devote herself to literary pursuits—founding *Story* magazine and a well-known series of anthologies, *Best American Stories.*) She joined the Socialist party, and three months before May Day had picketed Boston's State House when Woodrow Wilson spoke there. The President was opposed to women's suffrage, so Martha and twenty-one members of the Women's Party carried signs bearing such slogans as EQUAL RIGHTS and TAXATION WITHOUT REPRESENTATION IS TYRANNY. They were arrested and spent a well-publicized night in jail. Martha had her first taste of front-line action, and she liked it. By May Day she was ready for more.

Martha's cell was near William's, and they managed to shout to each other over the din of the rapidly filling prison. The guards caught on quickly to William's shyness and awkward courting, and began to tease him, saying that unless he behaved and stopped talking, they'd put Martha Foley in the same cell with him. Under the stress and strain, William's sense of humor failed him, and he took the "threat" seriously, shouting back angrily to the guards that they wouldn't dare insult him in that way—which, of course, they didn't. As the evening wore on, Martha was joined by a dozen more women, most of whom did not really speak English. Nonetheless she managed to keep them in high spirits, leading them in a militant suffragist singalong.

The Roxbury court convened the next day to consider 102 of the cases. After being identified by his arresting officer, William pleaded Not Guilty. While the average bail set for the prisoners was $500 to $1,000, William's alone was $5,000. His counsel protested, but Judge Albert F. Hayden refused to lower it—Sidis, he believed, was largely responsible for the riot. Martha too protested her bail—it was high, at $1,000 in cash or $2,000 in property. She eventually obtained a bail bond and was released.

Somehow, friends of the Sidises' had discovered William's plight and arranged for his bail. One of his Harvard classmates, Leverett Saltonstall, secured his release the following day. William's trial was set for May 13.

William's dramatic arrest produced a flurry of headlines: "Young Harvard Prodigy Among 114 Prisoners," "Boy Prodigy Among Red Flag Carriers," "Sidis, Harvard 'Boy Wonder' in Dock—Said to Have Borne Red Flag; Miss Foley, a Suffragette, Also Held." The *Houston Post* even remembered their city's erstwhile teacher: "Will Sidis Again in the Limelight—Former Rice Instructor Who Defamed Houston Girls, Is Now Red Flagger."

On May 13, Judge Hayden presided over the cases of sixteen of the Boston May Day rioters. William's testimony proved to be the most sensational, and it made headlines throughout the country.

Judge Hayden regarded the demonstrators with extreme distaste. For days he had been handing out jail sentences to immigrants with names such as Frank Szyolofky and Deomid Potimsky, and like most Americans probably believed the Red Menace would poison his country irreparably. Martha Foley had already been sentenced to an eighteen-month term, which she somehow managed not to serve.

William was identified by several policemen as the man who had carried the red flag at the head of the parade. A patrolman also testified that during the demonstration, when he asked Sidis why he was not carrying an American flag instead of a red flag, the boy wonder replied, "To hell with the American flag!"

The Boston cases, especially that of the former Harvard prodigy, excited enormous local interest, and the courtroom was packed with spectators. William took the stand late in the afternoon. His first questioner was the counsel for the defense, Thomas G. Connolly.

William, by all accounts, was sharp and quick—in the various battles of wits that followed, he proved himself a tough adversary. One reporter observed that while he was "nervous at times, he seemed to be little concerned with the serious charges on which he was in court."

After dispensing with a few preliminaries, Connolly began in earnest:

"Were you carrying a red flag?"

"I was carrying a red flag, two by three feet; it was a piece of red silk tacked to a piece of string."

"Are you a Socialist?"

"Yes."

"Do you believe in the Soviet form of government?"

"I do."

"Will you state briefly what the Soviet form of government is?"

"That will be a rather difficult thing to do."

"Could you give his Honor a description in one hundred words?"

William did it in sixty-one: "The Soviet form of government is the present revolutionary form of government in Russia. The word Soviet is the Russian word for counsel. The general principle is that those who do socially useful work are to control the government and industries of the country as officials of government do in general. The fundamental principle is that everybody is supposed to work."

"Would you say in that respect only those who do socially useful work?"

"I would state that only those who do work shall be entitled to control the government, but those who are in nonessential industries would not be counted."

"Do you understand that they intend to get control through industries in which they work?"

"So I understand."

"By force if necessary?"

"I understand every government implies a certain power to suppress opposition."

"That does not answer the question. You said before that the people want control of the industries of the country. I want to know whether you advocate 'by force' the control of the industries of the country, or by use of the ballot."

"I countenance the use of force only in case it should be necessary, and I base my statement on a comparison of the Declaration of Independence of the United States government, which states clearly that the people shall be governed only with the consent of the governed." William had thrown the proceedings for a loop—no previous defendant and Russian sympathizer had quoted the Declaration of Independence during his trial.

Connolly pressed on: "Who decides? The majority or minority?"

"The majority."

"Do you believe in economic evolution?"

"I do."

"Do you believe in a God?"

"No."

At this shocking admission, Connolly turned to the judge and in his client's interest, asked that the court establish what was actually meant by the word "God." Hayden replied, "God Almighty," casting little illumination on the matter.

William attempted to explain his position further: He said that the kind of a God he did not believe in was the "big boss of the Christians," but he did believe in something "that is in a way apart from a human being." To the further horror of Judge Hayden, William explained that he believed in the evolution of species as well as economic evolution.

Connolly continued his interrogation. Did William believe that Soviet ideals necessarily implied violence? No, replied William, there should not be any violence on the road to that goal. The Bolsheviks, he explained, believed in the control of industry, and the Socialists believed in the ballot.

Now Connolly brought out a piece of evidence that would become a regular part of trials such as these in the coming years: a red flag, the one the defendant had carried. William declared that the red stood for the common blood of humanity, as it does in the American flag. What, pressed Connolly, does the red in the American flag represent? "It stands for the common brotherhood of mankind," repeated William, adding, "I do not believe we should have idolatry in the world. I do not idolize the red flag—it is just a piece of red silk." Connolly held up the flag and asked William if he cared whether it was trampled and spat on. William repeated, "It is only a piece of red silk."

Next, William was cross-examined without event by the prosecution, whose questions were not nearly so probing as Connolly's had been. Connolly returned for redirect examination.

"For a man who believes in the Soviet form of government," he said, "you certainly did not use much force."

"I do not believe in using force," replied William simply. "And I did not say 'To hell with the American flag'—I never use such language." (This was true—William never swore, but when he wanted to, he always invoked the name of a lake in New Hampshire: Lake Chaugoggagoggamauchauggagoggchaubunagungamaug.)

"Do you," demanded Judge Hayden, "believe in what the American flag stands for?"

William stood firm. "I believe in certain ways for what it stands, in the sense of the Declaration of Independence."

"Did you and Martha H. Foley, the militant suffragist, organize the parade, or have charge of it?"

"I was not a leader of the parade—there were no leaders and as far as I know no permit was asked for."

"Didn't you think there would be trouble when you went on the street with a red flag?" persisted the judge.

"It did not occur to me. . . . Under the American flag I do not stand for the lynching of Negroes without trial."

Judge Hayden erupted, "We all know what the American flag stands for."

"Well I don't," interjected the feisty Connolly. "We have slavery here, fighting of armed thugs and everything else."

On this tense and confused note, the trial ended. The May Day offenders received their sentences, an average of six months in the house of correction. Only William and two others received eighteen months each—six months for rioting and a year for assaulting an officer, to be served at hard labor. William appealed, and was released on five hundred dollars bail. His paradise of seclusion had been shattered by his bold public protest, and he left the courtroom a notorious man, front-page fodder once again.

1. *William in high school. He qualified for admission to Harvard at age nine, but was not invited to attend until he was eleven.*

2. After William's return from the Rice Institute, a Boston paper portrayed him being pursued by a marriage-minded Texas female, with a preacher in tow.

3. William at sixteen, in his Harvard graduation photo.

4. This cartoon appeared in the Boston Herald *in 1914, shortly after William's graduation from Harvard.*

5. William, Harvard Law School student, by the statue of John Harvard in Cambridge, Massachusetts.

6. Portrait of William during his Harvard years.

3

4

In Cambridge, Mass. Taken

William by the
statue of John Harvard
near Memorial

5

EATS CRACKERS AND
MILK OR CHEESE THREE
TIMES A DAY

RIDES ON TROLLEYS
FOR RECREATION

BECOMES YOUNGEST
COLLEGE PROFESSOR
IN THE WORLD

6

7

8

7. *In front of the Institute, 1914. William, age sixteen, stands alone at left. Front row: Helena, Sarah, Boris, and Sarah's youngest brother. In the back row are five of the Institute's patients.*

8. *Solarium and greenhouses, Sidis Psychotherapeutic Institute.*

9. *The drawing rooms, Sidis Psychotherapeutic Institute.*

10. *William with Mrs. Whittemore—the Sidises' patron—in front of the Institute.*

10

9

11

12

In Portsmouth N. H.

William and his Brownie

13

14

15

11. Sarah and Boris at Portsmouth.

12. Sarah and Boris.

13. Self-portrait of William and his Brownie, 1916.

14. Helena, age twenty-two.

15. The Sidis family in Los Angeles, shortly after William's angry departure: Boris, Helena, Sarah.

16. A selection from William's collection of more than two thousand transfers.

17. Diagram from Notes on the Collection of Transfers.

18. William's perpetual calendar, which he invented at the age of six and manufactured twenty-five years later.

16

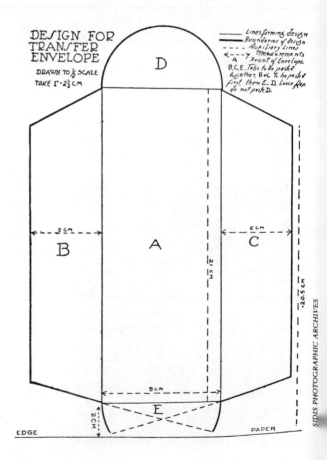

Perpetual Calendar

What day of the week was it —
    that July 4, 1776 came on?
    that Washington was born?
    that YOU were born?

What day will it be —
    that Christmas will come next year?
    Thanksgiving day, year after next?
    that next Election Day comes?
    when the Mortgage falls due?

Directions

For years 1900-1956, turn wheel till year desired appears.
Complete year's calendar is below. Week-day is in same row with date,
and below the month.

For 1700, use 1909
For 1701-1736, add 220
For 1737-1764, add 164
For 1765-1799, add 136
For 1800, use 1902
For 1801-1832, add 124

For 1833-1860, add 68
For 1861-1899, add 40
For 1957-2012, subtract 56
For 2013-2068, subtract 112
For 2069-2099, subtract 168
For 2100, use 1909

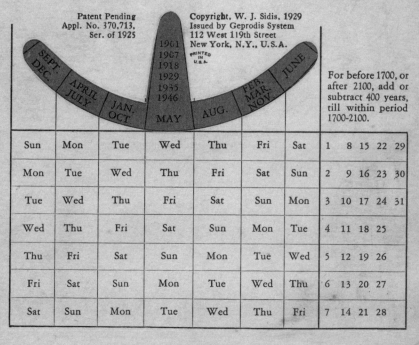

Patent Pending
Appl. No. 370,713,
Ser. of 1925

Copyright, W. J. Sidis, 1929
Issued by Geprodis System
112 West 119th Street
New York, N.Y., U.S.A.

PRINTED IN U.S.A.

1901
1907
1918
1929
1935
1946

For before 1700, or
after 2100, add or
subtract 400 years,
till within period
1700-2100.

Sun	Mon	Tue	Wed	Thu	Fri	Sat	1	8	15	22	29
Mon	Tue	Wed	Thu	Fri	Sat	Sun	2	9	16	23	30
Tue	Wed	Thu	Fri	Sat	Sun	Mon	3	10	17	24	31
Wed	Thu	Fri	Sat	Sun	Mon	Tue	4	11	18	25	
Thu	Fri	Sat	Sun	Mon	Tue	Wed	5	12	19	26	
Fri	Sat	Sun	Mon	Tue	Wed	Thu	6	13	20	27	
Sat	Sun	Mon	Tue	Wed	Thu	Fri	7	14	21	28	

SIDIS PHOTOGRAPHIC ARCHIVES

19

19. *William, age forty-five, with his friend Isaac Rabinowitz.*

20. *Martha Foley, the only woman William ever loved.*

HOUGHTON MIFFLIN COMPANY

20

11

Rebellion, Romance, and Reversibility

Boris Sidis was in a truly difficult position. Unlike his wife, who was an old-fashioned Republican, Boris had certain sympathies with radicalism. As a young man Boris had written fiery verse, which William translated from Russian at his mother's request. At first Boris was enthusiastic about the Russian Revolution, but after a few months had passed he dourly told Sarah, "Their slavery is going to be deeper than it ever was under the Tsar."

In 1919, the year of his son's arrest, Boris published a small book devoted to his own political views. In *The Source and Aim of Human Progress: A Study in Social Psychology and Social Pathology,* he described war as a "mental epidemic," a mass hysteria that fed man's most primitive impulses, his "fear instincts." The result of fear run rampant was mass hypnosis, which produced a population of robotic humans.

Boris condemned the Germans and the Allies with equal ferocity. He contemptuously wrote of "the great 'saving' mania," and its hypnotic effect: "Everything and everybody had to be saved. . . . Save Belgium, save the country, save Democracy, save your food, from potato peelings to the garbage can. The suggestion was irresistible, and the weak human spirit yielded and fell into a deep social trance. . . . Everybody was full of war. . . . Why wonder that when the air was full of the germs that the war malady spread like wild fire?" This pestilence, Boris declared, could only be compared with the crusade mania: "In this world-war nations fell to the lowest level of savagery. The frenzied, suggestible, gregarious, subconscious self, freed from all rational restraints, celebrated its delirious orgies. . . .

"No man," continued Boris, "is so low as to deserve oppression, no opinion so mean as to merit suppression." Every important step in human life could be traced to an individual or group of men "whose opinions were regarded as anti-social and dangerous, on account of their extreme radicalism."

But Boris now owned a mansion, ran a private practice. He had reaped the very sweetest fruits of capitalism, from seeds sown by his own fine mind, his hard work, his great ability. Boris was proud to be an American. He would fight, with the written word, those Americans who affronted the democracy he held dear, who perpetrated Red scares and the deportation of aliens. But though he supported his son's rebellious spirit, he could not support his sympathy with communism.

William had been emotionally and intellectually alienated from his mother for many years. Now, for the first time, he and his father stood divided. Boris and Sarah, too, were divided in their reactions to the scandal of their son's behavior. Sarah described their attitudes in the years preceding William's arrest:

"While this phase of his youth ran its course, Billy was loud in his denunciation of everything done by any human who was older than twenty-five, especially his parents. We were 'bourgeois,' he said, like he was the first boy who ever thought of using the term to describe his parents.

"Boris was entirely undisturbed. 'It seems quite normal to me,' he said. 'Youth that has no rebellion in it is not worth its salt. Remember when you rebelled and studied though your mother wanted you to marry the jeweler's son? Don't worry, this is good for him.'

"But it hurt me, to some extent. While my son was probably right in describing me as 'bourgeois'—I have enjoyed fame and money —it seemed to me very shallow of him to be so loud in his condemnation of his father, in whose image Billy was so molded."

For Sarah, the shame of the family disgrace, the tarnishing of the Sidises' image, the editorials in *The New York Times,* were an agony. To sully the image of "Dr. Science," and of the immigrant family risen from the slums—this was an unforgivable outrage.

For Boris, the argument was philosophical, ideological—rebellion was natural to youth, but communism was a wrong, an evil, philosophy. When he headed the May Day parade, William had gone to extremes Boris could no longer condone.

Elliot Sagall remembered Boris's reaction: "William became a radical. He and Boris had different philosophies. And Boris Sidis being a professor at Harvard . . . this was insufferable, to have his son in an anarchistic parade on Main Street! He was put in jail, and we heard his father used his influence to get him out. And he tried to cover it up."

William Fadiman recalled, "We were liberals, and so we understood. But we all felt that Billy had been set up because his last name was Sidis, and in Boston that was a very big name—Sidis of Harvard, etc. He had been set up to be leader of the May Day parade, so that the radicals would have publicity for their party. We thought he didn't quite know what he was doing. He was victimized to some degree."

Clifton Fadiman shared his brother's impression of Billy's credulity: "His communism, I think, was very naïve in character. I never got the impression that it was anything but a wild outburst of general indignation."

The events that followed William's trial are among the most confusing portions of Sidis history. Somehow Boris pulled the appropriate strings and kept his son out of jail, but William was not exactly a free man. As Helena described it, "He was cleared, sort of temporarily, but it took a number of years before they were able to clear him so he could even be in Massachusetts." According to a number of accounts, the case was eventually nol-prossed in the Superior Court, at the request of the prosecution; if this is true, it was probably the result of Boris's further efforts. It is also possible that Boris and Sarah did not inform their son when they achieved the nolle prosequi, as a way of maintaining control over him. This is likely, since William remained frightened of possible arrest for a good many years.

The ordeal that followed was a prison term nonetheless, in William's opinion. His parents swooped down on Boston, scooped him up, and took him to Portsmouth, where they set about to reform their boy wonder. Little is known of what happened in the year that followed. Sarah's memoirs, despite their meticulous detailing of her son's every childhood action, shrivel up and end here. The last completed chapter, "Billy Rebels," is nothing more than a smattering of cheerful anecdotes, without mention of the harsh conflicts that rent the family. William rarely spoke to his friends about this period of his life. Yet twenty-five years later he was still bitter—he submitted the following to a radical journal he coedited:

"RAILROADING" IN THE PAST

Lest anyone acquire the impression that sending conscientious objectors to asylums is a new trick, it might be of interest to note that the trick was known in the last war.

A CO [conscientious objector] who was too young to be called on to register till late in 1918, and who thereby escaped any actual draft call up to the time of the Armistice, was hauled into court on a trumped-up charge in May, 1919. The sentence was appealed (such procedure is normal in Massachusetts district courts); but, before the appeal could come to trial, he was kidnapped by his parents, by arrangement with the district attorney, and was taken to a sanatorium operated by them. He was kept there a full year—from October, 1919, to October, 1920—and kept under various kinds of mental torture, consisting of being scolded and nagged at (everything that did or did not happen was grounds for a tongue-lashing protracted over many hours) for an average of six to eight hours a day; sometimes this scolding was administered while he was loaded with sleeping medicine, or after being waked up out of a sound sleep. And the threat of being transferred to a regular insane asylum was held up in front of him constantly, with detailed descriptions of the tortures practiced there, as well as of the simple legal process by which he could be committed to such a place. He was unlawfully held in this sanatorium, but he could not escape while watch was being kept, for the criminal case was kept pending against him, and it was on the court records that he had jumped bail (being kidnapped, he could not appear for trial, or even know that trial had been called).

In October, 1920, he was taken to California, to prevent his communicating somehow with friends in his home city sixty miles away. He made his escape from there in September, 1921, by which time he appeared to be scared of his own shadow. The attempt to get him back to the old tortures was never given up, the parents resorting, from time to time, to various efforts to track him down and to persuade his friends to turn him over for "protection," especially when any misfortune is known to come his way. A particular effort to bring him under control of relatives was made about a year ago, but was highly unsuccessful.

Since, in most states, any two physicians can commit a man, without giving him a chance to defend himself, into a sanatorium or asylum, where he can be held incommunicado indefinitely, the danger of railroading of that sort is still very much alive. In any case where the prosecution is able to command the services of two doctors, the victims would then simply disappear without leaving any traces.

This bizarre little document is virtually the only account of this traumatic segment of William's life, and it leads one to ask many questions. Did his parents really dope him? Did they actually threaten to commit him to an insane asylum? How could William truly have been kidnapped and held prisoner? One of William's closest friends throughout his adult life, fellow radical Julius Eichel, addressed the question of the "imprisonment": "His father and mother had some power over him. As far as he knew they could turn him over to the police any time they wished—an old indictment was hanging over him. For many years he dared not go openly to Boston, for he feared arrest for that May Day activity."

In Helena's opinion: "Billy couldn't take any correction. I could; it didn't bother me. Billy said to me, 'You are like a reed, and you bend and then come upright again. I am like an oak tree, and I get uprooted.' And of course, I have learned to be a little diplomatic, tell little white lies. He was straightforward, and utterly frank, and would tell everybody just what he thought of them—and that's not the best way. He always told me I had a New England conscience and it would get me into trouble. But why would he say that, when he was far more conscientious than I was and far more honest? I have learned to lie, I don't think he ever learned to. My mother could lie. I don't think my father could very well."

According to Helena, all the family fighting was over petty issues. Sarah harped and hammered away at her son with a daily refrain of "Do it this way." Recalled Clifton Fadiman, "I think Sarah, like most mothers, wanted him to live like a mensch, you know, put on a tie and eat right—chicken soup and so forth. But he thought of all that as merely symbols of her dislike of him and he wouldn't have any of that. So I think what they quarreled about was life-style."

A major source of friction was William's appearance. At twenty-one he had bulked out considerably, and despite his handsome face, he was ungainly and sloppy. He had developed psoriasis and his sensitive skin made it difficult for him to shave. At a time when men wore suits and high collars, William was content with sneakers (without socks) and an unfashionable cap. Both Boris and Sarah criticized their son's garb, which was odd, since neither of them was much concerned personally about dress.

Helena, who was ten, adopted her parents' point of view about the May Day parade, and thought her brother had been foolish to get involved in it. But brother and sister remained close, and little Helena suffered acutely from the constant tension and bickering in the family. She was particularly upset by a mother-son spat that occurred just a few months after William's trial and "abduction." As she described it, "My mother got really red in the face. He had insulted her. She just sat down and said, 'I am insulted.' Then she went and sat somewhere else and said, 'I am insulted.' Then she went and sat somewhere else and said, 'I am insulted.' I was ten years old, and it was a big word. I didn't know what 'insulted' meant. I wondered what in the world my brother had said, but she wasn't the kind of person that you could ask. I never found out what it was about. Now my father would never have behaved like that. He might have yelled at Billy—he did—but she pushed him into it. I don't think my mother conscious-ly encouraged my father to turn against Billy. But people ask, 'Did she have enough power over my father to turn him against Billy?' She had plenty of power over anybody to turn them against anyone!

"Another time, in California, my brother and father and mother were fighting, I don't remember what about. Billy was sitting in a chair, suffering a very bad cold, or an allergy. A neighbor's dog, Patsy, used to visit us often; and that day Patsy ran over to him, and laid a paw on his knee, and looked up in his face. Years later he told me, 'That was the only sympathy I got there.' "

Not surprisingly, William parted ways with the Socialists and joined the Communist party. However, he quickly became disillusioned with the Communists. He observed that the Russian people had traded slavery under the Tsar for slavery under Lenin, and he was disgusted to see that the American Communist party was wracked by infighting, and its members were more loyal to the central power in Russia than they were to the United States. Horrified by Communist repression of individual liberties, he quit the party, and began to talk to radical friends about his vision of an American party: a party with no international ties, and with democratic, cooperative ownership of industries by workers, free from all governmental interference. Helena concluded, "As a Red, he was pretty much a pink."

William, like so many radicals, longed to go to Russia and see communism in action. He almost had his chance. President Wilson appointed Boris to an American "peace delegation" to Russia, and William was to go along as interpreter. Shortly before the departure date, Boris went to Washington to discuss the trip with Wilson, withdrawing angrily when he discovered that the President did not plan to bring home American troops still fighting with the Poles against the Russian revolutionaries. Though the trip fell through, the plans are revealing—if Boris and William planned to travel together, the bad blood between father and son could not have been beyond repair.

A reporter for the *New York Sunday News,* writing many years later, referred to this period of William's life with an astute observation: "He developed radical tendencies so extreme that even members of the Communist party lifted their eyebrows a bit. This political leaning was in itself strange. For the Communist, theoretically at least, works for his fellows while from all one can gather, Sidis worked for none but himself."

Sarah wrote, "Billy's communism did not last many months. His rebellion was part of the quick blood of youth. A few years after the Russian Revolution I asked him whether he thought communism was working. He replied, 'How should I know? Communism has never been tried.' " In writing off her son's behavior as "the quick blood of youth," Sarah failed completely to see that William remained passionately devoted to radicalism; her blind spot could only have increased the tension between them.

Other difficulties troubled the family. Helena underwent a series of ailments, and Boris remained very sick. He had never fully recovered from his bout with the Spanish flu, and in his weakened condition he suffered a mild stroke. Helena recalled, "Father was ill for a long time. He kept it to himself. I don't think my mother was terribly conscious of his illness. She was not terribly conscious of the fact that I was ill."

After a difficult year in Portsmouth, Boris was encouraged by his doctors to return to California. What William referred to as his "kidnapping," Sarah saw in an entirely different light, writing, "In his early twenties, after his flurry of revolt, Billy came out to California with us."

Because the Institute was closed, and because Boris and Sarah rented a relatively expensive home in San Diego, there were money problems on top of everything else. That winter Boris had his second, more serious, stroke. Remarkably, he continued to work, producing books and papers at almost his former pace.

William had two major forms of escape from the family tension. When he was not suffering "tongue-lashings," he took refuge in writing and in travel. He often borrowed the family car or boarded the bus, and toured the small towns that dotted the California coast. Sarah reminisced about his travels: "Helena always turned to nature, but it was the man-made world that Billy loved. He told me with a glow of the pleasure that he got in going into strange towns, and eating at little holes-in-the-wall with all the people who drive the trucks and push the typewriters that make the world go. Thus Billy, who had grown up among people who were above all intellectual, who made their mark on their time, fell in love with the type of person who leaves no record in this world, except in the memory of those who loved them. He once told me, 'Mother, a man who has lost his anonymity has lost a precious and irreplaceable thing.' Billy never left America. He joked about his provinciality, but was stubborn in it, and later when Helena and I traveled in Europe he flatly refused to go with us.

"Billy read a great deal about any town he planned to visit, its history and geography. Then he would go and explore it. 'I can really see a town,' he told me, 'because I am not in it, don't belong to it. And I have learned how to look so that I can see the town of fifty years ago, or one hundred years ago. I can see the Indian mounds and trails that were there first.'

"Not only did he love the history of these little towns, he loved the 'now' in them, he said. He gave far more time when he was grown to the language of the American people than he had ever given when he astonished professors as a child by learning Latin, Greek, Russian, and German. He wrote a dictionary of what he called the 'lingo' of this land. He prided himself on his ear for dialect, for accent." The "lingo dictionary" is long lost, but it was not to be the last time he would demonstrate a fascination with language not only "American" but essentially "uneducated."

In 1925, Richard G. Badger, owner of Boston's Gorham Press and publisher of most of Boris Sidis's books, brought out *The Animate and the Inanimate* by William James Sidis. Considerable mystery surrounds the book's publication. The preface was completed in 1920, when William was twenty-two. Why had William waited five years to publish it? Some, but not all, of Badger's books were vanity publications—was this one of them? Why didn't it receive a single review? Since the name William James Sidis was always good for a newspaper story, why was this major work completely ignored? How did it entirely escape the attention of Boston's reporters? Perhaps the press wasn't up to comprehending the work, and its level of brilliance was certainly no help to any reporter looking for a "genius gone crazy" story.

And how did the academic community miss it? In 1979, fifty-four years after its publication, a Columbia University graduate student, Dan Mahony, brought the book to the attention of Sidis's former classmate Buckminster Fuller. Fuller wrote the following letter to Gerard Piel of *Scientific American,* urging Piel to reprint the text: "Imagine my excitement and joy on being handed this Xerox of Sidis's 1925 book, in which he clearly predicts the black hole. In fact, I find his whole book to be a fine cosmological piece. . . . Norbert Wiener used to talk to me about him . . . and Norbert was grieved that Sidis did not go on to fulfill his seemingly great promise of brilliance. . . . I hope you will become as excited as I am at this discovery that Sidis did go on after college to do the most magnificent thinking and writing. I find him focusing in on many of the same subjects that fascinate me, and coming to about the same conclusions as those I have published in *Synergetics,* and will be publishing in *Synergetics Volume II.* "

Fuller's praise for *The Animate and the Inanimate* is not overblown. Indeed, the book explores the theory of black holes—collapsed stars so heavy and dense that their high gravity prevents even light from escaping—fourteen years before the publication of another work commonly recognized as the first on the subject. The second book suggesting the existence of these mysterious stellar objects was *An Introduction to the Study of Stellar Stucture,* written by Subrahmanyan Chandrasekhar in 1939. Sidis actually wrote his book five years before it was published in 1920; and he had formulated his ideas as early as 1915 during his stay at Rice Institute. Since William did not fraternize with scientists, he accomplished all this without knowing the latest theories making the informal rounds of scientific circles. He reached his conclusions using the same methods that his father taught his mother when she wanted to learn geometry as a young, uneducated immigrant—read the basic laws, and figure out the rest for yourself.

As the basis for *The Animate and the Inanimate,* William explored the possibility that all the laws of the universe are reversible in time, with the apparent exception of the Second Law of Thermodynamics. This is analogous to running a film backward—theoretically, all laws of physics would still hold true in a reverse-running universe, except the Second Law of Thermodynamics. This law is popularly known as the Law of Entropy; that is, the universe is proceeding on an unstoppable course toward total chaos and "heat death." All the particles of all the atoms in the universe will eventually bounce off each other, moving farther and farther away from each other, until they no longer collide at all; then nothing will move, nothing will live, and the universe will exist in a frozen tableau forever afterward. If one imagines this happening in reverse, there is no energy source to cause any particles to bind together in the ordered forms that make up matter —therefore, the Second Law of Thermodynamics is believed to be irreversible.

William offers the following image as a relatively simple introduction to his theory: If one were to watch a film running backward, for example a ball bouncing down stairs, it would appear that the ball were being "pushed" by each stair, up to the next one. Where would this "push" come from? Everything else about the picture would look normal—gravity, mass, and so forth. But there is no physical law yet to explain a normal stair "pushing" on a ball, so that a ball would inexplicably come to rest at the top of the stairs.

William suggested that the Second Law of Thermodynamics is not a law at all, but a probability. The fact that the Second Law of Thermodynamics seems always to hold true is more or less coincidence in our corner of the universe. Also, entropy is reversed in other corners of the universe—elsewhere, chaos is proceeding to order. And if the Second Law of Thermodynamics appears to dominate local events, then probability suggests that there must be reversals of it all around us that we haven't yet recognized.

In the book's preface, William credits his godfather, William James, and not his own father, with the discovery of "reserve energy." Following the observations that led James to suggest a "reserve energy," Sidis theorized that inanimate (dead) objects follow the Second Law of Thermodynamics, while animate (living) things reverse the law, and draw on a "reserve fund" of energy to mold the universe to their will. Life provided the reversal of entropy that Sidis's theory required.

William's theory remains highly speculative; there is no reason to believe that a reverse universe exists. Also, biological processes are no longer the mystery they were at the time of his writing. But while working on this problem, Sidis came up with other conclusions that are interesting to this day.

Cosmogeny is the study of the origins of the universe; the most popularly known theory today is called the "Big Bang" theory. In *The Animate and the Inanimate,* William proposed a "Great Collision" theory, wherein two large, inert bodies, containing all the matter in the universe between them, collided; this collision provided the energy that started the universe in motion.

As our sun hurtles through space to an eventual frozen death, it gives off energy. Somewhere in the universe there are suns that take in energy, and death becomes life. This other kind of sun Sidis dubbed a "black body," since it would be taking in all light energy, and therefore be totally invisible. This exactly describes a black hole. Should the Second Law of Thermodynamics eventually reverse itself in this "black body," it would then start giving off energy and become a sun. In this way, the universe would be in a perpetual state of ebb and flow, all energy being conserved.

Scientists all over the world are still working on a problem known as "Fermi's paradox," proposed by Enrico Fermi. If the universe is infinite, Fermi postulated, then everything possible must occur somewhere sometime; therefore, there must exist a planet where the inhabitants speak English. Why haven't we met them? Why haven't we met *anyone* out there? Young Sidis also said, "The theory of the reversibility of the universe supposes that life exists under all sorts of circumstances, even on such hot bodies as the sun." Like Fermi's paradox, Sidis's reversibility theory also requires that life must exist in every corner of the universe, in order to provide the necessary reversals of the law of entropy.

The theory is challenging, fascinating, and controversial on its own merits today. It was far more so in 1925; and it must be remembered that it sprang from the mind of a boy in his early twenties, who devoted only a portion of his scholarship to this book, because he was dedicated to such a vast variety of other intellectual pursuits at the same time. Had he dedicated his life entirely to cosmogeny, who knows what extraordinary body of work he might have produced?

Sidis himself called his work purely speculative in nature, since there was a dearth of observations available to prove or disprove his reversibility theory. How much faster might cosmology, cosmogeny, and particle physics have progressed had his ideas been examined by the scientific community? Sidis even went so far as to include a chapter on his own objections to his theory: "All that is attempted here is, not to prove this theory scientifically, or even to claim it as perfectly consistent with itself or with facts, but merely to indicate that there are . . . other possible theories than the one at present generally accepted by physicists, and yet not more absurd or more inconsistent with facts."

And in his preface, Sidis states: "At first I hesitated to publish my theory of the reversibility of the universe, but . . . I have decided to publish the work and give my theory to the world, to be accepted or rejected, as the case may be." As it turned out, Sidis's theory wasn't even considered.

William never spoke of his thoughts or feelings about being ignored. However, he ceased to write about mathematics, physics, or cosmogeny. He never again published a book under his own name. That he drew nationwide attention when he talked about girls in Texas, and none at all when he broke ground theorizing about the structure and laws of the universe, must have seemed to the boy prodigy a sick sort of joke.

When William was twenty-three, he and his parents had their final fight. According to his sister it was over an office job he lost for some trivial reason: "He didn't do something he should have done—maybe it was his clothes or his manners." Whatever it was, it was the last straw for William, and, as he put it, "He made his escape . . . scared of his own shadow."

Fearing arrest if he returned to Boston, he headed for New York. That city held a number of attractions for him, not the least of which was its new resident Martha Foley. William found his first refuge at the home of his aunt Bessie Fadiman. She gave him a small room, with the understanding that he could stay for a few weeks. Bessie was warm and welcoming toward William, although he was something of a nuisance. For one thing, his eating habits were bizarre. She was disconcerted to see him attack a plate of food one article at a time—first the meat, then the potatoes, then the peas, etc. This unusual approach dismayed nearly every host who served William dinner. Also, he followed his aunt around the house, complaining constantly about his parents. One of his bitterest refrains, she remembered, stemmed from his early childhood. William lamented that his parents had not taught him the rudiments of grooming, and to his great embarrassment he had found himself years behind other children in the simplest matters, such as tying his shoelaces or getting dressed properly. At the age of twenty-three, these humiliations still rankled (but not enough, evidently, for him to change his now casual approach to these matters).

Eventually William rented his own, cheap apartment, and settled into life in New York. He took a job as an interpreter with an agency handling Soviet business in America. He expanded his political contacts, and could often be found at the offices of the League for Industrial Democracy or at the American Civil Liberties Union. He formed what was to become a lifelong friendship with fellow conscientious objector Julius Eichel, a Brooklyn pharmacist who at the time of William's arrest was already serving a prison term for his pacifism. Eichel too listened to William's complaints about his parents, who by now had returned to Portsmouth.

The light of William's life was Martha Foley, whom he saw often. He confided the details of their meetings to Eichel, who wrote about the trysting twenty years later. "Sidis sought out his new flame and carried on a romance on Central Park benches. He was very naïve when he would tell this story of his lovemaking. The first time he had her to himself in Central Park he kissed her with a great deal of ardor. 'Why, you kiss like an experienced lover,' she said. 'Where did you get that experience?' And he naïvely answered, as he later told us, 'Why, can't you believe it comes as naturally to me as any other man?' "

An elated William secured a photograph of Martha, which he flourished at every opportunity. Cousin Clifton Fadiman saw it, as did numerous other acquaintances. "He would suddenly take it out, her picture. We might be talking about the price of eggs and all of a sudden he would say, 'Did I ever show you this?' And it was Martha."

William continued to drop in on the Fadimans, usually for a meal. His visits made the teenaged Clifton uncomfortable. "He would come to our house without any announcement—it never occurred to him to use the phone. Because we were his aunt and uncle and cousins we couldn't throw him out. 'Home,' as Mr. Frost's line has it, 'is where they have to take you in.' But he was a damn nuisance. His conversation was never submitted to the ordinary conventional rules. It was explosive. His voice would get very loud when he complained of his mother and father. He certainly never asked for any pity, but he often screwed himself into a state of excitement. In many ways his eccentricities were the consequence of his not having the conventional censor that we all have.

"I don't think he had anything like a regular job. He lived in third-rate little lodgings. He ate at the Automat. He was simply not an attractive man. He was quite large, about six feet tall, overweight, slovenly, with a mild skin disease. He was never ragged, but he didn't seem to change his clothes. Even we, who weren't dressed very well, felt somehow that this was somebody from the street—that's what my mother used to say. And she'd try to clean him up and give him food. He was an enormous eater. When he came to our house, it was straight antique Jewish hospitality. And he would eat anything put before him no matter how frequently it was repeated."

William Fadiman, too, commented on his cousin's clothing: "He dressed not oddly, but shabbily. His clothes were ill fitting and unpressed. Shoes were always scuffed and dirty. And he didn't bathe very often. He always wore a vest, summer or winter, which is curious. He wore a tie. He was quite formal, in a bizarre way."

But more puzzling to the Fadiman brothers than William's appearance was his attitude toward academic or intellectual matters. When Clifton ventured to discuss mathematics with his illustrious cousin, William turned on him furiously, saying, "I don't ever want to talk about that kind of thing!" According to Clifton, he referred contemptuously to "the intellect and the world of ideas, particularly mathematics. He didn't say it was nonsense, but he would not talk about it. We would ask him what he was doing and he would toss it off. My impression is that he didn't know what the hell was going on in the intellectual world; that he abjured everything that his father respected, everything about the academic, intellectual life. We thought he was merely passing his time in some second-rate lodging house doing nothing. And he read pulp science-fiction novels. I read them too—they were great. But you wouldn't think this great intellectual would like that sort of thing."

William was a little more forthcoming with William Fadiman. He spoke to him at length and with great enthusiasm about a novel he had been writing for several years, concerning the lost continent of Atlantis. Nevertheless, his basic stance was consistent. According to William Fadiman, "He abhorred being referred to as 'the genius.' If someone found out about him in the beginning of a relationship, he would get very choleric. He would get rid of and be furious at that person. He never swore, but he indicated as clearly as a man could that he was angry, that this was nobody's business but his own."

This, then, was the young man who had recently completed a major work in theoretical physics. In a few years he would publish it, a work so undeniably brilliant, so profoundly intellectual, and so heavily based in pure mathematics that his cousins, had they known about it, would have been very bewildered indeed. Said Clifton, "I never knew he had any interests."

Though William would publish *The Animate and the Inanimate* under his own name, it would be the last time he did, using pseudonyms forever after. He had begun his double life.

12

In Search of Solitude

During the two years that William spent with his parents, he had escaped the prying eye of the press. In 1922, when he was twenty-four, the *Boston Traveler* dug up enough material for a front-page story: "What Has Become of Sidis, the Boy Prodigy?" The article undoubtedly aggravated William, for not only was it riddled with inaccuracies about his childhood, but it accused him of cowardice: "Sentenced to jail, Sidis has neither served time nor appeared in the superior court to fight the matter out." The *Traveler* sought information about William's whereabouts from an unnamed "former friend," who supplied the curious information that Sidis was now a teacher in "a New York labor-Socialist school. . . . Previous to the May Day 'Roxbury riots' he had been teaching in 'Hesperia,' the socialistic school for children set up in the south end by Frank Mack and raided by the authorities in 1919." Since the article is full of erroneous information, some of this may be false. However, there was a Boston Communist named Frank Mack who was deported to his native Britain in 1922 after association with a radical school, and it may well be that William had again assumed the role of teacher despite his traumatic experience at the Rice Institute.

The former friend, evidently knowing nothing of William's love for Martha Foley, insisted that William was a woman-hater. He was equally certain that William did not know how to enjoy himself: "He has no conception of play or pleasure—outside his intellectual pursuits. Likewise he has no conception of beauty. I once showed him a remarkable picture of a mountain. 'Don't you think it's beautiful?' I asked. 'No,' he said, 'it's only a big hill.' "

Aside from this article, William received no publicity, and did not participate in any more political demonstrations that might land him on the front pages. His life was gradually becoming a happy one. He no longer had his parents or journalists to torment him, he had an active social life and, as always, an extraordinary intellectual life. His courtship of Martha had not progressed beyond the kissing stage. Although they remained close friends, she let it be known that she was not interested in anything more. Apparently, this disturbed William not at all, and he spoke about her to friends with the same enthusiasm as before. Perhaps he held out hopes for the future, or perhaps he was secretly relieved at the limits she set.

William eventually lost his job as an interpreter, and set out to look for work. Thus began a series of menial office employments that earned him enough to survive and little more—between fifteen and twenty-five dollars a week—but enabled him to preserve his precious anonymity. His real work, the writing of the books he loved, was done on his own time and without moneymaking in mind.

This comfortable existence was shaken on October 24, 1923, when William received a phone call from a friend telling him that his father had died that morning at Portsmouth, of a cerebral hemorrhage.

No one knows how William took the news, but he did not attend the funeral. His reason for not appearing, however, seems not to have been disdain for his father, but a refusal to see his mother. Since his departure from California, he and Helena had corresponded steadily, often in French. In his letters he explained that he wanted to visit her, but he couldn't abide their mother. Great as the tension had been between father and son, it was not enough to keep him away. The possibility of a painful run-in with Sarah was.

Boris Sidis's death came as a shock to his colleagues and to the public. He was only fifty-six, and even some of his best friends never knew how ill he was. He had published seventeen books and more than fifty magazine articles in twenty-five years, and at the time of his death was hard at work on another book, *The Psychology of the Folk Tale.*

Boris had requested simple and informal services, which were attended by family, friends, colleagues, and admirers from around the country. The funeral was held at Maplewood Farms, and Boris was buried on the estate. Obituaries ran in newspapers across the country, some describing him as the first American doctor to practice psychotherapy. In spite of Boris's distinction, his death was not the front-page news that his son's arrest had been.

Boris's estate was surprisingly small, considering his wide reputation and the wealth of his clientele. The expenses of the last few years —the trips to California, maintaining the Institute, and his illness— had told on the family bank account. He left his children about four thousand dollars each. Helena was to receive her inheritance at twenty-one, while William could collect his immediately.

Though it meant braving Sarah, William went to Portsmouth to claim the inheritance. Relatives and family friends looked upon his decision with contempt. Because he hadn't attended the funeral, some felt he had no right to take the money. Others thought he should turn his portion over to his mother, since she was a widow with an enormous estate to run and he was a brilliant young man who could easily make a fortune.

No one knows what passed between William and Sarah during

this visit, but Clifton Fadiman described an unfortunate meeting between mother and son during this period: "Sarah visited us, and he came in, apparently accidentally. And there was a real fight between them, in our home." Fadiman did not remember the cause of the argument—some trivial matter—but he did recall his aunt's aggression: "My aunt was a very arrogant, self-confident person. I think she had a deep sense of guilt. And highly aggressive and arrogant people like Sarah are hard put to accommodate their sense of guilt. So it expresses itself in more indignation and more anger and more fury, rather than reconciliation."

After this harsh exchange, mother and son ceased altogether to communicate. Helena now assumed the unenviable position of go-between and buffer for the two, living with her mother and visiting her brother on neutral territory at the Fadimans' home in New York.

In the previous year, Helena's situation had altered radically. She missed her brother, and though Boris had told her "your cousin Jack will be a brother to you," it wasn't the same. Shortly before her father's death, when she was thirteen, Boris had summoned her and announced that he wanted her to take over the running of the Institute. Sarah, though she managed the place brilliantly, got along badly with the patients. Boris no longer nurtured hopes that William would fill his shoes, and so he looked to his daughter, who began by helping him with his patients and his voluminous correspondence with European psychiatrists.

Despite her father's seeming confidence in her, Helena was extremely doubtful that the patients would accept a thirteen-year-old girl in a position of authority, and she suspected that her father privately shared these doubts. He had been adamant about her other options for the future: he didn't want her to go to college because, as she said, "He didn't think much of women's education," or, as she speculated, "He was so fed up with my brother that he didn't want to educate me." Furthermore, there remained his general contempt for universities. Helena was a budding poet, and Boris was convinced that if she went to college, her professors would "destroy her literary talent." Because of her series of illnesses, he didn't think she'd ever be well enough to go out into the world and get a job, and so he wanted to groom and prepare her to manage the Institute.

When Boris died, Helena realized what it was that she truly wanted: to go to college. She'd had no tutors and had never been to school, though with her father's encouragement she was well grounded in Plato and Aristotle. Still, that was hardly enough to prepare her for a college entrance exam.

Helena decided that she couldn't afford a professional tutor or a private prep school, so she studied for the exams at home. She and William had long corresponded in French, and now one of the patients tutored her further. Her cousin Jack Goldwyn came to her aid, coaching her in arithmetic, algebra, and geometry. Most important, Helena followed her mother's advice, the same advice Boris had given Sarah some thirty years before: If you can reason things out, you don't need to use your memory.

William was supportive if somewhat doubtful. He was worried that his sister would strain her health cramming, trying to fit eight years of grammar school and four years of high school into a single year. But in spite of everything, Helena prevailed. She flunked her first entrance exams to Smith College because she had never taken a written test in her life. The second time, she ranked third out of a hundred or more students. In 1924, Helena entered Smith College, but the stress of her remarkable achievement caught up with her. She fell so violently ill with flu that she missed the entire first year, but returned in 1925 to major in sociology.

After her father's death, Helena's relationship with her mother deteriorated. "My father died and I got the brunt," she reflected. Boris or William had always been there to leap to her defense, and now she had no protection against her mother's rages. "It is normal for a mother, when she loses a child as my mother did Billy, to transfer the attention to the remaining child. Well, she didn't." Helena hid from Sarah, retreating to an upstairs bedroom to study, "away from her yelling and giving orders."

Sarah was under an enormous strain, and it intensified the most abrasive aspects of her personality. She missed her husband terribly, she was completely estranged from her son, and she was shackled with a huge estate and its attendant financial burdens. Somehow, in her inimitable way, she managed. The staff was reduced to an absolute minimum, and when summer came, Sarah opened up Maplewood Farms as a tourist resort.

After collecting his inheritance, William resumed his active social life and his prolific writing in New York. He put a little of his money aside for travel and the rest he invested in bus stocks. He made a brief trip to California by bus, presumably to visit Martha Foley, who was working as a newspaperwoman in San Francisco. (She remained in California for three years, not returning to the East Coast until 1925.) William's customary cheerfulness was not dampened by her absence—he continued to brandish her picture and chatter about her to friends. Returning to New York, William got an office job, and he carefully guarded from his employers and coworkers the secret of his genius.

His task was to run a comptometer, which was the first wholly key-operated calculating machine. It was a far more difficult device to use than present-day adding machines, and some of the operations called for two hands crossing over on one machine, working two or more keys in different columns at the same time. William was highly skilled at his job—he frequently astounded employers by operating two comptometers at the same time, one with his right hand and one with his left, using his elbow for the space bar. As much as William abhorred calling attention to himself, his passion for doing excellent work overruled even this consideration.

On January 10, 1924, three months after his father's death, the *New York Herald Tribune* exposed William's identity in a front-page story:

Boy Brain Prodigy of 1909 Now $23-a-Week Adding Machine; Son of Late Dr. Boris Sidis, Who, in Knee Pants, Lectured to

Harvard Professors, Lives as a Clerk; Shuns Mother and Friends; Shrugs at Books, Theaters, and Girls and Prefers Job That Takes No Thinking.

At 26, the boy prodigy of 1909 has become a mere cog in the workaday world of 1924. For $23 a week he is working as a clerk in the statistical division of an uptown office. . . . About six months ago persons in New York who were interested in young Sidis tried to find a job for him. They finally succeeded in placing him with the concern for which he is now working, but not without difficulty, for he insisted on being given work that did not require too much thinking.

The reporter wrote of "the tragedy that young Sidis represents," castigating him for not attending his father's funeral and for cutting off contact with his mother. The most serious charges the reporter leveled against Sidis were of eccentricity, sloppiness, and indifference to common concerns:

As one of the tide of humanity that ebbs and flows at nine and five each weekday in New York, young Sidis is distinguished only by being less careful of his appearance than the average New York clerk. Chided recently for a seeming lack of ambition, he said:

"All I want is a little greater margin than I have, so I may put something aside for a rainy day."

"But don't you care about books, the theater, girls, automobiles, all the things that are denied you on twenty-three dollars a week?"

Sidis merely shrugged his shoulders.

Yesterday young Sidis was wearing a cheap brown suit, much too tight for his fleshy frame. He had not been shaved; his reddish moustache was a ragged fringe that appeared to have been whacked off with a pair of manicure scissors. His mop of mouse-colored hair was in need of trimming. His necktie was in a hard knot, that did not come within inches of his collar.

Not only did William affront by not being dressed properly, he offended by his lack of interest in "normal" pursuits: girls, the theater, automobiles. On the one hand, he was expected to be special—that is, to be brilliant, and above clerical work; on the other, he was expected to be "normal"—interested in ordinary amusements. The conflict between these two requirements seems to have escaped the *Tribune* reporter as it had so many before him. And, like so many of his brethren, he thought nothing of publicly humiliating William with a lip-smacking description of his badly trimmed moustache and his "mouse-colored hair."

The *Tribune* article prompted a snide editorial the following day in *The New York Times*. Entitled "Precocity Doesn't Wear Well," it began: "Parents whose boys show no indications of being or becoming intellectual giants can get consolation from observing what has happened in the case of the once much-advertised son of Dr. Boris Sidis, the Boston psychologist." After thus reassuring the parents of dull children, the *Times* gave a brief résumé of his activities in the intervening years, and concluded: "The mental fires that burned so brightly have died down, to all appearances. It may be, of course, that precocity now takes the shape of realizing that all is vanity, and ordinary successes are not worth seeking, but such philosophy is a poor result of the speed shown early in the race; and while young Sidis is no more to be criticized adversely than anybody else for not wanting what he doesn't want, it is hard not to regret that his marvels should have been confined to adolescence."

If he had been a man of different temperament, perhaps he would have sent a copy of *The Animate and the Inanimate* to the *Times,* or written a letter of complaint. But he did not. He probably thought that his great work of theoretical physics was not fit for such little minds, and disdained to argue with them. He wanted only his solitude, and now, exposed as a genius, he quit his job.

Indeed, the editorial writer of the *Times* had hit on a point of truth: For such a prodigy as William, "ordinary successes are not worth seeking." Where the reporter went wrong was in guessing the reason for William's indifference to these successes. It was not that the prodigy had realized, as the reporter thought, "that all is vanity." It was rather that he had had enough of callous reporters and an insatiable public, who seemed to believe that he owed them a debt just because he was a genius—who felt he was obliged to perform marvels with the regularity of a trained seal, and that if he did not, he ought to be criticized, pilloried, and humiliated. But a mind is not public property. William Sidis had only one debt—the same debt every man has to himself—to achieve his own happiness and fulfillment, using his mind to the best of his ability. To achieve this happiness, William chose an extraordinary path: to lie about his genius, that he might remove it from the public arena; to pretend he was ordinary; to maintain his privacy; and to follow his star alone, publishing under pen names and teaching small groups of students who would not betray him. His choice was a brave one, but he never became cynical about it, and he never lost sight of the stars he followed. While he hated academia and spoke harshly of the world of academics, he became more and more pedantic; while he pretended to dislike the intellect, he read and wrote ever more prolifically. The strain showed on Sidis—it accounted for many of his eccentricities and increased his reputation as a burnout and a failure.

A growing part of the Sidis myth was that he had indeed had a nervous breakdown. Different people placed it at different times in his life—some said it occurred during his childhood, others after the May Day affair. This rumor was so prevalent that even Norbert Wiener believed it, writing in his memoirs of "how great a loss mathematics suffered in his premature break-down," and adding that "the collapse of Sidis was in large measure his father's making."

After receiving his M.A. from Harvard, Norbert went in an entirely different direction from William's, and it is worthwhile to compare the paths the two geniuses followed. Norbert himself had suffered a painful crisis after his graduation from Tufts College at fourteen. He was physically exhausted and deeply pained by "one of the greatest realizations the infant prodigy must make: He is not wanted by the community." Not only was he, like William, a social misfit at Harvard, but a Jew whose mother, though Jewish, was anti-Semitic and concealed his Jewishness from him. Norbert was stunned by the revelation of his true race and crushed by the unexpected anti-Semitism he encountered at Harvard. Under these strains, his studies suffered.

Norbert studied biology at Harvard, but was not gifted in the field and was uncertain whether or not to continue. In his memoirs he wrote bitterly, "As usual, the decision was made by my father. He decided that such success as I had made as an undergraduate at Tufts in philosophy indicated the true bent of my career. I was to become a philosopher. . . . This deprivation of the right to judge for myself and to stand the consequences of my own decision stood me in ill stead for many years to come. It delayed my social and moral maturity, and represents a handicap I have only partly discarded in middle age."

Norbert didn't have the courage to rebel against his father, though he resented his father's decision bitterly. Unlike William, he never made a statement of this urge to rebel, but instead bit the bullet and entered into the study of philosophy, eventually managing to specialize in an area that he loved, that of mathematical logic.

William's rebellion, then, was a healthier statement of individuality than Norbert's obedience. On the other hand, Norbert enjoyed certain advantages in his emotional relationship with his father that William did not. As mentioned earlier, when a cruel article was published during Norbert's stay at Harvard, naming the college's four prodigies as social and emotional failures, Leo Wiener leapt to a passionate defense of his son, wrote letters of complaint to the magazine in question, and considered taking legal action. While the letters of complaint yielded nothing in the way of a retraction or an apology, that was not the point. Leo Wiener had acted on behalf of his son in a way that it never occurred to Boris to do. Boris constantly defended

William in theory, and defended his own method of education—but he never saw the value in taking a stand against an abusive or humiliating article, except in order to correct educational theory. He did not give his son the sense of personal protection that Norbert, however much his father bullied him, seemed to enjoy.

More important, Leo Wiener only occasionally paraded the proof of his theories' success—Norbert—to the newspapers. Boris, of course, advertised his boldly, blind to the harm it was doing to his son. Writer Kathleen Montour, in a 1977 article in *American Psychologist*, compared William and Norbert, and held to the common opinion that Boris Sidis was a villain who had made a tragedy of his son's life. Even with these strong views, she conceded the crucial role of the yellow journalism that haunted William: "Certainly, those who took pleasure in holding [William's] misadventures against him were as much to blame for his outcome as his father. For all that Norbert Wiener and William Sidis had in common, Wiener never had to deal with such unrelenting ridicule."

Norbert also cherished the frequent hikes and camping trips he took with his father. Boris and William had no equivalent amusement. Their intellectual discussions of mathematics, religion, and politics were deeply satisfying and stimulating, but father and son were never free of the feeling that Sarah hovered somewhere nearby, about to give orders putting them to work while bitterly resenting being left out of their discussions.

After completing his graduate studies at Harvard, Norbert spent six unhappy years. At Cambridge University he studied under Bertrand Russell, who found him pompous and told a colleague, "He thinks himself God Almighty." Poor Norbert was wildly insecure, and afraid he would be thought "a fool"—in his efforts to impress, he succeeded only in appearing as an arrogant, if brilliant, boor. Like William, he lacked the social graces, writing later, "I had no proper idea of personal cleanliness and personal neatness, and I myself never knew when I was to blurt out some unpardonable rudeness." The great difference between the two prodigies was this: Norbert never stopped worrying about whether he was tactless and out of step socially, while William had never learned to care.

Returning to the United States at the age of twenty-one, Norbert lectured at Harvard for a time. At his father's urging he became a math teacher at the University of Maine, where he was miserable. A series of unsatisfactory jobs followed. Norbert did not find any happiness until 1919, when he took a post teaching math at MIT.

Clearly, Norbert's observation still held true: Just because the boys were prodigies did not mean they had anything else in common. At the time that William Sidis took up a double life as his solution to the pains of his existence, Norbert settled into a respectable job at MIT. Leaving philosophy behind, he slowly began what would become a brilliant career in mathematics and science.

Equally important, Norbert began to court the woman who would become his wife, Margaret Engemann, a language professor. Norbert had had one previous girlfriend, of whom his family did not approve, and they humiliated him mercilessly until the couple broke up. "Family ridicule," he wrote sadly, "was a weapon against which I had no defenses." The fact that his family approved of Margaret and pressured him intensely to marry her disturbed both the young lovers, and made them unduly cautious. "A courtship that might end in marriage," he wrote, "could only be my own and could not represent a decision imposed on me by parental authority." Furthermore, Norbert believed, his parents saw Margaret as someone who would "serve as a ready instrument for holding me in line," and "they supposed that my marriage with Margaret would mean an indefinite prolongation of my family captivity." Happily, none of this was so, and theirs was a true love match. But there were other problems—the beginning of their honeymoon was spent at a depressing, musty New York hotel that had been the headquarters of the American Mathematical Society; and during their European honeymoon they were joined by Norbert's parents. Just when the couple most needed to be alone, Norbert faced the sorry realization that "I had become too emotionally dependent on my parents to ignore their summons."

In his autobiography, Norbert wrote frankly of this problem in his marriage, stating that it was many years before he overcame his parents' domination, and that their "policy of glossing over my emotional difficulties" made his struggle for independence all the more difficult. This problem, in a nutshell, is common to many prodigies, and like other prodigies, Norbert credited his marriage with defrosting him emotionally. He wrote, "I wish no reader to draw the conclusion that my emotional life has been restricted to my scientific career, or that I could live with any satisfaction without the loyalty, affection, and continued support of my lifelong companion. . . . I cannot express how my life has been strengthened and stabilized by the love and understanding of my partner."

Had Martha Foley returned William's passion as Margaret did Norbert's, perhaps the two prodigies would have had more in common in the long run. The same year that Norbert married, Martha definitely cast her lot with a man whom she had met in San Francisco, a troubled young writer named Whit Burnett. Unlike William, Whit had no interest in Martha's great passions—politics, socialism, and feminism —but he shared her other love, writing.

Martha returned to New York and set up housekeeping with Whit. He got a job at *The New York Times,* she at the *Daily Mirror.* According to friends, William treated this development as if it didn't exist. Martha still saw him socially, but without Whit, and William did not attempt to prevail over Martha—he simply avoided discussion of the interloper and carried on as before, but without the kisses. In 1927, Martha and Whit moved to Paris. William did not see Martha again for five years. As before, William bore his unrequited love cheerfully, continuing to talk about Martha and show the photograph that he carried for the rest of his life.

In the life of a prodigy, perhaps more than in the average life, a marriage or a requited love is the greatest single factor that can heal the old childhood wounds. William and Norbert's response to their childhood and teenage rejections and humiliations was to retreat into the painless world of ideas, where successes and satisfactions abounded.

A successful love affair could be the key to reentry into the world of feeling, bridging the gap between the cerebral and the emotional lives. This was dramatically true in the case of that other great prodigy, John Stuart Mill.

John Stuart Mill's father was a more ferocious version of Leo Wiener. Intensely critical and cold, James Mill lavished continual attention on his prodigy son, but never affection. Like Norbert, John did not rebel overtly against his oppressive father. Instead, his inner pressures led to a kind of nervous breakdown at the age of twenty. Outwardly, he went through the motions of his busy intellectual schedule; inwardly he was morose and empty. He had lost the ability to feel—neither poetry, nor music, nor even his favorite books, inspired any real emotion in him. He had lost his former zeal for the altruism his father had taught him, and no longer felt excitement at the thought of reforming mankind and bettering the lot of millions of Hindus. If he did not learn to feel in a year's time, John decided, he would commit suicide.

To his despair, he discovered that his mood did not crack under rigid self-analysis, the only tool his father had given him. Sadder still, he could not think of a single person to confide in. His father was the last person he would consider approaching—not only was John afraid of him, but he was also, paradoxically, afraid of making James Mill feel like a failure.

After suffering this depression for some six months, John's first breakthrough came when he was moved to tears while reading a sentimental book. A passion for Wordsworth's poetry followed, and a hunger for all things emotional. He recovered, and resumed his furious work pace. While he never declared any outright opposition to his father, he realized that he needed emotion to supplement his father's brand of arid, dour rationality. At the age of twenty-four, John met an intellectual, sympathetic, married woman, Harriet Taylor, and they began an emotional, though not a sexual, affair. When her husband died twenty years later, the lovers were finally married. Though less perfectly satisfying than Norbert Wiener's marriage, John Mill's unconventional love affair did much to synthesize his feelings and his intellect. Furthermore, the liaison was such an assault upon Victorian mores that it served as a satisfactory, if indirect, rebellion against James Mill, who heartily disapproved of his son's coveting another man's property.

Leo Wiener and James Mill were both unlike Boris Sidis in that they were verbally abusive of their sons, harshly criticizing the boys when they failed to conform properly. However, there is a crucial similarity that runs through the upbringing of the three—all of the boys reached young manhood with a feeling of helplessness and inability in regard to handling the practicalities of life, and all knew their parents were to blame.

John Mill's mother left her son's training so wholly to her husband that the boy never learned to take care of himself in trivial, domestic ways. James Mill regarded his son's ineptitudes with scorn. Wrote John bitterly, "The education which my father gave me, was in itself much more fitted for training me to know than to do. . . . There was anything but insensibility or tolerance on his part towards such shortcomings: but, while he saved me from the demoralizing effects of school life, he made no effort to provide me with any sufficient substitute for its practicalizing influences. Whatever qualities he himself, probably, had acquired without difficult or special training, he seems to have supposed that I ought to acquire as easily . . . he seems to have expected effects without causes."

What shades, here, of William Sidis's not being taught to tie his shoelaces! The mistake of these parents of prodigies, then, was to assume that their children, with their marvelous brains, would absorb the commonsense details of life as easily as they would their Latin declensions, and with less need of instruction.

Of these three prodigies, William, though by far the most outcast by society, and appearing to be the greatest failure, was at this stage in life finding the greatest happiness. He had hit upon a strategy—the double life—which served him well, and he was both productive and satisfied with his daily existence. If he had found a reciprocal love as had Norbert Wiener and John Mill, he too would have had the advantage of a richer emotional life. But more important, he had rebelled against his parents for all he was worth, and reaped enormous benefits from it. He had no morose depressions or restless years spent following his parents' plan—he was his own man, however odd, however eccentric, however unorthodox.

13

The Peridromophile

One of the most extraordinary events in William Sidis's extraordinary life was the publication of his second, and last published, book, a year after the appearance of *The Animate and the Inanimate.* A very small edition of *Notes on the Collection of Transfers* was published in 1926 by Dorrance and Company, a Philadelphia vanity press, with William's inheritance money. Most of the copies were destroyed in a warehouse fire, and today the book is extremely rare. This work is arguably the most boring book ever written, and as every bibliophile knows, the competition is fierce. It unquestionably placed him among the foremost ranks of literary eccentrics. Of course, literary history abounds with unusual books. Before Sidis arrived on the scene, there had been a volume entitled *Nothing* by Methelá which contained two hundred blank pages. In 1634, Charles Butler published *The Feminin Monarchi,* a history of bees written in phonetic spelling. In 1802, there appeared *A Pickle for the Knowing Ones* by Timothy Dexter, composed of a single sentence unmarred by even one instance of punctuation (in a second edition, all the punctuation was grouped together on the last page). And after Sidis's book, in 1939, there came *Gadsby* by Ernest Vincent Wright, a complete fifty-thousand-word novel written without the single use of the letter *e.*

William selected a peculiar pseudonym—Frank Folupa. Choices of pseudonyms are rarely arbitrary, and given William's near perfect command of hundreds of languages and dialects, it is tempting to look for meanings in his choice of a name. *Folle* is French for "crazy"; *lupa* is Latin for "she-wolf"—could William have been calling himself a crazy wolf? Certainly, anyone picking up *Notes on the Collection of Transfers* might find this an accurate pen name.

The work, as its title indicates, was devoted entirely to William's beloved hobby of streetcar-transfer collecting. His passion for public-transit systems began when he was a toddler. A pair of Harvard professors visited the Sidis home and found the two-year-old poring over maps of greater Boston. Little pink-cheeked Billy called to his mother, who had just brought him back from a shopping trip. He showed her the maps and pointed out a much shorter route to the area they had just left. When he was five, in 1903, he collected his first transfers; by the time he was in his mid-twenties he had more than 1,600. He corresponded with other collectors, swapped transfers, and even acquired foreign transfers by mail.

William successfully memorized hundreds, if not thousands, of transit routes throughout the United States. Among his friends and relatives, stories abounded of his startling ability to give transit advice. On one occasion, a friend of Jack Goldwyn's wanted to know about a train leaving Boston. "I said, 'Now look, Frank—I got a cousin who knows a lot of stuff, maybe he knows that garbage.' So I asked Billy, and he said, 'Sure, there's a train leaving so and so from Boston.' And he told Frank there was a dining car and a sleeping car." When a friend of Helena's wanted to go to Cleveland from Boston, she gave William the name of the street that was her destination. "He told her exactly what buses to take, and connecting buses and where to get them. She was just amazed. How he knew places all over the country, without having been to them, is really almost fantastic." In his spare time, William composed lengthy transit guides: *The Transfer Guide to the District of Columbia, The Transit Guide to the Northwest Suburbs of Boston,* etc. According to his friend Julius Eichel, "Most people had preconceived notions that similar city guides were already in existence. Nothing could be further from the truth. With painstaking thought and logic he had evolved a system whereby anybody could, by looking at the part of the city he wanted to reach, see at a glance what transit facilities to use towards that end. He was constantly studying city transit problems, and solving some quite elegantly, and that without ever having set foot in some of the cities."

There was a persistent rumor that William was offered a job by the Eastern Massachusetts Railway Company, who gave him their most difficult statistical problems to solve. As the story went, he spent an hour surrounded by blueprints, charts, and statistics and was found weeping over the documents. Figures, he purportedly told the company officials, made him ill, and he quit the job. It is difficult to say whether or not this tale is pure fabrication. He did tell his sister that the very sight of a mathematical formula made him ill, so perhaps it is true. On the other hand, where Helena was concerned, he was generous with this type of information. If she had a question, particularly about paradoxes (his specialty), he warmly gave her an answer. She seems to be the only one for whom he would make an exception. If he had the slightest sense that anyone was making an exhibition of his abilities, he would clam up completely and pretend uncompromising ignorance.

George Gloss, the owner of Boston's Brattle Bookshop, recalled a trip he made to Seagate, "an exclusive part of Coney Island. They had some kind of a streetcar, and they issued a transfer. Well, I came back triumphantly, and I said, 'I bet you haven't got this!' 'Oh!' William says. 'They just issued that. . . . ' And he knew all the details." Gloss knew William only slightly, but one incident in their acquaintance stuck out in his mind: "Once I took him home for dinner. As we were walking, he saw a subway or heard an elevated, and he was . . . *overcome* by it. I had never seen such a reaction. Excitement and admiration. Love. For the railroads and the railroad sounds."

In the introduction to *Notes on the Collection of Transfers,* William advises the reader to begin at the end of the book and work backward, in order to avoid the driest material.

This suggestion is sound advice indeed, since Part I consists of seven stultifying chapters, proceeding from the merely boring to the staggeringly dull. The topics covered are: I. Transfers in General; II. Transfer Privileges; III. Fares; IV. Reversibility; V. Fare Limits and Overlaps; VI. Circumstances of Issue; and VII. Systems and Subsystems. What, one cannot resist asking, remains? A great deal, since Part I represents only 69 pages out of 305.

Part II is titled Contents of Transfers, and delves deeply into the following subjects: VIII. Transfer Tickets; IX. Transfer Forms; X. Dating of Transfers; XI. Transfer Time Limits; XII. The Half-day on Transfers; XIII. Routes; XIV. Transfer-Issuing Units; XV. Conditions of Place; XVI. Miscellaneous Conditions; XVII. Standard Types; and XVIII. Coloring of Transfers.

Part II, despite the bludgeoning dullness of most of the material, contains bits of charm. A wry comment here and there; or a note of melancholy philosophy, when writing of obsolete transfers not immediately withdrawn from usage: "Such forms . . . which are vestiges of former transfer privileges, are called vestigial forms. . . . Vestigial transfer forms have the same interest as other vestigial remnants—objects, manners, actions, that are entirely disconnected from their present surroundings, and are simply survivals of a bygone past." If the reader makes it to Part III, Collecting Transfers (or has taken the author's advice and begun there), he will be amply rewarded, for at last the going gets good, so to speak. After a tolerable chapter,

Collection in General, the reader comes to one of the most interesting parts of the book, the chapter titled Derelict Transfers.

"What is a Derelict? By the expression 'derelict transfers' I mean the discarded transfers frequently found lying about, abandoned by their rightful owners." These abandoned transfers, Sidis stressed, form an important source for the dedicated collector, and their acquisition and treatment is described in rather tender detail:

Handling Derelicts. The collector picking up derelict transfers should do it as inconspicuously as possible, and should generally not let it be noticed that that is what he is doing. Although picking up a derelict for a souvenir to put in a collection is a perfectly legitimate action in itself, still it would hardly do to appear as one who picks up rubbish, or especially as one who is trying to pick up transfers to evade payment of carfare.

Wet transfers can be kept in a special pocket for a while, and will dry fairly rapidly. In any case, when unfolding a transfer, especially a wet one, care should be taken not to tear the transfer itself in the process. If a transfer is dirty, it is best not to keep it where it is liable to soil clean ones, especially if it is wet.

Wet transfers are often found adhering closely to the pavement, and there special care is needed to avoid tearing, especially if there is already a slight tear. Where there are attached coupons, these are quite likely to come off if care is not observed. Sometimes the process of detaching such transfers can be done very effectively, and quite inconspicuously, too, with the point of an umbrella, which can also be used to pick up the transfer if handled properly. [Sidis constructed his own litter stick—a stick with a pointed metal end attached to it, rather like the kind streetcleaners used.] Snow will very frequently keep them frozen in all winter, and many derelict transfers can be found under a deep layer of snow; these may be treated essentially as ordinary wet transfers, but great care should be used if they have to be taken out of ice, in which case it may be best to break off the whole piece of ice and let it melt.

The proper storage, labeling, and indexing of the collection is a matter of many pages, including detailed instructions on how to make envelopes in which to store the transfers, complete with a diagram.

The next chapter is titled Local Exploration, and details the advantages of transfer-hunting as an aid to gaining knowledge of a city; and indeed, Sidis makes a very good case for his thesis:

> The transfer collector, besides the information acquired from reading and analyzing the inscriptions on transfers, gets a thorough and firsthand knowledge of more details of his city and its vicinity than the average inhabitant would be likely to get . . . other inhabitants or visitors will not see the city so much as a whole. A city and its environs will thus appear to the transfer collector not merely as on a map, but rather as a dynamic map, one into which some life and motion has been put. . . . If a city is passed through on a train, the parts seen are anything but characteristic, since the neighborhoods about a railroad track are apt to be rather run down in appearance. The opposite will be true of the city as seen from an auto, which will be principally from the point of view of the boulevards. But the local transportation lines will take in everything, business sections and all other types of sections of the city and suburbs. . . . This in itself should be enough to lend some interest to the collection of transfers.

In the final and most intriguing chapter, Miscellaneous Items of Interest, William stated his case for the hobby, allowing that "it is hardly fair to assume that the reader will be interested in collecting streetcar transfers, since such a hobby is, to say the least, a rare one." However, he cited a number of advantages to collecting, such as that of visiting historical sites, and the pleasure to be derived from "arithmetical or statistical figuring . . . in connection with the calculation of car indexes."

As if this were not inducement enough, William wooed his readers with, of all things, "Transfer Humor": "According to this story a man applied for admission at the gates of St. Peter, and was told to go to the other place. He immediately replied: 'Gimme a transfer.' "

Another went: "It is said that a Harvard College student got on a streetcar, and wishing an extra ride, asked the conductor for a transfer. When asked where to, he said, 'Anywhere.' The conductor winked and said, 'All right, I will give you a transfer to Waverley.' The student was afterwards laughed at when he told the story, and was informed that the asylum for the feeble-minded was located at Waverley."

A little transfer poetry followed the jokes. First, an excerpt from the eleven-year-old William's ode to the opening of the Cambridge Subway. And then, "an extract from a verse in the form of a Mother Goose Alphabet to explain the letters on the cars of the Los Angeles Railway.

> *A is for Adams, well-known man of state.*
> *B is for Brooklyn, that borough so great.*
> *C is for Crown Hill, or Crooked, maybe.*
> *D is for Depot, where stops the Espee.*
> *E is for Eagle Rock, towards the north.*
> *F on the top of a car stands for Fourth.*

In conclusion, William wrote:

One thing in which the collection of transfers differs from other kinds of collection, is that such collection can never be commercialized, since trading in transfers is illegal, being presumably fraudulent even where there is no specific law in regard to transfers as such. Therefore, collectors must always be amateurs, collecting for the intrinsic interest in it; the professional collector cannot very well appear in this field, nor would it be desirable that he should. The collector of transfers will, therefore, not be faced by the problem of the stamp collector of issues printed exclusively for sale to collectors and not for circulation.

While any number of passages from *Notes on the Collection of Transfers* lend themselves to psychological interpretation, it is perhaps this last speech that is the most revealing. Since William's very genius was "commercialized" from his earliest childhood—by his mother in her eager display of him, by his father in *Philistine and Genius,* and most of all by the press, who used him for reams of good copy at the expense of his feelings and who continually urged him to commercialize his genius in adulthood by offering it up to society—the deep love of a truly, eternally amateur hobby is a symbolic cry for freedom from exploitation.

Kathleen Montour, in her perceptive article on Sidis in *American Psychologist* magazine, made the same mistake that many others had made in analyzing this odd book. She wrote, "Unlike *Notes on the Collection of Transfers, The Animate and the Inanimate* is a serious treatment of a scientific topic; it involves the philosophy of science. The contrast in the content of these two reflects the change that Sidis underwent, from scholar to cynical eccentric, hostile to intellectualism." In fact, there is nothing cynical about *Notes.* On the contrary, it is its very innocence that is bizarre; to present a passionate work about a hobby that would certainly appear absurd to most people, even if done pseudonymously, takes a little bit of courage and a great deal of enthusiasm.

Dan Mahony, a political psychologist who has been studying Sidis's writings, observes: "A hobby is a very idealistic activity. I think what Sidis is doing is exploring the borderline between work and play. The average person is an expert in their hobby; because they think it's a hobby, it keeps the academes at bay—if it's a hobby, it's not official and it's okay to have it. But there are experts in hobbies that are better than most college professors. You're free to think within your hobby. And Sidis is saying, 'In your hobby, you're free to be a perfectionist.' "

In September 1926, William began a monthly publication for transfer collectors, titled *The Peridromophile,* available at ten cents an issue or one dollar per year. This unlikely magazine ran for six and a half years, resurfacing under several more titles in the years that followed.

The first issues featured columns on predictably dry topics, such as the written matter (usually advertisements) featured on the backs of transfers, special "revival issue" transfers and their peculiarities, etc. A regular contributor to *The Peridromophile* was one Mr. M. W. Nash, who drew a monthly cartoon chronicling the adventures of "General Phorm," who cavorted with a transfer-stabbing stick and a collector's box slung over his shoulder. To add to the levity, there was a regular humor column, called "Rail-ery," featuring William's latest collection of bad transit jokes, such as the following:

> "Excuse me, does this train stop at Reading?"
> "Yes; get off one station before I do."
> "Oh, thank you."

> CONDUCTOR: This transfer has expired, madam.
> LADY: I don't blame it a bit. This streetcar is so poorly ventilated.

> Overheard on the Boston streetcar during the 6 P.M. rush hour:
> "We are in a jam. Heaven preserve us!"

> A man was seen walking a car track—an old, abandoned line—
> and gazing intently at the rails. A bystander called out to him:
> "Hey, what are you doing there?"
> "Why, I'm a detective!"
> "What are you looking for?"
> "The president of the streetcar company."
> "Well, you don't expect to find him here, do you?"
> "No, but I'm on his track, anyhow."

In 1927, one year after William launched *The Peridromophile* and authored *Notes,* the *Boston Sunday Post* published an article titled " 'Fourth Dimension Sidis' Becomes Peridromophile—Not as Bad as It Sounds, Though; Harvard's Mathematical Genius Collects Street Car Transfers." In a warm-hearted review of *Notes,* the reporter says, "Be a Peridromophile! It's the very latest fad—so new that only one man has taken it up. . . . Think of the strangest things you have ever heard of a collector amassing. And then decide that William James Sidis, the former Brookline boy prodigy of Harvard, has started the queerest collector's fad you or anyone else has ever heard of." The reporter gave special attention to the streetcar poetry and jokes, remarking amicably, "The readers must understand that transfer collecting isn't old enough to have gathered many good ones, so a little indulgence."

Sixteen years later a second article on the subject appeared in the *Baltimore Evening Sun.* Titled "Peridromophily and Mr. Willie Sidis," it was authored by one James P. Connolly. His column was subtitled "Bus Correspondent's Apology," for he had made an error in a previous column. While reporting on the passing of the Charles Street bus line, he had hobnobbed with some of the assembled crowd and was informed (or so he thought): "We're philomorphilists—like philatelists, only, instead of stamps, we collect streetcar transfers." Mr. Connolly considered the whole business a joke, but when he wrote a column about it, he received his comeuppance. The president of the Baltimore Transit Company sent him a copy of the Frank Folupa opus, thus setting him straight about the hobby, and its adherents' proper name. *Peridromophile,* he discovered, came from the Greek—the prefix *peri-* means "around" or "about"; the suffix *-dromos* means "running track" or "course"; and the suffix *-philos,* "dear, friendly, loving." In conclusion, wrote Connolly, "The *Evening Sun*'s Bus Correspondent herewith makes a sweeping apology to 'peridromophiles' all over the world. He is heartily sorry for ever having thought of them as 'philomorphilists.' " *Notes on the Collection of Transfers* was the subject of only these two reviews—not many, but curiously, two more than *The Animate and the Inanimate* received.

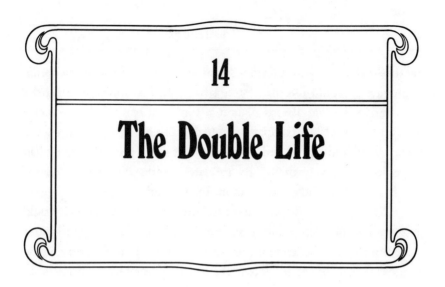

14

The Double Life

Despite William's dedication to his unconventional hobby, it remained just that—a hobby, an occupation for his spare time, a relaxation for his racing mind. He was busy at all times with at least a half-dozen serious writing projects, in addition to his regular workaday job. He appeared to have the energy and zeal of ten men, and the decade between his thirtieth and fortieth birthdays was his most productive. Despite his ceaseless activity, he was usually under financial strain, receiving small loans from friends.

After publishing *Notes on the Collection of Transfers,* he had invested almost his entire four-thousand-dollar inheritance into bus stocks. It was a sound enough plan, since many bus companies thrived in the 1920s. "His principles prevented him from living extravagantly," explained Julius Eichel, "but he was looking forward to the day when he could use the nest egg from his investment to start the cooperatives he was always planning. Financial manipulation carried on by the parent bus company resulted in his being squeezed out of his holdings, and he suffered a complete loss of his inheritance. He had not enjoyed a penny of it." By the late '20s the stocks were, in the words of Helena Sidis, "little more than wallpaper."

Consequently, William took job after job that he hoped would preserve his anonymity and leave him free to do his life's work after office hours. Yet he was unable to settle into a single, satisfactory employment. Most of his jobs were procured for him by friends, or came from passing civil service examinations, and paid fifteen to twenty-five dollars a week. (William scored so high on these exams that he was frequently offered managerial positions, which he turned down in horror.) Almost invariably, William lost these jobs after a matter of months.

One of his main difficulties in acquiring a job was his utterly nonconformist appearance. The following description, which was written by Eichel and applies to Sidis in his late thirties and forties, gives a good overall impression:

Sidis was as indifferent to his personal appearance as was Samuel Johnson in an earlier age. But he suffered more than Johnson for this, for whereas Johnson was the literary leader of the groups then congregating in coffeehouses, Sidis had no such admirers, and few could overlook his careless appearance and uncouth manners. The result was that first appearances would shut out his genius to those who met him casually. Sidis was about five feet, eight inches tall, stocky and broad boned, and weighed about 220 pounds. In appearance and habits he could have passed for a longshoreman rather than a white-collar worker, yet he insisted that the only work he was fitted for was that of operating a comptometer in an office. That incongruity made it difficult for him to get such office work, and that was at the root of his financial troubles. No one could complain about his work; it was accurate and efficient, and he would be asked to locate mistakes that others would make. If only he had paid more attention to cleanliness and his distasteful habits. But in spite of friendly advice he could not overcome such weaknesses. He wore a dirty old cap, musty with age. He always seemed to need a shave, although he did not cultivate a beard. His trousers were unpressed and dirty, and his shoes always remained unshined, when he wore shoes. In later years he wore ordinary gym sneakers, with socks in winter, and without socks in summer. His coat was ragged, with the lining usually showing where the stitches or wear had loosened it from the cloth. His tie was usually cut six inches from the knot, and usually dirty. In an age when dress and appearances count for so much, his carelessness was an obvious handicap.

Another extraordinary account of Sidis on the job appeared in *The Come As You Are Masquerade Party,* author Samuel Rosenberg's collection of essays. Rosenberg was told the following story by Edward T. ("Ted") Frankel, an auditor who worked in the same office with William:

In 1928 the National Industrial Conference Board, a research organization, hired Sidis to operate a Burroughs calculating machine for $25 a week. At first, he managed to keep his story secret, but when it was discovered that he knew higher mathematics he was immediately offered some advanced work with the promise of more money. But Sidis, who had been through the same situation before, stubbornly refused and stayed with his calculator.

"He was good with that machine," said Frankel. "So remarkably good, in fact, that his immediate supervisor, J. M. Robertson, became obsessed with the idea that Sidis was really performing all his calculations mentally and only pretending to operate the machine to throw him off the track! A hilarious

Charlie Chaplin comedy developed, with Robertson watching Sidis like a hawk but pretending not to, and Sidis pretending not to know that Robertson was watching him. But it was no match. Sidis ran that machine right under Robertson's nose so cleverly that Robertson never knew what in hell was going on."

While Sidis was employed at the NICB, according to Frankel, several experts in the organization tried to involve him in discussions of mathematics or philosophy, but he insisted angrily that he had forgotten everything that he had known. "But on one occasion he slipped," said Frankel. "Somebody showed him a new set of tables that had been prepared by some of our top experts as an aid in solving certain complicated statistical problems. The tables were useful but admittedly incomplete. Sidis studied them for a while and suggested a simple way of eliminating all the difficulties. It was obvious that he had forgotten nothing. After that brilliant demonstration, the pressure on Sidis to conform increased, he began to look and behave like a trapped animal, and he finally resigned.

"I really felt terribly sorry for him. He was like a child. He told me that he didn't know how to apply for another job and that it was useless to write letters of application because they were all thrown in wastebaskets. He really needed help. I spent many of my lunch hours going around to the offices of the big companies around Grand Central station trying to find a job for him. I told the office managers that Sidis was a wizard, but, since I knew that they would discover his story (people always did), I had to tell them that he was only interested in a subsistence job and that he would refuse any promotions. When they heard that, they said that they were definitely not interested. They didn't want to have a man like that around."

The following tale was told by Grace Spinelli, whose husband Marcos was one of William's dearest friends. Mrs. Spinelli said simply, "Frankly, we didn't care whether he bathed or not. Whether he ate one way or the other. We liked him for what he was. It had nothing to do with the surface behavior—we didn't care about that. My husband called him 'Pop,' because he said, 'He was my intellectual father.'"

Marcos and William struck up their acquaintanceship in an unconventional manner, according to Grace: "Marcos knew him before we were married. He met him on his job on Wall Street, where Sidis was working for a spiritual publishing house. My husband was out of work, and someone sent him there for a job.

"They met in the men's room. There was Sidis in the men's room with stacks of newspapers. He would buy them in the subway and lock himself in. He'd be in there for hours, reading his papers. And they just happened to say hello to each other. And Bill said, 'What are you doing here?' And Marcos said, 'Well, I'm applying for a job, but I don't know anything about finances.'

"You know how it is. Somebody refers you to somebody. Marcos eventually got the job through a friend, but he was embarrassed. He said, 'What am I gonna do? I don't know anything about math.' Math was his weakest subject in school. So Sidis says, 'I'll help you out.' I don't know what he did. He showed him something. But Marcos was still worried. And William said, 'I'll help you. Don't you worry about it.' By eleven o'clock, Sidis was through with his work. And of course he didn't have to use adding machines, but if he did use the adding machines, he added with both his hands, all his fingers— an adding machine for each hand. Sometimes he could do the thing quicker than the machine could do it. By eleven o'clock in the morning he was through, but he wasn't allowed to go home. He had to stay there, and then he did whatever he wanted to do, because the work didn't keep piling in. Probably he was writing one of his newsletters. The rest of the staff wouldn't have anything to do with him. They thought he was weird.

"And once, the office was moved from one room to another, and they asked him to move his machines. He wouldn't do it. He said, 'I can't do it. It's not good for my health. It's too heavy for me.' They insisted that he move his own typewriter and machine, which in those days were heavy, not as streamlined as they are today. And Marcos said William took hold of a stick and said, 'You come near me, I'll hit you.' It was a matter of principle, and he was not going to do anything for which he was not employed. He stuck to his job."

If he would not do more than he was hired for, neither would he pretend to dawdle over his work and stretch it out throughout the day. Often, he completed an entire day's work in twenty minutes, and in another twenty he would do Marcos's work and pass it to him under the table. His habit of retiring to the men's room with a collection of newspapers offended his fellow workers, who complained to their boss. Like the bright student who finishes his schoolwork in twenty minutes and is left twiddling his thumbs in class, William was deeply resented by his coworkers and his employers, and thus lost job after job. When Helena begged her brother to seek another type of employment, he told her, "I just want to work an adding machine, so I won't have to use my mind on it—I want to use my mind for other things."

There were a great many of these "other things." One was an organization William founded with a friend in 1929, which he called the Geprodis Association. The meaning of the word *Geprodis* is a mystery. There was a fourth-century Scandinavian tribe called the Gepidae. Or, perhaps the word was an acronym, or a word in one of William's invented languages, such as his childhood Vendergood.

This association was formed to promote a variety of enterprising business projects, potentially to be run on a cooperative basis. With his passion for constitutions and legal documents, William drew up a fifteen-page "Syllabus Program of the Geprodis Association." He had mellowed considerably since the days of the fascistic Hesperia Constitution, and this latest, idealistic system attempted to meld communism and democracy. Small groups, no larger than twenty-five, made policy decisions, electing delegates to make decisions in higher-up groups of twenty-five, and so on. Contributions from members outside the organization were welcomed, but moneys made by the businesses under the

Geprodis umbrella were to be recycled back into the cooperatives—personal profit to any great degree was discouraged.

Despite his visions of expansion, William never got his cooperative venture going on a large scale. He did, however, manage to start a few small businesses under its wing, and published newsletters and other written matter. He wrote a lengthy revision of *Robert's Rules of Order*, emphasizing the replacement of traditional parliamentary procedure with group rules tailored to the aforementioned small groups of twenty-five or less. This work, which remained unpublished, was circulated in mimeographed form and was called the "Geprodis Code of Group Procedure."

The organization's first order of business was to market the perpetual calendar that William had invented at age five. In the years since, William had improved on the device. The difficulty with all perpetual calendars existing at that time concerned leap years. To calculate a day of the week on a leap year involved the consultation of special tables and charts, thus making the devices cumbersome and troublesome to use. William was among the first to conquer this problem, incorporating leap-year calculations into his pocket-size, easy-to-use device. He applied to the U.S. Patent Office, saying that he believed himself to be "the original, first and sole inventor" of the improvement, and was granted his patent.

William and a partner, Joseph Resnick, next set about promoting the calendar, employing the services of attorney Hobart S. Bird, who would later see William through a serious legal crisis. Bird negotiated sales contracts with bookstores and private distributors, and in six months the Geprodis Association had sold 1,500 calendars at ten cents each. Sales were brisk in New York, Boston, Cleveland, and Chicago.

Sidis and Resnick started a monthly newsletter, the *Geprodis Organization News,* which advertised *The Peridromophile,* William's transit guides, and the perpetual calendar. It also advertised two unusual services. For twenty-five cents, Sidis's "City Information Service" would supply all the transit information necessary to travel door-to-door between any of fifty major metropolitan cities. For fifty cents, one could purchase the "Itinerary Service," which provided an itinerary for railroad travel anywhere in the United States or Canada, including any local transit information necessary at the starting point of the journey. The partners then started the Geprodis System Translation Service and the Geprodis Manuscript Library. The latter was based on a clever idea for the circulation of unpublished manuscripts on a lending-library basis, and it must have appealed to any number of struggling authors. The Association printed an attractive circular that read:

WRITERS! ATTENTION!
IF—YOU HAVE BEEN UNSUCCESSFUL IN GETTING YOUR WORK PUBLISHED
IF—YOU WOULD LIKE YOUR WORK TO HAVE A FEW READERS WHILE WAITING FOR A PUBLISHER—HERE IS A CHANCE
The GEPRODIS MANUSCRIPT LIBRARY, now being organized, is looking for *unpublished* manuscripts only, preferably by *unknown* writers, for the purpose of introducing them to the public by lending them out on a circulating library basis.

Your work can become known to readers—possibly even to publishers in this way.

You will get a small royalty—a nominal sum, but more than if your manuscript remained totally idle during the same period.

The GEPRODIS MANUSCRIPT LIBRARY is not intended as a regular means of income to its writers. It is intended to bring their work before the public, and serve as a practical test of popularity of works which might otherwise get little or no consideration from publishers. It is intended to rescue from oblivion much good work which is at present passed over by publishers' critics. . . . You can lose nothing by it, and you stand a chance of gaining recognition which might otherwise be more difficult to obtain.

There is no record of the success of these various projects. The calendar seems to have done moderately well over the years, but judging by the comments of Sidis's friends, he was never out of financial straits for long. Either his projects were unsuccessful, or he invested what money he made into such a myriad of new enterprises that he saw little profit. For a brief period, he reported on the progress of the various projects in the *Geprodis Organization News*.

The Peridromophile, William explained in the fourth issue, had long endeavored to maintain a neutral editorial policy; given the nature of its contents—transfer trivia—this was not exceedingly difficult. However,

> A neutral policy was more difficult in the case of G.O.N., its purpose being almost a propaganda purpose by its very nature; and yet, in accordance with Geprodis policy, this paper has become an explanatory organ rather than one which presents definite opinions.
>
> It has been alleged by critics that it is impossible, in any statement of facts, to avoid completely all trace of the writer's opinion; and this is undoubtedly true. But nevertheless, this does not mean that it is impossible to avoid going out of one's way to air the writer's opinions; and omission of out-and-out editorials is certainly a possibility. At any rate, such is the variety of new journalism that Geprodis proposes to create.

William, the subject of hundreds of opinionated, if not downright slanderous articles and editorials, longed to maintain the utmost objectivity and neutrality when he placed himself in the position of journalist or author. This ardent concern showed itself fully in William's next magnum opus: a 1,200-page revisionist history of the United States.

15

The Tribes and the States

At the same time that William was collecting transfers, running his half-dozen Geprodis projects, and working a nine-to-five job, he was composing a massive manuscript: two volumes describing America from earliest prehistory to the twentieth century. Unfortunately, only six hundred pages—the first book, called *The Tribes and the States,* and a single page of the second, *The Peace Paths*—have survived. The tone in which the first volume is written reflects William's desire to be a perfect, neutral observer and reporter.

The single remaining page of *The Peace Paths* gives fascinating insight into his purpose in the epic work of *The Tribes and the States.* William wrote:

Through all this it is hoped that the reader will never lose sight of the fact that it is all intended to be a story—that it is in no instance the result of any deliberate research—that the atmosphere is lost if you begin to scrutinize evidence in detail—that, even if any considerable part of it turns out to be untrue, the saga can be the basis for a new (and let us hope, finer) tradition of the origin of American ideas and ideals.

This tale is hardly an epic of America, and is not intended to be such; but it has the broad legendary type of basis on which such an epic—if one is ever composed—should rest. Kipling once expressed the sources of Homer's epics as follows:

> *When 'Omer smote 'is bloomin' lyre*
> *'E'd 'eard men sing by land and sea,*
> *And wot 'e thought 'e might require*
> *'E went an' took, the same as me.*

Our own sources are precisely that; and we claim no better investigation of authenticity, than just that. It is, after all, not a history, but a story, even if some history has crept in unwittingly.

We may also warn the reader against supposing that the story deals with "Indian lore," just because it starts with mention of that race. The very concept of "Indian lore" implies an unbridgeable gulf between the history of the red race and the white people of this continent; and the tale of the Peace Path is an effort to bridge that gap. It deals neither with the red race nor with the white race as such, but deals with America, whoever its people may have been at any time.

Though this tantalizing snippet was written for *The Peace Paths*, the basic point of view is the same as that expressed in the stodgier introduction to *The Tribes and the States*. Since this latter book is so vast in scope, covering as it does prehistory to the year 1828 in six hundred closely typed pages, it is impossible to go into its contents at any length here. Furthermore, much of it is dry, scholarly, and labored.

According to friends of William's who read it, the second volume was written in a far more popular, accessible style.

Since the entire work contains not a single footnote, a frustrated scholar might conclude that the book is in large part speculative fiction mingled with fact. Certainly William was thumbing his nose at academia when he said, "it is in no instance the result of any deliberate research . . . the atmosphere is lost if you begin to scrutinize evidence in detail," but William was simply too meticulous a scholar to have made the entire thing up.

However, in William's opinion, the percentage of verifiable truths contained in this book is not nearly so important as its point of view toward American history. William treated his subject with loving detail. The surviving book constitutes an impressive, intelligent, and coherent revisionist history of the American population. The task of verifying William's stories belongs to historians. A number of modern scholars have dedicated themselves to proving similar theories, and none has heard of William James Sidis. An excellent work, complete with footnotes and an extensive bibliography, is Bruce E. Johansen's *Forgotten Founders,* published in 1982 by Gambit Publishers. Johansen, in a concise 126 pages, reaches conclusions remarkably similar to Sidis's.

William's basic premise is that American history properly begins before the landing of the *Mayflower.* The inhabitants of America, William stressed, had developed enormously diverse cultures. In 1930, the following remark sounded a note that would come into vogue only in the 1960s and '70s:

> The mere fact that their white conquerors have lumped them all together under the incorrect heading of "Indians" does not make them all alike . . . any statements about customs, forms of government, etc. applying to one red nation would be likely to be false as applied to their neighbors. . . . The tribes of Indians are considered, not as savages or barbarians who created nothing of

importance, but as the real founders of the best and most important parts of modern American institutions.

The Tribes and the States, William acknowledged in the introduction, was full of controversial material:

There are points of difference from the established text-book view of history, such as: picturing America as a country where popular revolts have been the rule rather than the exception, and even as the origin and inspiration of such revolts throughout the world; describing George Washington, not as the hero of the American Revolution as he is ordinarily considered, but rather as one who had little sympathy with democracy, and finally overthrew by conspiracy the republic the Revolution established; the existence of a First Republic (John Hancock being its first president) representing the American Revolution, and a Second Republic representing a political counter-revolution. . . . All these will doubtless be difficult for the average reader to swallow. . . . To those who have been used to reading into American history the idea that the administration is always right, or that the people always follow the governing power, or that it is un-American for the people to take the law into their own hands, this version of American history might prove somewhat of a shock. . . . But let us also hope that the new point of view will make the reader "think it over"—that it will excite his interest, and make him reconsider much that he has taken for granted about his country.

William made no effort to publish *The Tribes and the States,* though he did circulate copies to his friends under the guise of a secret society he had founded, the American Independence Society (AIS). There was a close link between the book and the organization, as the society claimed to be the modern exponent of the political philosophy presented in the revisionist history. Since it was a secret society, no account can be made of the membership or its activities—although it appears from surviving correspondence to have been limited to friends and friends-of-friends in the New England area (William had by now moved back to Boston from New York).

William wrote a detailed program, or manifesto, for the AIS, along with an account of its origins, a credo, poetry, and other intersociety memoranda. In the AIS's credo, William wrote:

> We believe that the right of equality, as stated in the Declaration of Independence, does not mean that all persons are exact duplicates of one another, and does not, cannot, imply any sort of forcible leveling, discipline, or regimentation; for such leveling action can provide no equality except that of equal submission to a superior authority, which is in itself the most flagrant denial of equality, liberty, pursuit of happiness, as well as of the requirement of consent of the governed.

Instead, William took "equality" to mean "that no person should derive either reward or punishment from any accident of birth or from any acts of other than himself; . . . that no person should be granted superior consideration before the law by reason of possession of wealth, control of organizations important to the life of the people, or for any other reason whatever."

This view of individual liberty differs from the ideas William expressed in his constitution for the utopia of Hesperia, wherein every citizen would in effect be a government employee. Clearly, William's ideas had changed since that first pubescent credo, and since the days of his May Day parade arrest. William probably saw his treatment then at the hands of the authorities and his family as a form of censorship, and he gave that subject special attention in the AIS credo.

William made it clear that he did not consider himself unpatriotic because he advocated a new order; on the contrary, he wrote that government by consent of the governed made rebellion just the patriotic thing to do whenever the authorities got out of hand. Harkening again to the Declaration of Independence, he stated that a "government has no rights whatever as against its own people—not even that of self-defense."

While William was trying to make his position clear, he simultaneously took great pains to obscure it. His AIS was so secret that it met in abandoned subway tunnels, and was organized so that no member ever knew the identities of more than nine other members. And whenever he referred to his writings in correspondence, he made it very clear that he was not the author—that he had "heard" from his friends in the Okommakamesit Indian tribe that a meeting was scheduled on such and such a date, or that a new historical fact had been "told" to him for inclusion in his book, or that a certain "John Shattuck" had written some freedom songs, with radical lyrics put to the tune of "Fair Harvard."

In fact, there is no indication that William ever met with anyone of Indian blood. Rather, he selected carefully from among his friends, and "initiated" them into the tribe. With his great love of codes, rituals, and secrets, forming a club of modern-day Okommakamesits suited him to perfection. He liked to hint to friends that he was in touch with a line of direct descendants; and there was a boyishness in his dedication to these rites and rules, adhered to with all the passion of a Tom Sawyer or a Huck Finn. When William told his friend Isaac Rab that members of the group met in the subway, Rab replied acerbically, "Do you meet in telephone booths, too?" William expanded on this theme in conversation with George Gloss, explaining that members met on the subway line from Harvard Square to Park Street, signaling to one another with a secret sign.

William also liked to hint that the tribe was a large underground organization, but his friends suspected otherwise. Of the Rab family members, William deemed only fifteen-year-old Ann worthy of initiation. Said her younger brother Bill, "He didn't select me. I think I was a little too frivolous. My father, no, because he was far too logical. But my sister was closer to him. I was play. She was business."

And so, Ann went with William to an Okommakamesit meeting, expecting to join a large group. To her enormous surprise, the gathering was in a home on Beacon Hill, and consisted of only four or five "Beacon Hilly people—very Waspish. Cultured. Refined. I thought they would be people like Bill!" The next surprise was that the main topic of conversation was an informal discussion of the different types of solitaire; William knew twenty or thirty kinds. When a puzzled Ann tried to question William, he just laughed. She was never invited to another meeting, but she continued to receive excerpts from *The Tribes and the States*. Ann concluded that the tribe was similar in spirit to the Druids of England. "They're certainly not the descendants of the original Druids, and Bill certainly wasn't an Indian. But he was a spiritual descendant of the Okommakamesits."

Julius Eichel, too, was invited to be an AIS initiate. "My wife, Esther, and I were the subject of one of Bill's initiations. It lacked atmosphere—only the three of us were present—and we did not show too much enthusiasm for the event. He had a secret sign which we could exhibit to the initiated, a method of indicating danger by sign language, and an oath to remain true to the principles of the organization. We were willing to go through that for the sake of getting things started, but they never seemed to prosper. We eventually resigned from the organization. His secrecy was too much for us."

To one degree or another, many of William's friends and relatives thought he suffered delusions of persecution. Given that his political activities were so radical and that most of his acquaintances did not know the extent of them, his fear, as Eichel said, "had some foundation" and may have appeared exaggerated at times when it was legitimate. Even bearing this in mind, however, there is no doubt that William had a strong streak of neurotic fear in his makeup. As Clifton Fadiman stated, "He was very radical. He was afraid of authority, he evaded all symbols of authority. And because he'd had a traumatic experience, the May Day arrest, he was scared. So there was both evasion and fear. But I think the fear was part of a generalized fear of living, of the world in which the rest of us live—that world seemed to him to be full of threatening objects. I think he was afraid of everything. Not in the sense of being a physical coward. Rather that the human race was an alien kind of life that he couldn't adjust to."

As a result of his obsession with anonymity, William's friends were often confused. Obviously he was the prime mover behind his publications, but what could they say to his protestations? In several letters to Eichel, William stressed that he had not authored *The Tribes and the States.* "I have got hold of three more copies of *The Tribes and the States,* and sent them to you, as you ordered. I do wish it to be understood that, as the pamphlet states in the introduction, it is not to be considered the work of any individual, but of an organization. I may have helped on it, but I certainly do not wish to be considered the author, as there are lots of things that I would not care to take personal responsibility for; so please do not represent the pamphlet to anyone as my work."

His efforts reached comic proportions. He circulated a newspaper purported to be written by the Okommakamesits, called the *Penacook Courier.* This paper demonstrated his interest in languages and dialects, as it was written in the English dialect spoken around New England at the time of the Revolution. The *Penacook Courier* pretended to be a current periodical of that time, with datelines of January 1621, June 1774, etc. He wrote to Eichel, "That tribal organization just surprised me by sending—from some place in New Hampshire I never heard of before—an historical newspaper written in American, and which seemed to be good and exciting stuff. Hope they can keep it up."

The *Penacook Courier* told stories from *The Tribes and the States* in journalistic form. Although the language reads humorously, William tried to communicate his revisionist ideas seriously. Under the protection of the anonymity provided by the fictional authorship, William felt free to write about his most controversial historical interpretations. George Washington, generally viewed as a national hero, was to William an enemy of the democracy being built by the Americans. From the *Penacook Courier,* this flash: "Congress just appointed a commander-in-chief for the buncha rebel fighters beseigin

Boston. He's George Washington, who's botherin Congress by too much Tory talk, so they're gettin ridda him that way an sendin him to Cambridge. He's gotta bitta reputation for knozin fightin."

William was understandably shy of openly inciting rebellion himself, though that was clearly what he was hoping would follow from the spread of his American independence ideas. He was particularly inspired by a rebellion against Sir Edmund Andros, governor of New England. Andros frequently marched his Redcoat troops through the streets of Boston as a show of power. On one spring day in 1689, wrote William in *The Tribes and the States,*

> Andros marched proudly down the Cornhill, but, on turning the corner into King street, suddenly found himself face to face with a defiant mob. . . . The governor shouted orders to fire into the crowd; but the crowd's reserves in the buildings started pouring out into the street . . . and the militia were seized and disarmed before they could have time to take aim. Sir Edmund Andros himself was also seized by the crowd, and . . . he was promptly hustled in [jail], while Bradstreet, the last Puritan governor, was found and hailed as the new governor of Massachusetts, and he was installed in the Province House the next day.

William's commentary on this rebellion aptly sums up his hopes and motivations for the fledgling American Independence Society:

> It has very rarely happened in the world's history that a powerful administration was so speedily and completely overthrown; and it probably could never have happened without the self-reliant population guided by a secret organization unknown even to the rebels, such as was the case in Massachusetts then. Once again New England proved itself a center of the fight for liberty.

William had always loved the New England legend of "The Gray Champion" in Nathaniel Hawthorne's *Twice-Told Tales.* In

1938, he penned a curious document in which he obliquely hinted that he was the actual incarnation of the mysterious Gray Champion, "an earthly representative of [his] spirit." According to this legend, the Gray Champion was a mythical character who appeared at key moments in the history of the young American nation. He would incite the patriotic spirit in the hearts of Americans and then vanish into thin air when his leadership was no longer required. William's version of the legend has it that "The Modern Gray Champion" was present at the Andros Rebellion, and again at the Boston draft riots of 1917. William also credited the Gray Champion with founding, in 1936, a movement that bears an unmistakable resemblance to William's own AIS group.

16

Friends and Relatives

William's elaborate, absurd ruses of anonymity, which probably fooled no one, were absolutely necessary to his peace of mind. If he made his friends promise not to name him as the author of his works, he would never, he hoped, attract the attention of an inquisitive reporter. And he could continue to disseminate his radical ideas. There were other, stranger ruses. In one letter to Eichel he stated, "Took another Civil Service exam, and was informed that I passed the state clerical exam, and am No. 254—not so encouraging." How could William James Sidis possibly score as low as 254th on a Civil Service exam? Either he botched it on purpose, so as not to draw attention to himself, or he was having fun with Eichel.

Two months later, in January 1935, Eichel wrote sternly to

William: "We hope that you are still employed. If it depends on ability, you should be able to hold down your job. As for having a reputation which you cannot live up to, this is a burden which many of us with less ability must be willing to shoulder. None of us is perfect, not even on demand. If we get along at all it is because of luck and the willingness to struggle with responsibilities that are thrust on us." Less than a month later, William began a letter to Eichel with a rare reference to his childhood drama: "Not so good now. Was fired Jan. 31—as I said, having a reputation makes the situation completely hopeless. Really fired for not being a mental calculator."

What story lay behind this remark? Probably, once again an employer or fellow employee discovered that they shared an office with the former wunderkind, and in the ensuing tension William lost his job. Of William's many ruses, his denial of his mathematical genius was the most outlandish, and the most intensely adhered to. Friends and relatives nearly all tell the same tale:

"He would always deny that he had any ability for anything but running a comptometer" (Eichel). "He completely denied any knowledge of math" (Ann Feinzig). "You know the greatest phobia he had? He absolutely resented anybody who told him that he was a good mathematician. He resented being referred to as an expert, or anything like that. He would deny it" (Rab). "Of all things, he didn't want anything to do with math . . . because that was his talent. He resented it. It was one of the things that had been exploited. This is what he led us to believe" (Grace Spinelli). In Helena's opinion, this distaste for mathematics "was probably something in Harvard itself and not anything my father did. Because he also took an aversion to law. And he always maintained that he was a normal person and not a genius —and he didn't want people coming to his place and asking him questions."

William made exceptions for certain of his friends. Helena enjoyed talking about mathematical paradoxes, so they discussed them at length, and he seemed to relax completely and relish the subject. He willingly gave legal advice, especially to Julius Eichel, who was on trial for draft resistance. He helped Ann and Bill Rab with their math homework, though as before, he could never explain how he arrived at his answers. Said Ann, "It could be that he really couldn't tell me how, or he just didn't want to acknowledge the fact that he could. Now if it came to something like a historical theory, he would just say, 'Well, it's a story. Either you believe it or you don't.' " If the topic was a less sensitive one, he could be a gold mine of facts. Len Feinzig, Ann's husband, recalled, "I did a paper on the Federal Reserve Bank and he had information in his head I'd have to spend hours looking up."

William discussed *The Animate and the Inanimate* with his sister and with both Isaac Rab and his son, Bill, though he rarely discussed it with anyone else. It's not surprising that the Rabs were privy to conversation that William withheld from others—they were among his favorite friends. He visited them nearly every Sunday, appearing on their doorstep unannounced. Much as they loved Bill Sidis, the family could not always welcome him. As Bill Rab explained, "There were two or three occasions in which we were expecting company, and it would have been very awkward. Because Bill was not the kind of guy who would fit into a social group. He never came announced, and I don't think he had a phone. So a few times we pretended not to be home."

For the most part, the visits were a pleasure for one and all. The head of the household was the distinguished Socialist Isaac Rabinovitz (the family took the name "Rab"), whose wife and two children, Bill and Ann, were great friends of William's. "Rab," as Isaac was affectionately called, held an informal weekly salon in his home, dubbed "The Headquarters" by Boston leftists. The atmosphere was lively, yet William's privacy was respected completely. No one ever pressed him about his childhood or referred to his genius. He was often invited to stay for Sunday dinner, when he would discuss politics with Rab, Indians with Ann, and physics with Bill, who was in high school. Bill's colorful memories of these visits prompted him to say, "I wish I could go through it all again—believe me, I'd take notes."

"On the brightest sunny day," he reminisced, "William always wore a three-piece suit, usually dark, and he'd always carry a raincoat or an overcoat over his arm. I don't think he ever untied a tie—he'd just take it off, over his head. He wasn't dirty, though that's the impression that everybody got. Not unkempt, but careless. He reminded me of a Buddha. Well rounded. He always had his jacket open with his vest buttoned tight. And he always had an ear-to-ear grin, without showing his teeth.

"He would arrive with his vest pockets full of illustrated cartoons and jokes clipped out of the *Boston Post.* And he'd have his pockets pretty well oriented, so he could always pick out the right joke. And if he told you one that he thought was funny, he couldn't hold back at all—he'd let it all out! He loved a good laugh."

William Fadiman had a slightly less charitable attitude toward his cousin's sense of humor. "He laughed at his own jokes. He would break out before he finished. He was one of those people who start telling you a funny story and then start laughing. It isn't funny at all, but they think it's hysterical."

In addition to his joke-telling, William's proficiency at crossword puzzles was legend among his friends. Bill Rab remembered the informal competitions that occurred in his home: "He and my father used to have good-natured contests. Once in a while, my father, with a sense of humor, and Bill, with a sense of humor, both with their own self-assuredness, attempted to do *The New York Times* crossword puzzle. My father would do it in ink, right off the bat. But Bill—Jesus! He would just look at the thing. He had that photographic memory and didn't have to write down too much. Maybe one letter instead of a word, sometimes in the middle so he wouldn't lose his place, while he was doing the Downs. But it was mostly done mentally. Then my father would quiz him. 'What have you got for thirty-six across?' It was just that one of them hoped he would catch the other in a mistake. They'd ask each other, 'How did you arrive at that word? Where did you get that information?' And they'd surprise each other."

From time to time William helped Bill Rab with his homework.

"I was particularly stupid in chemistry. I had problems with it in school. But Bill's approach made it hold some scope. It helped me out a hell of a lot." William also taught Bill Rab how to make a hectograph. Hectographing was one of the earliest techniques for copying written material, and laborious as it was, William spent hours making copies of his newsletters by this painstaking process, which Bill Rab described:

"He had a little pie tin, like a shallow cookie dish, and he put in a gelatinous yellow material, an eighth of an inch deep. The process is similar to a ditto. You type or draw through a carbon onto a piece of paper, put it face down in contact with the hectograph jelly, press it, and leave it for a few minutes. When you lift it up, the analine dye would have transferred to the hectograph jelly. Then you put another piece of paper on top of it, rub it a couple of times, lift it up, and you've got an image, the original. It came out purple, just like conventional ditto. This was good for twenty copies or so. That's how he did every bit of it. He had a very tiny one for postcards.

"I took him up in the attic of my house, where I had a simple chemical lab. He and I made my first hectograph up there. We had to make substitutes since I didn't have all the chemicals. I remember saying, 'How come you're using this when you wrote such-and-such down on the formula?' And he derived a molecular composition of a particular chemical and explained how it would serve the same function. And believe me, he had a wonderful way of expressing this. But to him this was pure play. Fun. He explained other things that kids love—the nature of light refraction, and how the molecular structure of crystals and liquids created different optical illusions. And it wasn't just chemistry. I'd ask, 'Why is grass green?'

"And there was history. I was in my junior year of high school and I had to write a book report, and I chose the Boston Tea Party. And Bill says, 'Oh. . . . ' And I said, 'Do you know anything about it?' He replied, 'Oh, I know a little bit about it.' I pumped him, and he gave me a little story about the political and economic relationships that were behind the concept of the Boston Tea Party. And I discovered that my school textbook was a highly edited version of the original book, with certain aspects eliminated. So I wrote my report. I got an F! So I said to myself, 'Holy Jesus! I know I'm right. It all makes sense. If anything, I should have been given credit for doing original research, rather than having stuck to the pat thing.'

"My father went up to school. He was really buddy-buddy with Walter Donne, my headmaster; they were Latin School graduates. They had quite a discussion. I was sitting in the anteroom. Donne came out and he says, 'Look,' pretty much man-to-man, 'we're dealing with a teacher who only knows one thing, what the textbook says. I'll let you write the report over again, with another teacher.' All this was my father's doing—he was very forceful in his arguments, he had a hell of a lot of charisma. This incident didn't make me cautious of Bill. Not at all. If anything, it conditioned me never to accept anything on face value just because it's printed."

Though most of his friends didn't know it, William wrote a great many short stories, all of which are lost. He did not show them to many people, but one of the exceptions he made was for Bill Rab, who liked the stories immensely. He read two that were centered on Atlantis, and several that could be classified as science fiction. Bill Rab considered them all "well written. . . . They didn't have the flavor of contemporary science fiction; they weren't sophisticated in that respect. But they were convincing, real good stories in themselves. My favorite, favorite, favorite—far and away—was a science fiction story similar to a Jules Verne concept of a time machine. Now Bill didn't give any preliminaries, any scientific orientation as to why the thing worked. I wish I knew then what I do now about time warps, black holes, parallel existences, because it was pretty much in that vein. It's about a contemporary man who gets a concept of how to go back in time, I'm not certain about the future. But he was able to go back in time, and picture the social relationships as they once existed. In other words, it was a vehicle for social comment. I didn't realize that as a kid, I took it as just a well-written story. I had that manuscript for a long, long time—I just wanted to read it over and over again.

"Starting in Lorraine, Ohio, this man took several trips into the past, through colonial and Indian days, through the Ice Age, and back through geological eras." According to Bill Rab, there was one problem in the story's construction that greatly irked William: "This time capsule was not physically removed from its original geographical location. In other words, if we were to transport back a hundred years, at this moment, we would appear at a very precise longitude and latitude. So the operator of the time capsule had to do research in order to assure that when he went back in time he wasn't going to wind up in the middle of a mountain, or some body of water.

"I don't know of anyone else who read those stories. My sister wanted to do her homework at the time, so I don't think she read them. Bill didn't want me to pass them around. It never entered his head that the ideas would be stolen—it was the possibility that it might get to a newspaper somehow, to some kind of journalist. I was terribly worried about that too."

The company of the Rab household constituted only a small part of William's social life. Before he moved from New York to Boston in the early 1930s, William saw a great deal of his sister, who was studying sociology at Columbia University. He saw nothing of his mother, who was busy running the Portsmouth mansion as a tourist resort. She lost virtually all of her capital in the stock market crash of 1929, including her daughter's four-thousand-dollar inheritance, which Helena had been pressured to let her mother invest. Soon Sarah would make a small fortune playing the stock market, more than recouping her losses; but for a time she was in difficult straits.

After Helena graduated in 1929, and before the crash, she and her mother had taken a trip to Europe. Helena, at her brother's request, looked up Martha Foley at the Paris *Herald Tribune* office, met her, and liked her enormously.

Martha and Whit Burnett were married in 1931, and had a son in November. That same year, they also gave birth to the first issue of *Story* magazine, which was devoted to publishing the short stories of both established and struggling young talents: William Faulkner,

Ernest Hemingway, Sinclair Lewis, and Willa Cather, among others. In 1932 Whit and Martha returned to America, bringing *Story* with them and launching its soon-to-be illustrious American career. They were on their way to popularity, if not fame, and a few years later were well known enough to appear in *Current Biography,* which described Martha as "a little woman who wears tailored suits and horn-rimmed spectacles and looks like a pleasant young housewife."

Martha had lost none of her charm for William, and although her marriage to Whit was difficult—according to Martha, he was often arrogant and petulant, and they fought—she was not tempted to reconsider William as anything more than a former friend. According to Julius Eichel, they saw each other only once more: "When she returned from Europe with the baby, he wrote asking permission to visit her. He discounted the husband altogether—was not interested in meeting him. Actually, he considered him an interloper who had best be forgotten. He had Martha Foley all to himself at that meeting; he was permitted to fondle the baby, and he had to take leave for-ever. . . . I know that Sidis was deeply disappointed at the cold reception and forever sad at the parting. Sidis admitted that her love might have achieved wonders with him, for whereas he might be stubborn with others, there is nothing he would not have done to please her. He carried her photograph with him from 1920 until the day he died, and was always anxious to be asked about it, and would flourish it in the face of any newcomer to arouse a curiosity which he was fast to satisfy on demand. That was the only lady he ever loved, and would admit it, just as readily as he would admit that she did not love him."

There was nothing "he would not have done to please her." Even, he told Eichel and other friends, break the vow of celibacy he had taken at the age of fifteen. Recalled Eichel, "To direct questioning, Sidis admitted to me that he had no desire for any sex experience. Intellectually, it was distasteful, and he could not think of submitting to that experience unless Martha Foley would demand it. He would do anything to be near her." Helena affirms this: "We talked a lot about Martha. I'm very sure he was celibate. A relationship, for him, wouldn't be dependent on sex—he would want people who were as intellectually minded as he was. He did tell me that he never got married because our parents fought so much.

"He reminisced about some of the girls at the Rice Institute. . . . And according to his friend, Marcos Spinelli, he used to do plenty of flirting with the girls in his office, and they smiled back—when Billy told me stories about it, he'd get a twinkle in his eye and he'd laugh. He had a way of going around that Constitution of his."

William paid regular visits to the Spinellis' apartment in Jersey City. Said Grace, "I never met any of William's friends. The only name I remember is Martha Foley. Marcos used to tease him about his platonic affair with Martha, and he loved it. Marcos would say, 'Come on, come on, show me the picture,' and they'd chuckle. And they'd go through this little routine every time."

In 1980, Martha Foley's posthumous memoir, *The Story of STORY Magazine,* was published. William received only a single mention, and parenthetical at that. After explaining that her mother had dedicated a volume of verse to her—the first of many such dedications to Martha—she wrote: "(The second was a volume on higher mathematics, by William James Sidis, the famous and tragic prodigy who was the first boy ever to pay court to me. [The first part of this sentence is incorrect—*The Animate and the Inanimate* was not dedicated to anyone; perhaps Martha was given an inscribed copy, and she remembered incorrectly some forty years later.] Ready to enter Harvard at the age of nine, he was held back until eleven, became a university professor at fifteen, pioneered discoveries in the fourth dimension, became the focus of international attention, and had his life blasted by notoriety.)"

William settled into his bachelorhood, devoting himself, as ever, to his work and his friends. Few of William's multitude of friends knew each other; many assumed they were his only friends. The Rabs believed this; and certain relatives held the absolute conviction that they were the poor genius's only link to society. Some lived in New

York, others in Boston. William bounced back and forth between the two cities for several years, finally settling in his beloved Boston in the early thirties, evidently no longer afraid of being jailed for his May Day "crimes."

When in Boston, he periodically dropped in at his cousin Elliot Sagall's home, generally for a quick meal. Like all of William's hosts, the Sagalls vividly recalled their guest's eating habits: "He would eat one dish at a time. He would eat the vegetables, then he would eat the potatoes, then the meat. If there was a box of candy, he would finish the whole box." Conversation was usually light, but occasionally William spoke of his dislike for his mother. "Many times," recalled Elliot, "he would come and visit and go out the back door when she came in the front door. But he never spoke of his father."

William frequently arrived unannounced at Jack Goldwyn's home, wearing rubbers and carrying an umbrella, even in fine weather. Jack and his wife, Polly, have fond memories of these visits—they even accepted William's eating habits, which they referred to as "methodical." William never spoke to the Goldwyns of his parents. Said Jack, "I never heard him speak in anger about anyone. Billy reminded me so much of his father, but his father's talents were harvested properly by my aunt Sarah. Now, this Martha Foley, I never saw her, but I was hoping that he would marry her, because she could organize him better."

William told the Goldwyns little of his intellectual life. Jack "pulled a few things out of him"—that he had written a book on Euclidean geometry and another on Atlantis. He never spoke to them of American Indians, or pacifist politics, or streetcar transfers. They had never heard of *The Animate and the Inanimate*. The main topic of conversation was William's quest for employment. Jack told him, "Billy, the first thing you do is . . . well, shave! Be a little bit more acceptable. Take care of your clothes. Look more presentable."

Jack and Polly loved William's visits, and are proud that he felt comfortable in their home. "He was a very fine person," insists Polly. "He never bragged. Very humble, gentle, tender. I loved him, but I always felt sorry for him. I felt sorry because here is a genius, and he's ahead of the world." Added Jack, "He was always happy! He'd sing songs, and he had the lousiest voice. He'd sing, and recite poetry and hum. Yes, he was a very happy person. He loved people. He had no malice in him—just honesty and integrity." Like the rest of William's relations, the Goldwyns were certain that he visited no other relatives. Said Jack, "He never had close contact with any relatives except us—we were the only ones who were any fun. Other relatives didn't tolerate him. We were the only ones he visited."

Clifton Fadiman was one of the few relations who was convinced that William visited largely to get a good meal and to discuss trivialities. "I don't think he really trusted us," said Clifton, "but I thought he had no one else to talk to. In all the time I knew him, Martha was the only one I ever heard him speak of outside of his family."

Making the rounds of family and friends for meals and companionship, William had his favorites. Along with the Rab family, the Spinellis were probably the most beloved. After moving from New York to Boston, William sent Marcos a constant stream of letters—unfortunately, all of these have been lost. But Grace Spinelli's recollections give us a picture of one of William's favorite friendships.

Marcos was a little-known novelist who wrote more than one hundred books. William read every one of his friend's novels, and gave him a single book as a present—*The Psychology of Laughter* by Boris Sidis. Besides literature, the two men talked politics. When Marcos, who was an Italian immigrant, applied for his citizenship, he was asked, "Who was the first President of the United States?" Primed by Sidis, Marcos responded with an elegant lecture about federated America pre–George Washington, startling the judge no end.

The Spinellis, of all William's friends, showed the least concern over his habits and appearance. Grace said, "He was uninhibited in his own way. He belched openly. He wouldn't take a bath. He smelled badly. He wore sneakers with no socks and he would scratch his legs in the summer. We thought, 'Well, he's a brilliant young man and he lives the way he wants to live, so what?' "

The question of whether or not William bathed is an exceedingly controversial one among his friends. Many swore he never bathed, and that the stench was brutal. Mrs. Rab once tried to draw a bath for him, and he was infuriated. Occasionally, some poor unfortunate would be delegated by a group of friends to speak to William about bathing. Many insisted that though he was slovenly, he was always clean. Other themes are more consistent. He never told the Spinellis when he was coming, preferring to appear on their doorstep. And he ate his food one item at a time, following the meal with an entire quart of milk, which Grace would sneak out and procure when he arrived, just to please him. He never smoked, never drank liquor, and never drank coffee—just milk, and occasionally a cup of black tea.

Naturally, William showed Marcos some of his writings, and Marcos took a special interest in an essay on floods. He gave the article to his agent, along with a few of William's newsletters, without telling his friend. By accident the papers were returned directly to Sidis, who was shocked and enraged. Marcos insisted, "Really, I was only trying to help you. I thought there was a chance for publication; and you wouldn't be labeled the Wonder Boy." William forgave Marcos, but insisted, "We will never talk about this again."

William's attitude toward the publication of his writings was highly idiosyncratic and variable. He was furious with Marcos; yet in 1934 he wrote to Eichel, "Last summer I started in to write up a 'Grammar o th'American Lingo,' and last Sunday I was talking to someone in the Bronx who is going to take it up with Simon & Schuster as to arranging for publishing it." Three years later he made an effort to have portions of his Atlantis manuscript published by the McClure Newspaper Syndicate.

William's friends came from all rungs of the social strata, and his remarkably active social life included a rare diversity of types. In addition to men such as the struggling novelist Marcos Spinelli and the dedicated Socialist Isaac Rab, there were a number of well-to-do sophisticates. One of these was Creighton Hill, head of the editorial department at Babson's Statistical Office in Wellesley Hills, Massachusetts, and a wealthy resident of Beacon Hill. Creighton was devoted to William and made unsuccessful efforts to have *The Peace Paths* published. Coming to the conclusion that what William Sidis needed most was a regular social life—since, like the rest of William's friends, he assumed he was the only one—he organized a once-monthly meeting, at which Sidis was to lecture on any subject he chose. (William already lectured a few times a year to the Vagabond Club, a group of teenage boys organized by Isaac Rab.) Creighton was too busy to attend, but he put together the core group of three or four selected from his friends and employees at Babson's. They were instructed never to ask William about his personal life. The classes began around 1935, expanding to as many as eight members, and continued until shortly before William's death nine years later.

The group usually met evenings in the office of Shirley Smith, who ran a rental agency in Boston; and occasionally at the home of a Babson secretary, Margaret McGill. The members paid fifty cents per evening, which sometimes added up to as much as four dollars. According to these ladies, the meetings were a combination of lecture and party. There were always refreshments—peanuts or cookies (once, when a full dinner was prepared, William ate nothing but baked potatoes the entire evening)—and William would begin by lecturing. The topic was generally American history, Sidis-style. He never read from notes, though he occasionally handed out portions of *The Tribes and the States* or *The Peace Paths*. Shirley Smith described a typical meeting:

"We would mill around and say, 'Hello, Mr. Sidis. How are you?' It was a small, comfortable room. And we had all ensconced ourselves. And then he'd stand up, near a table decorated with the peanuts and candy. He had a terrific sweet tooth.

"It was very characteristic of him to make his points by nodding. Although his voice was somewhat soporific, I don't think we ever went to sleep—it was interesting. And it was not too long. And then, presently, he would come to the conclusion. Meantime, he had been dipping into the peanuts. He'd work closer and closer to the table and then reach out and grab them and stuff them into his mouth, and keep right on talking. Afterward, we had soft drinks and cake."

According to Margaret McGill, "We called him 'Mr. Sidis,' but once in a while we'd slip and call him 'Bill,' on an especially festive occasion. On the whole it was very informal, except when he was talking. And if it got too long, we'd hold out a bag of peanuts. He'd just automatically reach for it—and that's how we'd get him to slow down or rest. But I don't think he realized it, because he was so intent on what was going on in his head. He really was an extraordinary person.

"He had a peculiar way of standing, as he would deliver a talk to us. He'd stand on one foot, and twist around, and bend. It sometimes got a little stuffy at the meeting and we wished that Bill would take more baths. It could get to be pretty bad. He had no use for conventions at all. If it was hot in the summer, he'd cut off his shirt sleeves —he went to his office jobs like that.

"After the lecture, he sometimes tried to make us sing. I can't carry a tune, so I sat down in the corner and laughed. He made up songs, too, even though he couldn't sing either. And he made up guessing games, and some of them were good. He was almost like a small boy in his pleasure in getting us to do these things. We never did anything as absurd as wear funny hats or anything like that. But he grew on you. He was a curious mixture of a small child and a very superior person."

William dropped in on Shirley occasionally at her office, and she took him to lunch around the corner. She kept a careful eye on him as they crossed the street; he was so deeply engrossed in whatever he was discoursing on that he barely noticed the oncoming traffic. Though they were frequent lunch companions, Shirley never visited Bill at his home. Very few of his friends did, so careful was he about his privacy.

One of the few visitors was young Bill Rab, who made two trips to the room on West Canton Street. "It was a typical rooming house, with the bathroom down the hall. There was a bed in the corner, a desk, and bookcases; and orange crates to supplement the bookcases.

It was never brightly lit, and the two light bulbs were always bare. It was stark. The wallpaper gave you the feeling that it was the cover of an old, old manuscript—aged, and aged, and aged. He had a little shelf over his hot plate, on which he kept the staples. Underneath it he had a cabinet, in which he kept the packaged staples. There was a little anteroom—it couldn't have been any bigger than four by six. It was probably just loaded with manuscripts. He had as many folders filled with manuscripts as he did books. He had a few Western scenes from magazines thumbtacked on the wall—by Remington—that's all. The room wasn't disheveled. It was just a bare minimum.

"And he had two typewriters. A conventional Miracle typewriter, and a Lichtenstern. That was an interchangeable-face typewriter—like the IBM balls. It was a very compact thing—it folded down so you could put it in a silverware drawer. It looked flimsy, but he did all his work on it, at least all his foreign-language work. He could type in Russian, in German, and in Spanish. He was a great protagonist of Esperanto, which he taught me."

As a host, William was predictably negligent. He did not care for conventional greetings, was reluctant to say "Hello" or "Goodbye," or to shake hands. He rarely gave gifts to anyone, with the exception of Helena, to whom he brought boxes of candy. He once stunned Julius Eichel by producing a box of candy and offering it.

William, nearing the age of forty, was fully as eccentric as Samuel Johnson, but except for trouble keeping a job, and his attendant worries about money, he hummed along happily, always productive and usually contented. On August 15, 1937, William's carefully built fortress of anonymity was attacked. A local newspaper, the *Boston Sunday Advertiser,* published an article about the former boy wonder —the first offensive article in more than a decade. And for the first time in his life, the former boy wonder did something other than retreat further into that fortress—he fought back.

17

Invasion of Privacy

The article in the *Boston Sunday Advertiser* was titled "Sidis, Genius, Discovered Working as Boston Clerk" and subtitled, "Child Prodigy of 1914 Shuns Publicity."

Genius in a tawdry South End boarding house. Genius driven by some strange mental quirk to seek obscurity in dullness and mediocrity.

That is the story of William J. Sidis, child prodigy and mathematical wizard, who yesterday was discovered working as a clerk in a Boston business house.

William J. Sidis, now thirty-nine, was once declared by a

group of eminent scientists to be a coming innovator in the field of science, with potentialities as great as Einstein and as brilliant as Marconi.

Yet yesterday a Sunday Advertiser writer found him in a small room, wall-papered and dark, where for the past five years he has lived unknown, unsung, uncaring.

HE LOATHES GENIUS

Master of Latin and Greek when he was barely large enough to mount a bicycle, Sidis prefers that room to the more palatial quarters that might have been his, according to a source close to him.

He hates to be a genius.

He prefers to be a clerk.

The writer yesterday stood in the street before Sidis's home. On either side were identical rows of red brick turret-front houses. From them, as he watched came men and women on their way to work—shipping clerks, waitresses, laborers. Next door a Chinese laundryman nodded now and then to a passing acquaintance as he industriously ironed shirts. In the middle of the street a man fed bread crumbs to a flock of pigeons.

Each day, five days a week, the man who was graduated from Harvard University in 1914 when he was barely sixteen years of age, comes out his door—like the laborers, like the others —and goes to work.

He runs an adding machine.

Publicity shy since his early youth, Sidis avoided questioning. While an embattled landlady stood grimly at the foot of a staircase, Sidis remained on the first floor landing. He made but one statement that could be recorded.

Asked for an interview, he snapped in a high voice:

"Decidedly not!" Then he shut his door and cajoling, arguing and flattering failed to move the Horatia at the staircase.

He Lives in South End Lodgings
Keeps Job Secret

The people with whom Sidis lives say he is a quiet, well behaved man. He has few friends "none of them very close to him, though," and for relaxation he writes books about streetcar transfers.

A large, heavy man, with a light moustache, Sidis is reticent to an extreme point. So afraid is he that his brilliant gifts will be uncovered that in the five years he has lived in the South End house he has never told the other people in it where he works.

Opportunities galore offer themselves to him, but Sidis consistently turns them down, it was learned. Only recently, a friend took him to an office, where he applied for a clerk's job.

Recognizing him the prospective employer exclaimed:

"Why you don't want a job like that! You ought to be on the Boston planning board."

But Sidis doesn't want the planning board type of work. He showed that clearly in 1918, when at the age of 20 he was a professor at a Texas college. He quit the position, returned to Boston and unobtrusively went to work as a clerk. . . . From time to time enterprising newspapers rediscovered him, but Sidis evolved a way of fooling them. He simply threw up what ever job he had and moved to another city.

His shyness toward the press had been evidenced at the time he was nine, when he astounded scientific leaders of the day with a learned lecture on the fourth dimension.

At that time he would turn and flee, old time reporters here recalled, whenever approached.

And so today—unless he has moved since this was written —he lives in the tawdry South End room, with its flower-covered wallpaper, and writes treatises on floods and streetcar transfers.

He lives a clerk, unsung, unknown, uncaring.

Mobilized at last by over thirty years of wrath, William sued the *Advertiser* on four counts. Because few documents pertaining to the case are extant, we know only what the first count was: libel. As a result of the article's publication, Sidis claimed, he "had been held up to ridicule, and had suffered great anguish of mind, and his reputation had been seriously injured, and he otherwise suffered great loss and damage."

This daring step—exposing William as it did to the possibility of further publicity—had barely been taken when a far larger bomb fell on his fortress.

On August 15, 1937, *The New Yorker* magazine made William the subject of a lengthy article in its "Where Are They Now?" series. It was the most publicity to which William had been exposed since he was front-page news in *The New York Times* at age eleven, and this time the publicity was far from favorable.

The article was titled "April Fool!" and was accompanied by a small cartoon of William in knickerbockers lecturing to the Harvard Mathematics Club. The author of the article was given as one Jared L. Manley, a regular *New Yorker* writer; but that name was actually a pseudonym for the famed humorist James Thurber, who was on the staff of the magazine.

"April Fool!" began with the standard rundown of William's childhood accomplishments, with an eye to the development of neuroses. The prodigy's youthful fear of dogs was mentioned, and Manley / Thurber wrote, "Those who remember him in those years say that he had something of the intense manner of a neurotic adult." The article contained a great many factual errors, including the claim that William had attended Tufts College, which was actually Norbert Wiener's alma mater.

The usual story of a nervous breakdown at Harvard and treatment at Boris's sanatorium was copied, after which "[William] began to show a marked distrust of people, a fear of responsibility, and a general maladjustment to normal life." To William's famous graduation quote, "I want to live the perfect life. The only way to live the perfect life is in seclusion. I have always hated crowds," was added this commentary, "For 'crowds' it was not difficult to read 'people.' " A brief account of the years preceding the May Day arrest followed, and a lengthy explication of the trial and William's testimony. Much text was devoted to *Notes on the Collection of Transfers,* with several excerpts from the book.

The New Yorker had traced one of William's New York City landlords, Harry Friedman, and Friedman's sister, a Mrs. Schlectien, who refused to pass on his current address, though they still forwarded mail to him. A few particulars of William's life were extracted from these individuals: " 'He had a kind of chronic bitterness, like a lot of people you see living in furnished rooms,' Mr. Friedman recently told a researcher into the curious history of William James Sidis. Sidis used to sit on an old sofa in Friedman's living room and talk to him and his sister. Sidis told them that he hated Harvard and that anyone who sends his son to college is a fool—a boy can learn more in a public library. . . . Once the young man brought down from his room a manuscript he was working on and asked Mrs. Schlectien if he might read 'a few chapters' to her. She said it turned out to be a book on the order of 'Buck Rogers,' all about adventures in a future world of wonderful inventions. She said it was swell."

The conclusion of "April Fool!" read as follows:

William James Sidis lives today, at the age of thirty-nine, in a hall bedroom of Boston's shabby south end. For a picture of him and his activities, this record is indebted to a young woman who recently succeeded in interviewing him there. She found him in a small room papered with a design of huge, pinkish flowers, considerably discolored. There was a large, untidy bed and an enormous wardrobe trunk, standing half open. A map of the United States hung on one wall. On a table beside the door was a pack of streetcar transfers neatly held together with an elastic. On a dresser were two photographs, one (surprisingly enough) of Sidis as the boy genius, the other of a sweet-faced girl with shell-rimmed glasses and an elaborate marcel wave. There was also a desk with a tiny, ancient typewriter, a World Almanac, a dictionary, a few reference books, and a library book which the young man's visitor at one point picked up. "Oh, gee," said Sidis, "that's just one of those crook stories." He directed her attention to the little typewriter. "You can pick it up with one finger," he said, and did so.

William Sidis at thirty-nine is a large, heavy man, with a prominent jaw, a thickish neck, and a reddish moustache. His light hair falls down over his brow as it did the night he lectured to the professors in Cambridge. His eyes have an expression which varies from the ingenuous to the wary. When he is wary, he has a kind of incongruous dignity which breaks down suddenly into the gleeful abandon of a child on holiday. He seems to have difficulty in finding the right words to express himself, but when he does, he speaks rapidly, nodding his head jerkily to emphasize his points, gesturing with his left hand, uttering occasionally a curious, gasping laugh. He seems to get a great and ironic enjoyment out of leading a life of wandering irresponsibility after a childhood of scrupulous regimentation. His visitor found in him a certain childlike charm.

Sidis is employed now, as usual, as a clerk at a business house. He said that he never stays in one office long because his employers or fellow-workers soon find out that he is the famous boy wonder, and he can't tolerate a position after that. "The very sight of a mathematical formula makes me physically ill," he said. "All I want to do is run an adding machine, but they won't let me alone." It came out that one time he was offered a job with the Eastern Massachusetts Street Railway Company. It seems that the officials fondly believed the young wizard would somehow be able to solve all their technical problems. When he showed up for work, he was presented with a pile of blueprints, charts, and papers filled with statistics. One of the officials found him an hour later weeping in the midst of it all. Sidis told the man he couldn't bear responsibility, or intricate thought, or computation—except on an adding machine. He took his hat and went away.

Sidis has a new interest which absorbs him at the moment more than streetcar transfers. This is the study of certain aspects of the American Indian. He teaches a class of half a dozen interested students once every two weeks. They meet in his bedroom and arrange themselves on the bed and floor to listen to the onetime prodigy's intense but halting speech. Sidis is chiefly concerned with the Okommakamesit tribe, which he describes as having a kind of proletarian federation. He has written some booklets on Okommakamesit lore and history, and if properly urged, will recite Okommakamesit poetry and even sing Okommakamesit songs. He admitted that his study of the Okommakamesits is an outgrowth of his interest in socialism. When the May Day demonstration of 1919 was brought up by the young woman, he looked at the portrait of the girl on his dresser and said, "She was in it. She was one of the rebel forces." He nodded his head vigorously, as if pleased with that phrase. "I was the flag-bearer," he went on. "And do you know what the flag was? Just a piece of red silk." He gave his curious laugh. "Red silk," he repeated. He made no reference to the picture of himself in the days of his great fame, but his interviewer later learned that on one occasion, when a pupil of his asked him point-blank about his infant precocity and insisted on a demonstration of his mathematical prowess, Sidis was restrained with difficulty from throwing him out of the room.

Sidis revealed to his interviewer that he has another work in progress: a treatise on floods. He showed her the first sentence: "California has acquired considerable renown on account of its alleged weather." It seems that he was in California some ten years ago during his wanderings. His visitor was emboldened, at last, to bring up the prediction, made by Professor Comstock of the Massachusetts Institute of Technology back in 1910, that the little boy who lectured that year would grow up to be a great mathematician, a famous leader in the world of science. "It's strange," said William James Sidis, with a grin, "but, you know, I was born on April Fool's Day."

William was horrified, enraged, and hurt. Some of his friends didn't speak of the article, out of deference to his feelings. Others, such as Julius Eichel, offered condolences: "Esther and I read the article that has so upset you in *The New Yorker,* for it was widely advertised. I knew that it would make you feel miserable. I had no notion that the reporters would add to your troubles by hounding you."

When Norbert Wiener read the story, he was stunned. Of all people, he understood all too well the mortifications that a child prodigy endures. *The New Yorker* piece offended him enough to warrant two pages of discussion in his autobiography. He called the article "an act of the utmost cruelty," pointing out that Sidis had "ceased to be news for nearly a quarter of a century . . . the question of the infant prodigy was not a live issue, even in the public press, and had not been for some time, until *The New Yorker* made it so." He thought it offensive that the editors of the magazine rationalized and justified their story "by the claim that the actions of people in the public eye are the object of fair newspaper comment." In Wiener's opinion, Sidis in adult life "was a defeated—and honorably defeated —combatant in the battle for existence" who, as a result of the article, "was pilloried like a side-show freak for fools to gape at." Wiener concluded:

"I suspect certain members of *The New Yorker* staff of muddled thinking. In many literary circles, anti-intellectualism is the order of the day. There are sensitive souls who blame the evils of the times on modern science and who welcome the chance to castigate its sins. Furthermore, the very existence of an infant prodigy is taken as an affront by some. What, then, could constitute a better spiritual carminative than an article digging up the old Sidis affair, at the same time casting dishonor on the prodigy and showing up the iniquity of the scientist-prodigy-maker? The gentlemen who were responsible for this article overlooked the fact that W. J. Sidis was alive and could be hurt very deeply."

If the public mockery were not enough, William rankled under the added outrage of having been spied upon. He had certainly not granted an interview to anyone he might have suspected was a reporter. How, then, did *The New Yorker* secure its story? Speculations as to who "leaked" William's tale abound. Shirley Smith and Margaret McGill are convinced that the mole was none other than John, a member of their study group.

Cheery, sociable, and a close friend of Creighton Hill's, John was above suspicion when he brought a female guest to one of the meetings. The members occasionally invited guests, as did William, and there seemed to be nothing strange in it when John brought along a good friend. According to Shirley Smith, she was the daughter of an editor at the Random House publishing company. She sat quietly during the meeting, and did not exchange a single word with Sidis— she certainly did not interview him at that time.

Shirley and Margaret became suspicious only when *The New Yorker* article came out, and John behaved guiltily. According to Shirley Smith, "We were ready to murder him after that. He admitted that he was afraid to come to any more meetings. As far as I know, he never met Sidis again."

It is not known whether Shirley and Margaret passed this information on to William; nor is it a certainty that John's friend was the "interviewer" referred to in the story. Nor is it known whether a reporter actually saw the inside of William's room. William always maintained that the entire article was a combination of imagination and old stories about him, and that no stranger had gained access to his room.

In any case, no amount of sleuthing on the part of Sidis or his friends could change the fact of the article's publication. Frustrated and angry, William had come to the end of his tether with reporters. Armed with a good deal of rage and years of legal training, he set about to sue *The New Yorker,* on two counts of invasion of privacy, and one count of malicious libel. He sued for $150,000. James Thurber, in his autobiography *The Years with Ross,* called the suit "far and away the most important legal case in the history of the magazine, and the only one that ever reached the United States Supreme Court."

Sidis commenced his suit in the New York Federal Court on July 7, 1938. He had turned forty thirteen weeks before, and the little joke he habitually made on his birthday—about April Fool's Day—had been spoiled by the publication of the article. His friends never heard him make it again.

William employed the firm of Greene & Russell, and according to his friends he prepared many of his own briefs. In his complaint, Sidis stated that as the result of the article's publication he had been held up to "public scorn, ridicule and contempt, causing him grievous mental anguish, humiliation, and loss of reputation" and "for a long time to come will be severely damaged and handicapped in his employment as a clerk or in any other employment and in his social life and pursuit of happiness." Furthermore, "the plaintiff was besieged in his residence by reporters from the newspapers and the press of the country and was forced to remain in seclusion and was rendered unable to attend to the duties of his daily occupation." This last must have been a terrible torture for William. It had been twenty-five years since reporters beat down his door en masse. But however strong his urge to pack up and leave, to run away from this onslaught, the courage of his convictions was stronger, and he stayed to fight the case.

William objected to a series of specific points in his first complaint. Besides the falsities about his education and nervous breakdowns, he added one interesting objection: "That plaintiff is in the habit of withholding from his employers an alleged extraordinary mathematical ability which defendant's said article states that plaintiff possesses, and thereby not rendering service to his employers to the best of his ability." Of course, William was right in essence—he was a responsible employee, and always performed to the best of his ability.

But in treading this ground, he must have been prepared to state, before a judge and a jury, that he possessed no mathematical prowess.

The New Yorker's attorneys, the renowned firm of Greenbaum, Wolff & Ernst, responded that the facts of William's life were matters of great public interest, importance, and concern. They had not damaged his reputation, because he "was not favorably known among people generally and did not have a good reputation, but on the contrary had the reputation for being peculiar and eccentric." Besides, they argued, *The New Yorker* magazine had offered to print any letter William cared to write in his defense, but he had refused to avail himself of the offer.

Judge Goddard in the lower court and Judge Clark of the Circuit Court were highly sympathetic to William; nonetheless Goddard rejected his suit for invasion of privacy. Clark stated his opinion:

"It is not contended that any of the matter printed is untrue. Nor is the manner of the author unfriendly; Sidis today is described as having 'a certain childlike charm.' But the article is merciless in its dissection of intimate details of its subject's personal life, and this in company with elaborate accounts of Sidis's passion for privacy and the pitiable lengths to which he has gone to avoid public scrutiny. The work possessed great reader interest, for it is both amusing and instructive; but it may be fairly described as a ruthless exposure of a once public character, who has since sought and has now been deprived of the seclusion of a private life." In spite of this sympathy, Judge Clark concluded, "Regrettably or not, the misfortunes and frailties of neighbors and 'public figures' are subjects of considerable interest and discussion to the rest of the population. And when such are the mores of the community, it would be unwise for a court to bar their expression in the newspapers, books, and magazines of the day."

William was not to be daunted. He changed attorneys, and was next represented by the firm of Sapinsky, Lukas & Santangelo, whom he employed to appeal the case; this time he asked to appeal as a "poor person." After red tape which dragged on for several years, the appeal was denied, and William was charged court costs of $31.45. In 1940, the U.S. Supreme Court listened to arguments and refused to hear the case.

"The article," wrote James Thurber, ". . . was to become forever celebrated in legal and publishing circles everywhere because of the important precedent established by the courts, affecting all so-called 'right-of-privacy' cases. . . . A decision in favor of Sidis would, to summarize it briefly, result in continual and multitudinous cases of public figures suing the authors and publishers of newspapers, magazines, books and encyclopedias. The opinion of the judges could be condensed into eight words: 'Once a public figure, always a public figure.' . . . The great importance of the Sidis case lies in its having become the principal authority in all similar cases in which the right of privacy is claimed by a person who is, or once was, a notable public figure. It was to save *The New Yorker* from a similar suit. . . ."

Thurber, writing over a decade after the courts' decisions, expressed his disappointment that the judges had not grasped the article's intention. "The general tenor of the article was called 'amusing and instructive' but nowhere was there any indication whatever of what I thought had stood out all through my story, implicit though it was —my sincere feeling that the piece would help to curb the great American thrusting of talented children into the glare of fame or notoriety, a procedure in so many cases disastrous to the later career and happiness of the exploited youngsters." Thurber expressed no regret at having disturbed the career or happiness of a vulnerable, and very much alive, individual.

Determined not to give up, William continued the suit—the libel charges remained standing—and he pressed on.

In the meantime, William had experienced a small victory— perhaps one that gave him the courage to continue his battle against *The New Yorker*. In 1941, he won his suit against the *Boston Sunday Advertiser,* and received a settlement of $375.

18

The Pacifist and the Transfer Wars

William's time-consuming legal activities didn't make a dent in his productive output. He churned out newsletters, manuscripts, and correspondence with a greater vigor than ever before. With only his cumbersome hectograph equipment, he produced a volume of work in five years that surely would have taken another man twenty.

Increasingly, the newsletters written when he was in his forties dealt with pacifism. Violent in his opposition to all war work, William despised the CO camps that were the fate of conscientious objectors during World War II if they wished to escape imprisonment. He regarded them as little more than concentration camps. As he told Helena, "Those who do war work while refusing to fight put the 'fist' in 'pacifist.' " As the war progressed, William developed a passionate devotion to a work plan of his own devising for objectors, which he called Volunteer Urban Self-supporting Projects. The VUSP, he dreamed, could be a national, cooperative venture centering on any number of industries, with none of the profits going to support the war effort. In the interests of receiving government sanction for the project, he wrote reams of letters to politicians and laymen, sent out petitions, and poured out newsletters. The VUSP's first project, he hoped, would be a series of urban transit guides.

The *Penacook Courier* gave way to the *Continuity News*, begun in 1938 and published under one of William's favorite pseudonyms, Parker Greene. It bore the mottoes "The Past Is the Key to the Present," and "We Attempt to Explain Rather Than to Advocate." In one of the first issues he used the word *libertarian* as a solution to the quest for "a new name for government with limited powers."

The content of the *Continuity News* was what we think of when we use the term *libertarian* today. Sidis railed against Roosevelt's New Deal, "with its idea of making money appear bigger by shortening the measure." He criticized the New Deal for introducing fiat or paper money into the economy and entitled the following commentary "Screwball Economics": "The main point common to the various brands of screwball economics is the fanatical belief that, given proper juggling, there is no difficulty in making something out of nothing, and that the particular candidate for office could do it if elected."

The *Continuity News* was followed by *The Orarch*, beginning in December 1938. *The Orarch*'s motto was "Grant to Others All Rights You Would Have Others Grant to You." Each issue bore the same disclaimer: "Issued by the Boston Liberty Group. This paper is issued by a group, and is not the property of any individual." Its contents were similar to that of the *Continuity News*, with more emphasis on conscientious objection and the evils of racism.

William published *The Orarch* for five years. During this period he formed a group that he dubbed the Liberty War Objectors Association (LWOA), "a CO organization based on individual rights as grounds of opposition to war," and released an assortment of constitutions and articles under its auspices.

Beginning in September 1943, William served as associate editor to Julius Eichel's CO newsletter, *The Absolutist*. William wrote a weekly column again under the pen name Parker Greene, in which he plumped for his pet VUSP, attacked current government programs for objectors, and stressed the point that he opposed the draft on the grounds that it violated individual rights. This was a position few COs emphasized. Wrote William, "Where pacifist organizations have so far been merely opposed to war on the basis of humanitarian sentimentalities, the LWOA bases its objections solidly on the destruction of civil liberties involved in war." And, "The VUSP plan is not a plan for 'humanitarian' work. . . . An absolutist cannot be a consistent 'humanitarian' oozing love toward all and sundry; for he must refuse to do war work even if it consists of 'saving life' instead of 'taking life.' "

William was opposed to the martyring of COs who went to prison. While a great many of his fellow COs supported these martyrs, he felt that a successful draft dodger had made a far better choice so long as he continued to seek a remedy (preferably the VUSP) to the situation that sent COs to prison. This stance made him unpopular with numerous fellow pacifists, who found a jail term and a hunger strike more romantic than a plan for alternative CO work.

Eichel, as William's editor, grew increasingly peeved, and their longtime correspondence grew ever more strained and pettish. Eichel wrote in November 1943: "There is a certain amount of tolerance we must exhibit even when we are absolutely sure the other fellow is wrong. . . . I admire your unbending devotion to principle, and often wish I could stand my ground as unflinchingly as you do in the face of great opposition, but our sheet will lose in influence if we make mountains out of the molehills of personalities." William replied hotly, "Once and for all, it is a choice between me and censorship. . . . As I have said before, I do not think that everyone who can mumble 'I hate war' should be immune from criticism. In many ways the interests of 'pacifist' politicians and those of absolutism are constantly clashing, and I don't feel we should deliberately lie down to let those leaders rule our thoughts. To my mind, even FDR has a better claim to sincerity in his 'I hate war' than have some who claim to be pacifists. . . . If that be treason, make the most of it."

Matters worsened with each passing issue of *The Absolutist,* as Eichel edited portions of William's columns, and William threatened to resign and start his own paper. Finally he announced that he had begun a "censorship strike." Eichel maintained his temper beneath the barrage of letters, and finally agreed to print William's column in its entirety with a disclaimer. This suited William admirably, and in his next letter to Eichel, he wrote, "I might have something on Anne Hutchinson, the Puritan martyr who suffered for the right to knock respected leaders. She was my inspiration in the 'censorship strike'; I have often looked at the old site of her house; and she has rated about three pages of *The Peace Paths.* Expect me Christmas weekend."

The truce did not last long. A month later Eichel wrote to William, "It was a mistake in the first place to agree to an associate editor so far away. Perhaps we could have gotten along better if you were closer. Now it is out of the question. You can write for *The Absolutist* if you wish but there will be no guarantee that it will be mimeographed." Hostilities heightened, and in the January 18, 1944, issue, Eichel took a low blow at Sidis. He announced that the paper was dropping the promotion of VUSP, and wrote, "For further information . . . readers will be referred to William James Sidis." Eichel knew very well what it meant to William to keep his real name a secret, and especially never to allow it to appear in print; this was certainly a hostile act, intended to wound.

In February 1944, William finally managed to put out his own four-page CO newsletter, as he had threatened to do for so long. Titled *The Libertarian,* it was devoted solely to his favorite CO topics, and to taking a number of digs at Eichel and his policies. It was edited by "Parker Greene," and bore the motto, "That Government Is Best Which Governs Least—Thomas Jefferson." William sent a copy to Eichel.

In the accompanying letter, William noted that "the VUSP plan is changing, and it is withdrawing from political controversy.

"I have always hated politics in general, and am coming to the conclusion that pacifist politics is as poisonous as any other variety of politics. . . . I hope you are satisfied [with the direction we are now taking]—but it makes little difference whether you are or not. Use your own discretion as to whether to continue me on your mailing list or not. My own suggestion is, don't do it. I am not especially interested in the welfare of prisoners—there are so many other angles that I find more important."

In April 1944, the vituperous correspondence reached a climax. In William's final letter to Eichel, one that ended a friendship of twenty years, he wrote, "In case you do not know it, the dodo was a bird which, when faced with men armed with clubs, walked up and openly challenged the hunter. Result—there are now no dodos. To my mind, such is the attitude of most of those whom you are holding up as heroes. I could feel more admiration for someone who frankly did a good job of dodging. And it makes no difference if you take that as personal antagonism—I would still feel the same if I had never met you."

Eichel retorted, "I have received your letter referring to dodos, and I feel it is about time I spoke out frankly on your social attitude towards others. Everyone seems to be aware of your lack of consideration, and I take it for granted you are aware of the same fault. . . . If human beings must be compared to birds, besides dodos there are ostriches who think that by sticking their heads in the sand they are completely hidden from view." Sidis and Eichel ended their friendship on this bitter note.

As for *The Libertarian,* its primary function had been as an organ enabling a crabby William James Sidis to bluster at Julius Eichel. In issue number 2, Parker Greene announced that "the VUSP is withdrawing from all political controversy," and *"The Libertarian* is taking this opportunity of saying goodbye to its readers. . . . A refund is being sent to all paid subscribers."

William seemed to be going off the deep end when it came to his CO politics. The contrast between his first essays on conscientious objection and plans for alternatives to the work camp system, and the ones he penned for *The Absolutist,* is striking. The strain of his ongoing lawsuit, and his constant financial duress might have accounted for this difference. Another factor probably played a considerable role in this change—William's deteriorating health. Although he refused to be bothered about it, he had very high blood pressure. Even if he had been willing to go to a doctor, he lived in an era that had no effective medications for his condition.

Though William pursued his CO activities with his usual burning intensity, spending countless hours hectographing newsletters, engaging in correspondences, and arranging his secret meetings and initiations, it was not the only—nor even the central—activity in his life.

For almost two years—from January 3, 1941, to September 18, 1942, William wrote a weekly page in a Boston magazine, *What's New in Town.* The column was titled "Meet Boston," and ran under yet another pseudonym, Jacob Marmor. It is not known what salary he was paid—probably very little since he continued to complain of financial difficulties. The magazine did volunteer to advertise his perpetual calendars, the sale of which brought in a steady trickle of income.

Of all William's writings—from those about higher mathematics to streetcar transfers to American histories to French poetry to pacifist propaganda—"Meet Boston" is the most readable, the most accessible, the most professional. It is a cheerfully patriotic and varied collection of trivia about the city William Sidis loved.

The column's first appearance was topped by a headline in the Robert Ripley tradition: "Strange but True." William saw and reported with the eyes of a true Boston-lover. He fueled the ever raging New York–versus–Boston debate, writing of the "insular Manhattanite," and he peppered his columns with items such as the following:

"According to the census of 1930, there were about 2,700 cows resident in New York City. And only 90 in Boston. Which would seem to prove that Boston is nowhere near as much a cow-town as New York. Or does it mean that the larger population of New York consists mainly of cows?"

William's choice of trivia was often fascinating. He told the story of Benjamin Franklin's leaving one hundred dollars in his will to his native town of Boston, to be put out at 6 percent compound interest for a century, then used for a work of public benefit. At the end of that period—in 1890—the one hundred dollars had grown to forty thousand dollars. The money was used to build Franklin Park, which is the same size as New York's Central Park.

William had collected a great deal of material about his home-town of Brookline. "In colonial times it was reputed to be the hangout of idlers who, so ran the belief of the more 'respectable' townspeople in 'the Village,' never did any work, but spent their time 'puttering about.' And so this region is still called Putterham."

Naturally, William slipped many of his pet interests into the column. He plugged his transit guides. He announced that "the small and obscure habit of peridromophily" had been organizing, and its national headquarters were now in Boston where it issued the hobby's only organ, *The New Peridromophile.*

William went so far as to quote a work by the ubiquitous Parker Greene titled *American Descriptions,* an unpublished book "giving some interesting descriptions of incidents in America." One such incident occurred when William (alias Parker Greene) saw a refraction mirage from the window of his Cambridge office building. In fact, he had been extraordinarily fortunate in seeing more than one. The first experience had proved so exciting that he watched the sky daily from his office window, hoping for the precise concurrence of light and timing that would bring the seemingly magical image into view again. William knew everything about the proper conditions for the appearance of such a spectacle. As Helena explained, "Of course, it's very rare, and you have to be very observant and know a great deal about meteorology. Billy knew plenty about meteorology, inside and out. He knew the time when the winds and clouds and everything else would be just favorable. He explained it to me in detail. But I was so mad when one of those reporters wrote up the thing. He said that my brother was some kind of an oddball, who used to spend most of his lunchtime looking up at the sky. The other people in the office didn't understand it, either. He was always looking up."

The following week, Jacob Marmor ran a correction of a minor error that had appeared in the preceding article, and offered "Our apologies to the author of 'American Descriptions.' " William's idea of a really good joke, it seemed, was to apologize pseudonymously to himself, using yet another of his pseudonyms!

While William battled *The New Yorker,* which fought to prove him a pathetic, useless wreck of a man leading a burnt-out life, he was producing professional, well-received pieces of journalism.

In "Meet Boston" William decided to tickle his anonymity funny bone. The following excerpt is William's only, not-too-veiled, reference to his Harvard days, and those of fellow prodigy Norbert Wiener:

> Over thirty years ago, Tufts College turned out the youngest college graduate on record—age fourteen. He would appear to have been the only extra-young college graduate in America who specialized in mathematics; for, though another boy shortly afterwards was reputed to be a mathematician, there was nothing authentic about such reports, which were 100% pipe-dream. The Tufts graduate now teaches mathematics; the victim of the press hoax is unable to even understand the subject. Case of mistaken identity.

At no time during his busy life did William neglect his hobby. He continued to publish transfer-collecting newsletters, to correspond with other enthusiasts, and to run a "transfer deposit bank" called the

"Transfer-X-Change," whereby collectors could make deposits and withdrawals through the mail. For fifty cents a new collector could purchase a sample pack of fifty transfers from the bank. William's own collection consisted of well over 2,000 items. Some correspondents claimed collections as large as 50,000 transfers strong, representing over nine hundred cities. However, all was not bliss in the world of transferania. Far from it.

An undercurrent of tempestuous unrest seethed among America's transfer collectors, all of whom were easily as dedicated as Sidis, if their correspondence and publications are any indication. Rival publications and organizations sprang up like mushrooms, hurling accusations and invective at one another. At times, the atmosphere of frenzy reached such proportions that it is a wonder William had time for the other pressing affairs of his life: his *New Yorker* lawsuit, his weekly "Meet Boston" column, his American history classes, his pacifist newsletters, and his books. The depth of feeling shown by some of the correspondents is not unlike that which emerged in the Eichel-Sidis exchange. The letters to William, and editorials in the major rival newsletter, *The Transfer Collector,* give the flavor of life in the transfer trenches.

The editor of the *Transfer Collector*—or TC as it was popularly known—was an impassioned character named Charles S. Jones who operated out of Ardmore, Pennsylvania, and appeared to rule his neck of the woods with an iron transfer. He editorialized loudly and passionately, writing that "TC tolerates no slackers. . . . If you are not in a position to give time and effort to your collection, we suggest that you seek some other less diversified avocation. Peridromophily is not a lazy man's hobby." (The word that William had coined in 1926, as Frank Folupa, had been appropriated by all like-minded hobbyists.)

Relations between *The New Peridromophile* and the *Transfer Collector* had begun amicably enough. Jones respectfully referred to Sidis as "one of the 'patriarchs' of transfer collecting." The publications shared subscription lists as early as 1930. William even wrote the occasional article for the rival organ, using his own name and referring to "the Folupa book on transfers." In 1932, the *Transfer Collector* interviewed William on the subject of a slump in the hobby, and printed his response, again under his real name: "I think we should go after new recruits, and get them organized somehow to keep them from back-sliding too quick, then we could slowly work some of the old hands back into the game." In 1933, the papers "merged." William had just moved to Boston, and decided to stop publishing *The Peridromophile*. He sent his complete set of back files to the TC, and generously donated a hectograph kit to Jones.

However, the passage of time saw increasing tensions among collectors. William had launched his *New Peridromophile* and there was bad blood between the two publications. In 1939, Jones turned the full force of his wrath on William in the April edition of the *Transfer Collector*:

TEMPEST IN A TEAPOT

On page 1 we stated that only one dissenting vote had been sent in on the question of a national organization. That vote was sent in by a person who has been opposed to almost every constructive plan that the TC has proposed in the past two years. We refer to one Parker Greene, who, with his magazine, has attempted to overthrow everything that we of the TC and the [Peridromophile Society] have worked so long and hard to accomplish. This gentleman comes forward with the mistaken idea that we are attempting to establish some sort of an autocracy, with your editor and Mr. Reinohl as co-dictators. If Mr. Greene had taken the trouble to read the constitution more carefully, he would have seen that there was no basis for any of his foolish accusations. The entire matter sums up to the fact that we are not organizing in a way suitable to Mr. Greene—a way which failed miserably under his leadership some months previously—and that there are no immediate plans for city transfer groups. However, this gentleman has no one to blame but himself, if our plan does not meet with his approval. An offer of cooperation, tendered Mr. Greene by our Mr. Reinohl last November, met with not even a courteous reply. Can the blame for this be laid at our door?

As for Mr. Greene's plan to hold a counter-meeting of those opposed to our society at the World's Fair, we are afraid he will have to be twins—if he wants any company!

The following week's editorial again pointed to Sidis/Greene, as an "instigator of riot." Jones cautioned that Greene and his ilk should "either cease their action or come into the open with their fancied grievances, or they will find themselves definitely out in the cold."

While Jones was obviously something of a madman, it cannot be denied that William had willingly entered the fray, and it is curious to consider that he did so with nearly the same intensity he dedicated to dangerous and important issues, such as conscientious objection. In fact, he had no option in the matter—his mind raced at an astounding speed that could not be turned down or off, regardless of the issue involved. Perhaps, in fact, memorizing lists of thousands of bus and streetcar routes throughout the country with every variation and alteration, in all their overwhelming detail, was for William a kind of quiet, low-key occupation, a lulling pleasure to be enjoyed much as the average man would muse over a baseball score, try to piece together the words of a popular song, or drift into reverie about his plans for Saturday night.

One transfer buff in William's circle guessed that there were about two hundred serious collectors in the United States. William received letters from several teenagers ("I am a very serious railroad fan of fifteen, with no 'kid stuff' about my hobby," wrote one from Brooklyn), but only a few were from women. One collector wrote to William, "I believe Mr. Dunlop of Cicero has left the hobby. He told one collector 'that he wanted to devote all his time to his wife' —of all things!" For some collectors, such as this one from Cincinnati, the hobby occasionally resembled a drinking problem: "One doesn't take to collecting transfers overnight—it grows on you. I can't recall offhand just how I started. It was about five years ago. With each year it accelerated until the present, and I'm up to my neck now."

Although William used his actual name in some of his transfer activities, he also used several of his pseudonyms, and he never let his subscribers know just who was running the papers. One collector broke the ice and wrote to Mr. Greene, "Are Frank Folupa, Parker Greene, Mr. Sidis and Transfer-X-Change one and the same person?" Another, from St. Louis, discovered the truth: "I am writing this letter as a congratulation. I didn't learn until a week ago that it was you whom the transfer collectors of the world have to thank for that brilliant work *Notes on the Collection of Transfers*. You have missed your due all these seventeen years by not revealing that you wrote that splendid book." He had discovered William's true identity by chatting with friends who worked at the transit company offices. A company official mentioned Folupa / Sidis as "the founder of the hobby." The collector concluded glowingly, "I think much credit belongs to you for your long struggle to establish and organize the hobby."

Most collectors did not share this relaxed attitude toward William's aliases. In 1941, William wrote a long Code of Ethics for Transfer Collectors, in which he addressed this topic: "A transfer collector is entitled to use a pseudonym for the purpose of making contacts with other collectors; and other collectors are bound to respect his right of privacy in this regard. A collector may adopt a new pseudonym as often as he finds reason to believe that the privacy of his pseudonym is being threatened; and collectors are bound not to discriminate in any way against collectors using or changing a pseudonym in the hobby."

The Code of Ethics was controversial, and William circulated it widely among his fellow collectors. It consisted of twenty-six points, several of which were strict and dictatorial. "Peridromophily," he wrote, "must not be made to extend to anything but the collection of local transit transfers. . . . Collectors who have other hobbies besides peridromophily should be careful to keep the collection of transfers separate from all other hobbies, and not to classify them together for any purpose." William went into detail explaining what was and was not admissible as part of the hobby—overlap fare receipts were, tickets were not. Derelict transfers were admissible and should never be overlooked just because they had been thrown away.

William stressed that violators of the Code of Ethics would be punished, if judged guilty by the Peridromophile Federation, although he did not say what form this punishment would take. Moreover, recipients of the code who belonged to the federation were "bound by this code upon its issuance." Nonmembers who read the code, then corresponded with members, "shall be considered as having accepted this code and consented to being judged in accordance therewith for any offenses against transfer collectors' ethics."

The code caused quite a stir, and William received a variety of letters in response, many written by incensed collectors. The St. Louis collector did not find "the whole Code of Ethics to be wrong. The exchange of transfers need be governed by certain moral considerations. . . . But the idea of any group or individual be he yourself, PS, NP, Jones etc. dictating what should be collected or how it should be displayed etc. is foreign to me. I believe in individual taste governing." One collector wrote, "Baseball fans are not told how to root or when to root—I'll do it my way, you do it yours." The most strident voice wrote, "I see you, as all dictators do (like Hitler does) passed your Code of Ethics even though some of us voted against parts of the code you didn't alter it any, that will not do, The PF is, I believe to follow the lines set by democracy governments. . . . Now why does the PF cloak themselves in darkness? Just who heads the PF is a mystery— I associate this with *fraud*—are they afraid of their lives if they make themselves known? Yes, I demand an answer. And another thing— why the Jawbreaker of a name permidromophile—my thought is whoever thought up a name as that should be committed to an insane institution. Awaiting your answer to redeam yourself and do see what you can do to revive the art of collecting transfers."

Charles Jones also objected to William's anonymous Peridromophile Federation, writing, "It is a rather soul-less occupation, writing to an organization rather than to another individual." But his true resentment toward Sidis lay in another area, one he finally revealed after years of hinting. "I feel personally that collectors should be permitted to correspond with other collectors as individuals rather than through the auspices of a central group. Such collectivism borders on the verge of Communism—a political science with which at least one of your members is familiar." The postscript to the letter read: "The member of your group whom I charge with Communistic tendencies is, of course, your leader, William Sidis. I refer to a 1937 issue of *The New Yorker* which contained a short biography of this person."

One of William's most poisonous correspondents also hailed from St. Louis. A typical missive from his pen read, "Dear Mr. Greene: I received the package of wastepaper, dignified by the name of transfers. When I say wastepaper, I mean just that, nothing but common stuff, such as New York City and Boston. All Boston transfers I ever saw looked like they were picked up out of the gutter. Boston has some of the lousiest transfers of any city. I don't recall what I sent you, but it couldn't have been as bad as what I got back; if that's the way your transfer exchange works, you can have it."

The collector had his own transfer club in St. Louis, but he wrote William, "By the way, the second notice of dues I sent you was just a formality, and is of course to be ignored by you, since we don't expect you to join. Speaking for myself, I don't give a damn if you ever join again," and then, in a fit of pique, dealt William the lowest blow one streetcar transfer collector ever dealt another: "No doubt you are a bus lover, tsk, tsk! What a pity, oh well!"

Indeed, the vicissitudes of the hobby seemed worse, at times, than those of an antiwar struggle or a lawsuit against *The New Yorker,* but William bravely fought his battles on all fronts. There was only one battle that William would not fight face to face, one battle from which he still thought it wisest to withdraw in silence: the battle against Sarah Sidis.

19

"America's Greatest Brain"

n the years following Boris's death,
Sarah and Helena continued to run Portsmouth as a summer tourist
resort. The clientele consisted of people driving by on the road and
word-of-mouth recommendations. It was a grueling life for Helena,
who was pressed into heavy service by her mother (much as Sarah
herself had been as a girl). From eight in the morning until eleven
o'clock at night she made beds, swept floors, and waited on guests. For a
few years there was a maid, but eventually the maid left and Helena did
everything. Her health was still delicate, she was still studying hard, and
she was taking her first jobs as a social worker and a teacher.

In 1933, Sarah bought property in Miami Beach and began to
build apartment houses. She had recently played the stock market with

considerable success, and while the Sidises' standard of living was hardly luxurious, Sarah was able to make several trips to Europe. Her business acumen was excellent, and by 1936 she was doing extremely well in the market and expanding her Florida investments. Each winter, Sarah and Helena migrated to Miami Beach, returning in the summer to run the resort. Though Helena didn't have to please tourists in Florida, she nonetheless found her life harder than in Portsmouth, "where we had a big house. If my mother started yelling, why, I'd just go into one of the other rooms."

Helena's jobs periodically separated her from Sarah. At various times in the 1930s she worked in Connecticut, New York, and the Boston area, often in close proximity to her brother. When necessary, he traveled considerable distances to visit her, his only concern being the fear of running into his mother. In the '40s, Helena spent several summers in a Brookline lodging house only a few blocks away from William. When Sarah visited Helena, William refused to stop by and risk a run-in until Helena arranged for their mother to be gone in the evenings. Then William came over every night, while Sarah stayed away—months passed like this, and mother and son never met. Despite the humiliation this must have been for Sarah, she never admitted to it in her autobiography.

When Helena and William were separated, they corresponded voluminously, William sending batches of jokes and funny clippings with every letter. All but two letters are lost. One was written to Helena in Miami in 1936. She had requested information about the constellations to be seen in the Florida night sky. According to friends' reports, William had a complete star map in his mind's eye, and could describe the conformation of the stars at any given place in the world at any given time. He modestly began his letter, "I hardly think I could give you a good star description now—it is so many years since I followed that up." He then proceeded to give an impeccable description of what to look for and when to do it, and illustrated this with a drawing of several constellations.

He displayed a similar modesty in the second letter, which began,

"Sorry to hear you are down with the chicken-pox. However, you need not worry about your letters infecting me—I had it in 1923; and did Martha [Foley] laugh when I phoned her and told her about it! As to your Portuguese dishes, I don't know why you consider me an expert on anything Portuguese, but I'll try." William then proceeded to give a precise and clear explanation of Portuguese pronunciation, with a list of examples—obviously, Portuguese was on the tip of his tongue, just as any language was.

It was in the first letter, the one with the star map, that William made the only surviving written reference to his mother. After a longish discussion of the weather in New England (one of his favorite topics) William wrote, "Had an awful nightmare about Miami a couple of weeks ago—but maybe that is best left undescribed. You probably know what is down there that I am so scared of."

While William admitted his fear to his sister, he usually showed his anger to his friends. George Gloss remembered: "He expressed over and over again a hatred for his mother. He said she was 'horrible.' He also spoke very bitterly of the time his parents tried to rehabilitate him in their sanatorium." According to Ann Feinzig, "There were occasions when people would say, 'Perhaps you should see your mother,' or 'Perhaps you should become reconciled.' And he really got infuriated. A good fury, too. He was a gentle person, but certain things would rouse him, and if you mentioned anything about reconciling with his mother! He used the word 'hate.' 'I hate my mother and I don't want to talk to her! I don't want to talk about her!' He would really become very, very tense and very, very angry if you mentioned her. I never heard him mention his father."

What fell to Helena, then, was the terrible task of trying to satisfy her mother, who wanted not only a reconciliation with William but to renew her domination over his life. She constantly relayed messages through Helena: "She'd say, 'Make him do this and tell him to do that . . . ,' but I couldn't make him do anything. And Billy would say to me, 'She'll never change.' She was expecting me to be able to iron out the situation between them, which I couldn't. All her life she wanted to make up, but there wasn't any point in her trying. Billy would never accept.

"It was hard to talk about this with my brother; in fact, we didn't. I wanted him to get over this feeling about my mother. I wanted them to get together, because it was very hard for me to be a buffer between them. My mother never stopped talking about Billy, hoping I could have some influence on him—but nobody could have any influence on him.

"She criticized me all the time, found fault in everything I did. You could never do anything right with my mother, she was a perfectionist. I always thought she was still taking it out on me that my father and my brother and I had left her out, because she didn't fit in."

Besides the problems over William, Sarah remained quite a handful for Helena. "She always demanded a lot of company, and I wasn't enough for her. I was teaching summer school and I couldn't give her all my time. I called up some of my ex-students, and asked them to mother-sit."

By all accounts, Sarah worsened as she got older, becoming increasingly demanding, impatient, and abrasive. According to Helena, her mother was still considered a very beautiful woman; she told her daughter she had received many, many proposals after Boris's death, but never considered remarriage. There were rumors that she'd had an affair with Dr. Herbert T. Kalmus, the inventor of Technicolor and an old family friend and patient, or, implausibly, with Howard Hughes, whom she met in Miami Beach—but if she did, it did nothing to soften her personality. When she reached the age of seventy, her relatives began to notice a slight mental deterioration. She was slowly developing senile dementia, which took the form of obsession about certain subjects, and incessant rambling. She stopped reading and stayed up all night playing solitaire.

Earlier, in 1936 when she was sixty-two, she decided to write a book about William's childhood and her views on child rearing. She wanted a collaborator, and Helena sent one of her brightest students, who found Sarah maddeningly obstinate and impossible to work with. The very idea was pathetic—mother and son were completely estranged, yet she continued to revel in the glory of his childhood, and to write the same early chapters over and over and over. When the book reached the point where William left the family, she returned to the beginning and began again, rather than face the hard fact of her failure to earn her son's love and respect.

William introduced most of his best friends to Helena, who in turn invited several of them to visit Portsmouth. Marcos Spinelli boycotted any contact with Sarah Sidis out of loyalty to William, but his wife, Grace, met her once. She said, "I could see why Sidis would have disliked her. Helena was very gracious, but Sarah was a very, very aggressive woman. I remember that she was short and chubby and she still spoke with an accent. A very dominating woman. I remember she had definite ideas about food—she had to have cottage cheese. She spoke with very positive, nonargumentative attitudes. You just couldn't argue with her. And this is where I got the feeling that, although people say it was the father's idea that you could develop a child genius, I thought it was hers."

Ann Feinzig, too, met Sarah once. She recalled, "I was perhaps twenty-one or twenty-two, very pensive, and I wanted to say things Bill would have said. And I did say something to Sarah that I probably shouldn't have. She replied that people were very unkind about the way Bill was raised, that he was born exceptional, and that there was no way he could have had a normal childhood. She was defending herself and her husband. She told me at length about how Bill taught himself Greek as a gift to his father. And she talked about how reporters grabbed him and while one held him down, the other took his picture." This diversion from the Boris-and-Sarah party line, that they made a genius out of an average boy, was most unusual. Sarah never admitted to anyone else that she thought her son was "born exceptional," and perhaps she switched attitudes as a defensive posture, or revealed to Ann a change of outlook that was not part of her public image as a genius-creator. And while she defended herself by citing the stories of cruel reporters, she didn't tell Ann how she had regularly dragged her son to teas and dinner parties against his will, to show him off to her friends.

Sarah's complaints about William were so numerous that Helena found it difficult to describe a single example. "It would be easier to say what she didn't complain about," said Helena. However, one persistent area of aggravation was money. With a mind like his, why did her son worry about finances, and whether or not he would keep his latest clerking position? Even the ever loyal Helena was angered by her brother's refusal to accept high-paying work, particularly during the Depression.

"For one thing," said Helena, "I felt that if he would only get a job that was more what people would expect of him, reporters would leave him alone. And his colleagues at his office jobs didn't like him because he did the work so fast. For some reason, he just wouldn't conform and do it slowly. He was offered plenty of jobs. He never told me about them, but I would find out from other people.

"I got really mad at my brother one time. I was very disgusted with him. He was offered twelve thousand dollars, which was an awful lot of money at that time. The Boston Subway System heard all about what he was doing with the transfers and everything else, and they wanted him to straighten out some of their problems. He refused, and I didn't find out till later—he didn't dare tell me. And my mother wanted me to give him some money! She said, 'You must give him something.' I was very upset and angry. I was living . . . not very well —in a furnished room. And I wasn't being offered any million-dollar jobs. I was willing to go here, there, and everywhere for a job; it was the Depression and I accepted anything. But he wouldn't do it. He wanted to go to Boston, he wanted to be in certain places. Well . . . then my mother got mad at me and I got mad at her. . . . And the upshot of it was that I gave him some of my own money. I tried to have him do a little something for me in exchange—he typed some of my poems. But it made me so mad that he wouldn't work when he could. On the other hand, I didn't know that he was ill. His blood pressure was very high, and he never told me."

There was a similar incident that particularly upset Helena. Barney Sagall, one of Sarah's nephews and Elliot Sagall's father, was a dentist practicing in Revere, Massachusetts. In 1942, he wanted a problem solved that involved occlusion of the teeth, which he recognized as a mathematical problem, and not a dental one. Though he had access to the finest minds at MIT and Harvard, he was convinced that only William could figure it out. As Barney told it, "I once offered to subsidize William if he would do some research for me in the medical dental field. But no go. He wouldn't. I offered him a wicked salary. And he wouldn't do it."

Helena elaborated: "At that time William was earning very little money. This problem that my cousin needed solved involved the striking surfaces of the upper and lower teeth. Barney told me, 'Only William can do it, only William. I offered him three thousand dollars. I think he could have done it in half an hour, two hours maximum. It was worth three thousand to me.' That's worth at least forty-five thousand dollars today, for only a couple hours' work.

"And I got a little mad at him. After all, he said he needed a job. I said, 'It's only half an hour, Billy, for heaven's sake, why don't you?' He said, 'No. I don't want to do it. The numbers would just make me sick.' "

The story is almost paradoxical. He would talk to Helena about mathematics, or help Bill Rab with his math homework; but he could not take a job of complex figuring without risking emotional and physical illness. The amount of money his cousin offered would have funded all his newsletters, co-ops, groups, and meetings—but it wasn't worth the mental suffering he would have had to endure.

There is no doubt that he was perfectly capable of the calculations involved. The *New York Sunday News* printed the following story when William died, and it proves that his mathematical mind was no less sharp as an adult than it had been as a boy of eleven:

Once a friend of his laid a copy of Einstein's final formula for relativity on the table near Sidis while they were dining in a chop suey house.

When he saw the Einstein formula he drew back slightly without a word as if he were puzzled. He was reading the figures upside down from three or four feet away. Then out of a clear sky he said without emphasis:

"That's a seven."

What he meant was that the friend had copied one little figure wrong in Einstein's formula. He had set down a quantity to the sixth power when it should have been to the seventh power. The power was indicated by a small number written above and to the right of a letter on the lengthy equation.

But if the friend thought Sidis would enlighten him on the theory of relativity he was mistaken. Sidis's mind had long since refused to contemplate anything deeper than the problem of who stabbed the Count in the latest detective novels to which his last years were devoted.

The reporter for the *Sunday News* understood little of Sidis's motive for stopping—it was not, of course, inability, but aversion of a painful, neurotic origin.

Naturally, what conversation William did have about mathematics with his sister or the young Rabs was limited by their knowledge. The only person for whom Sidis made an exception, discussing high-level math almost freely, was Nathan Sharfman, a friend he made during the 1930s through the Rabs. Perhaps this was because Sharfman and Sidis had something very uncommon in common. Like Sidis, Sharfman was an exceptional intellect who rejected academia and worked as a cab driver in Boston. He was a protégé of the famed philosopher Alfred North Whitehead, who taught at Harvard between 1924 and 1936. Whitehead guided his student's brilliant career at Harvard, where Sharfman had a teaching fellowship and was studying for his doctorate;

Whitehead proclaimed him to be the hope of American philosophy. Sharfman married a beautiful young girl and had a child, and it seemed he had a magnificent life and career ahead. However, he took to drink, lost the wife, and made an outrageous drunken scene at a dinner party at the Whiteheads' home, throwing his steak on the floor and insulting everybody. One of his best friends, British writer Dr. Paul Saunders, reminisced: "He broke all contact with Harvard. They gave him up, and he ended up driving a taxi. I can see him now, in front of the Copley Plaza Hotel, sitting there in his cab, slumped over the wheel with his hideous little black pipe in his mouth, and I thought, 'Oh, my god! That's the chap that Whitehead thought was the hope of American philosophy!' When he met Sidis he was breaking up with his wife, and with Whitehead.

"I remember the first time Sharfman brought Sidis round. I went to the door, and he pushed Sidis in ahead of him, saying, 'This guy's the best goddamn brain in the United States.' That was his introduction. Sidis sort of leaned back and said, 'Oh, don't be silly, Nat,' or something like that, something very lame. And Sharfman gave him another push, and he came into the room and sat down. For some reason I thought, It's not going to do any good to flatter this chap, or make a normal reply to the most brilliant brain in the United States! So I said, 'Sit down, will you have a cup of tea?' He thoroughly enjoyed a cup of black tea. When I offered him wine, he turned it down rather contemptuously.

"Then we had a general conversation. Something made me hesitate to plumb the depths of this brilliant mind, as it were. Inevitably, we got to talking about Boston. I lived in the west end; like all bohemians in those days, in the slums. But it was a nice apartment, and I had a very large library, three or four thousand books. These interested Sidis, of course, and he rather hesitantly asked me what most of them were. I said, 'I'm in English Lit., but I'm stuck at a horrible war job now.' So we got to talking. He was very cautious, putting in a word now and then, when all of a sudden—this is the first meeting —he began to expatiate on the significance of Boston, as far as Indian origins in the United States went, about what he'd assumed from geological phenomena, and the area that had been cleared in Back Bay, and what was discovered when layers of clay were removed, and so on. I don't know where he got this information. He must have talked for well over an hour, without interruption. Then Sharfman said rather brusquely, 'Well, what proof have you got?' and Sidis shut up like a clam. He said, 'I'm just a simple person. I don't make any claims. These are just my surmises. I hope you won't take this too seriously.' From there he went on and spoke about girls—not erotically, but as though he was trying to change the subject.

"Sidis and Sharfman were very fond of each other, but Sharfman's relationship with Sidis was quite unusual. He spoke to Sidis in a brusque manner that I felt would normally offend him. Sometimes Sharfman would rib Sidis. He'd say, 'Alright, how's the genius working today?' and things like that. It would upset Sidis terribly. Or Sharfman would start on some paean about Sidis, and Sidis would say 'No, no, no, no—that is not so!' Sidis didn't want to be treated as an exhibit; he resented being called 'America's greatest brain.' He'd reply with words to the effect of 'I'm not a prize guinea pig, you know.' Actually, it's amazing that he tolerated Sharfman, he seemed to have a certain awe of him, as a lot of people did."

In no other relationship did he tolerate that kind of teasing. Apparently, William was willing to put up with a lot for some actual intellectual camaraderie. Paul Saunders was witness to some high-spirited conversations between the two ex-Harvard men. As he explained, "Sharfman was a brilliant man, and when he was not in liquor he was a reasonable debater. Once he tried to bring up the matter of the high points of music, and Sidis wasn't receptive. But they discussed mathematical phenomena and philosophy a great deal. They argued about it a lot but the trouble was, it was a noncombat. Sidis would always back down and let Sharfman have the floor. It wasn't a backdown in ideas, ever—it was a backdown in the sense of 'Well, I'm not going to argue about it.' Sidis was a little bit autocratic in his reaction. When he was speaking he'd gesticulate a bit, he liked to perform a point. But you never knew when he was going to shrivel up. He repeatedly said, 'Well, I wouldn't know—I don't claim to be an authority on things like that.' Of course, he did claim to be an authority. He would expatiate for endless periods about something when he got under way, and you could tell he thought he was pretty good. But if you said, 'Well, of course, Bill, you know much more about this than I do—' he'd say, 'Oh, not necessarily, not necessarily!' He thought he was being modest, but in many respects he floored you with his erudition, even when he was trying to curb it. The Indian prehistory is what most impressed me, and everybody; along with his profound geographical knowledge and his mastery of tongues. You wondered where he found this information. I didn't know right away he'd been a prodigy. When I asked Sharfman about it, he just said, 'Oh, you don't know that fellow. I'm telling you, Paul—that is the greatest brain in the United States.' "

William never went alone to visit Saunders, he always accompanied Sharfman. On a few occasions Sharfman, who was having an affair with a married woman, used Saunders's bedroom, leaving Sidis and Saunders in the library. "Sidis never commented, never said a word about what they were doing in there," said Saunders. "And I found it a bit uncomfortable without Sharfman. Sidis was a bit awkward, and he'd relapse into silence, sipping his tea. I can see him now—he used to sit with one arm over the back of the settee, sipping his cup of black tea. He would get up occasionally and go over to the bookcase and take a book out, and ask me about it. Then he would take out another. I'm one of the few people who has a complete twenty-volume *Golden Bough*. He'd take a book like that, and he'd know where to turn to. He'd turn some pages and say, 'Did you ever hear of this phenomena?' And for a moment he'd be the pedant. Then he'd relapse into his modesty again. I think he thought of my place in a vague way as a haven of refuge, since all the walls were surrounded by books."

Many of the friends who visited Paul Saunders were leftists. As he put it, "Everybody was Marxist then, but I never thought of Sidis as a Marxist. I never was one, but my Marxist friends used to come and have all-night sessions in my place, right under a big picture of George the Fifth! I knew Sidis was a pacifist. But of course Sharfman, who was Jewish, was absolutely for the war, and they argued about it. [Sidis, of course, was also Jewish.] Sidis's attitude was, 'It need never have happened. . . . If there hadn't been such decay in society, the war wouldn't have arisen.' In other words, he didn't argue that we should try and stop it, he went back further than that—Hitler shouldn't have existed. A lot of pacifists then were secretly pro-German—I never got that impression from Sidis, I just thought he was a very, very pacifist sort of person. I don't mean he thought Nazis shouldn't be stopped, but he thought there were complications and ramifications that took place years and years before that made this terrible war possible. He was concerned with what had happened before."

William's historical perspective toward the war upset a number of his friends. Helena was also upset, since she believed in all-out war against the Nazis. They had their only real falling-out over this issue. Still, Helena was convinced that her brother's sympathies lay with the Allies. She explained, "Although Billy always claimed to be 'neutral,' he was like the Quakers during the Revolutionary War—one knew where his sympathies lay. He favored England, and after the fall of France he sent me this joke:

"Two Germans met in Paris. Said Karl to Fritz: 'Have you a good job here?'

" 'Yes, I have a fine job. I sit on the Eiffel Tower and wait for the English to wave the white flag,' said Fritz.

" 'Good pay?' asked Karl.

" 'Not much,' Fritz answered, 'but it's for life.' "

According to William's theory of geographical / political continuity, a people tended to repeat its political history over and over again. For example, the Russians replaced their Tsar with brutal Communist dictators; Americans continually strove for the proud democracy that was their first form of government; and the Nazis were another manifestation of the evil Kaiser's reign.

Back in 1936, on the November 4 that saw Roosevelt reelected to a second term, William had written to Julius Eichel, "You seem to be wondering about what the remedy is for the troubles across the sea. I am afraid that, first, I have no remedies ready at hand for anything, though I think I have a vague idea as to how to strike out in the case of America; second, there probably is no remedy 'over there' and the best thing we here can do is simply write off the so-called European civilization as a total loss and proceed to take care of our own troubles. And it won't be through governmental channels, so that yesterday's returns, for example, is a highly irrelevant matter, and the political campaign is simply a circus we like to have every so often. (As a circus, it wasn't so bad.)"

If being a conscientious objector during World War I had been radical and dangerous, it was considered even more un-American during World War II. William had been classified 1-A for a time, and was eventually reclassified 4-F, though it is not known why. Perhaps it was his high blood pressure and/or weight. Thus, while he was free from the onus and risk of being a draft dodger, he was a part of the very small American minority to oppose United States involvement in the Second World War.

William's political activities had already attracted the attention of the FBI. In 1940, one of the bureau's agents—who remains anonymous under the Freedom of Information Act—wrote two letters to Bureau Chief J. Edgar Hoover describing his meetings with "Peridromophilists," whom he believed to be dangerous radicals. He wrote, "There is a new group . . . the 'Boston Metropolitan Transfer Group' and the leader of that outfit has been arrested for several various picketing and communistic disorderly conduct charges. His name, or one of them, is 'William Sidis' but he has others also. He is not associated with the Peridromophilists which I know, though he is trying to win them over." In his second letter, three months later, the informer had discovered William's alias of Parker Greene. "I checked the article in *The New Yorker,*" he wrote, "and he is therein written up as a most 'promising' 'Red.' " Though William's wartime antidraft activities were far more radical than his transfer-collecting activities, the FBI made no further inquiries.

Despite the enormous amount of time and attention William gave to his pacifist activities, they were still being juggled along with a multitude of projects, not the least of which was the lawsuit against *The New Yorker*. In 1939, William wrote a letter to Eichel grumbling that his case was withering for lack of proper attention from his lawyers, and inquiring whether Eichel could help him find new counsel.

The case took several disappointing turns. William wanted a jury trial, but was unable to secure one. In 1943 his lawyers made an unsuccessful effort to keep the "right of privacy" issue alive by pointing out that Sidis was an infant when his life in the public eye began, and consequently could not have waived his right of privacy; nor had he, as an infant, ever sought publicity. When this tactic failed, William had no recourse but to press his suit for libel alone.

Once again William changed attorneys, employing Hobart S. Bird, who had served him in the past by assisting with his applications for the perpetual-calendar patent. On the defendants' side Harriet F. Pilpel, a member of the firm of Greenbaum, Wolff & Ernst, took over the day-to-day work on the case, for Morris Ernst.

Bird and Pilpel threw themselves into a hearty and time-consuming exchange of insulting red tape, and matters heated up once again.

Pilpel observed that more than five years had elapsed since Sidis served his original complaint, during which time the case had "had a complicated and busy history." Why, she asked, had Sidis waited so long to press the issue of falsity in *The New Yorker* article? Furthermore, she objected that he had done so "in the broadest possible terms, despite the fact that obviously a great many of the hundreds of statements about him must be true." Bird answered irately, "Must be true! Indeed! Unless publication in *The New Yorker* makes it ipso facto true, there is no warrant whatever for assuming that there is any single statement in the article that is obviously true." Much debate followed over whose job it was to detail the libelous portions of the article, the responsibility falling finally to the prosecution.

Sidis, said Bird, was the victim of *The New Yorker,* which injured him "without justifiable motives or good ends and with a reckless and careless disregard of the plaintiff's reputation and feelings." In short, he stated, the magazine had libeled him by causing the readers of *The New Yorker* to believe the following statements to be true of the plaintiff:

1. Was a reprehensible character;
2. Disloyal to his country;
3. A supporter of enemies of his country;
4. An insulter of the American flag;
5. A criminal;
6. A fugitive from justice;
7. A loathsome and filthy person in his personal habits;
8. Of having suffered a mental breakdown;
9. Of being afflicted with phobias;
10. Of being a neurotic person and having a deranged mind and having received treatment as such;
11. As one pretending extraordinary intellectual attainments and being a genius, yet in fact a fool, incapable of making a decent living and living in misery and poverty.

The New Yorker published its article with "evil design and wanton cruelty," wrote Bird hotly, leaving Sidis "greatly mortified and humiliated" and having "suffered greatly in his peace of mind and sense of dignity." To what extent these briefs were written by Bird, and to what extent by William, will never be known. William probably did prepare much of the material, since he was so deeply dedicated to the case. When the *Boston Transcript* went out of business, he obtained the morgue file on himself through an employee and gave it to his attorney, to dispute *The New Yorker's* defense that they had obtained their information from accurate newspaper articles. When the case ended,

William insisted upon having the morgue material returned to him, and he destroyed the entire file.

On March 24, 1944, the case was put on the calendar for trial. On April 3 and 4 of 1944, William was called to the office of Morris Ernst, who represented *The New Yorker,* and was asked to give his depositions.

Ernst was one of the most respected attorneys in America; he had become famous a decade earlier by defeating the U.S. Customs Office's ban on James Joyce's *Ulysses.* Now Ernst personally undertook the confrontation with William Sidis.

To the astonishment of his friends, William purchased a new suit for the occasion. These depositions are not among the records of the case in the Federal Court files, but were found among the papers of William's lawyer, Hobart S. Bird, by his daughter Caroline Bird Menuez. Mrs. Menuez made some efforts to publish a sensational article about William after his death, and used the vividly colorful depositions as the meat of her essay. Because it is the only source extant for these transcripts, it is not certain that her reconstruction of the conversation between Ernst and Sidis is 100 percent accurate. Nonetheless, William's statements have a ring of truth about them, and one can easily imagine him taking part in the following extraordinary exchange.

Mrs. Menuez wrote that William went to the meeting with the intention of proving that he was just "an ordinary person" and not a genius; nor had he ever been one. He denied all allegations of extraordinary achievement, and pointed out that he had graduated from Harvard cum laude, not magna cum laude.

According to Menuez, Ernst and the rest of the examiners had "a pack of papers and photostats of his record a foot high on the table, and they began questioning him about the facts contained therein." They first asked him if he spoke any foreign languages, to which he replied no. Aware that he currently held a job as a translator, the lawyers asked William what his present employment was. He replied, "Translating."

"What languages?" they inquired. "French?"

"Yes."

"German?"

"Yes."

"Spanish?"

"Yes."

"Russian?"

"Yes."

"Italian?"

"Yes."

"Portuguese?"

"Yes."

"What do you mean by saying that you don't speak any foreign languages?"

"I don't speak them, I read some of them."

"Didn't you write a book when you were a child, entitled *The Animate and the Inanimate*?"

"I don't remember."

Ernst turned to a page of the book, pointed, and said, "Isn't that a mathematical formula?"

"I don't know what a mathematical formula is."

"Did you write that?"

"If I did, I didn't know what I was talking about."

"Does a mathematical formula make you sick as alleged in the article?"

"No."

"Well, what is the fourth dimension, anyway?"

"All I know about it is what I've read in the newspapers. The newspapers at one time said it was spiritualism, then later they said it was mathematics. I don't know anything about it. People who do say it's not an abstruse subject."

"Did you ever attend Tufts College?"

"No."

In answering a question, William made a slight grammatical

error, and Ernst asked, "Do you want to correct your grammar, Mr. Sidis?"

"No," William replied, "I prefer to speak American."

Turning to the topic of his early childhood, Ernst asked him how long he stayed in the Brookline elementary school.

"About three months."

"Why did you leave?"

"I was kicked out."

"Why?"

"I was never able to find out."

"Did you have any trouble with the teachers or students?"

"No."

"Did they say you were incorrigible?"

"No."

"What studies did you take?"

"Just the ordinary things they take in school."

"Then did you go into the Brookline High School there?"

"Yes."

"How long did you stay there?"

"Well, perhaps a year."

"Why did you leave?"

"I was kicked out."

"What for?"

"I was never able to find out."

"Did you ever translate the *Iliad* from Greek into English?"

"No."

"Did you ever read the *Iliad*?"

"I may have looked at it."

"In what language did you read it?"

"I don't remember."

William was then handed a two-page typewritten account of some episodes from his childhood and asked to read it carefully. He took a quick glance at it, and returned it to the interrogator.

"Have you read it?" he was asked.

"I have looked at it."

The interrogator began to read from the paper, when William interrupted, "Hold on, it doesn't say that"—the interrogator had made a slight error. The questions continued.

"Did you ever study mathematics?"

"I never studied anything." William replied truthfully.

Ernst was discouraged by the depositions. Clearly, William was willing to fight tooth and nail to prove that he was ordinary, and would do so in front of a jury. Such a battle, fought by so great a genius, would be bitter. *The New Yorker* had no desire to allow the libel portion of the suit to go to trial. Rather than proceed, they offered William a settlement out of court.

William accepted. Consequently, wrote Menuez, the deposition was never filed. There is no record of the sum; friends believe it was between five and six hundred dollars. James Thurber wrote: "The libel charge, at first held in abeyance, was decided as late as 1944, in favor of Sidis. The judgment was small, for the libel, whatever it was, had been a minor slip and not intentional denigration."

The New Yorker considered that it had won, naturally regarding this tiny payment for libel as negligible. But William was jubilant. He had fought on and on, and caring little for money, had won at last on a matter of principle. For William had been libeled from birth— he had been libeled for forty-six years. From the age of fifteen, he had run from the sensation-mongering press; and, finally making his stand, he had won. A meaningless victory to the rest of the world, but a great triumph for William James Sidis.

Margaret McGill saw William for the last time a few days later. He arrived to teach his history class wearing his new suit, to the delight of his friends. William, who had never spoken a word to them about his past or his life, told the group all about the article and the lawsuit, explaining point by point the manner in which he had been libeled.

William did not regard the issues of libel and invasion of privacy as separate. He wrote to Eichel on April 10, "I got a settlement from

The New Yorker of the seven-year lawsuit I had pending against them. I feel that it was at last some sort of victory in my long fight against the principle of personal publicity."

According to Caroline Menuez, when William went to New York to receive his settlement, Morris Ernst invited Sidis and Bird into his office for a few words.

Said Ernst, "If you should come to New York at any time, come in to see me. And if you ever need any money, come to me, and I'll give it to you without any obligation. I'm a rich son of a bitch, and I'd just like to give my money to a fellow like you."

William's exact reply to this distasteful speech is unrecorded, but it must have been negative, for it prompted Ernst to say, "I'll give you one thousand dollars right now for any article you write of any length on any subject. You will not have to use your own name. I will not disclose the fact that you are the author." William refused.

"But why?" pressed Ernst.

"Because I wouldn't trust you," replied Sidis.

When William left, Ernst grumbled to Hobart Bird, "He's a sick boy."

20

A Superior Spirit

By the standards of Morris Ernst and those of most of the people the world deems successful, William James Sidis, the most intelligent human being alive and a twenty-dollar-a-week comptometer operator, was "a very sick boy." Certainly he was a very eccentric, and in many ways a neurotic, man. But at the core of his mind he was remarkably healthy and strong. "There is no question about it," said Bill Rab. "It's a wonder he could bear up all those years, under the forces of exile . . . his self-imposed exile."

In a literal sense, however, one that neither Ernst nor anyone in William's life was aware of, he *was* a very sick man. By 1944, William's debilitating blood pressure had been worsening steadily for at least a decade. The outward manifestations were few. He had become exceedingly overweight, yet Helena described her brother as "pink and laughing." He had occasional difficulty breathing, especially when climbing stairs.

According to Julius Eichel, William's room in a Shailer Street rooming house was "an attic which was very cold in winter." Consequently he caught a cold in the winter of 1943 and never quite shook it off. Since William had won a settlement of at least five hundred dollars in April 1944, it is strange that he did not leave the rooming house for more healthful lodgings. On the other hand, it may have been a matter of pride. Though reporters had hounded him since he began suing *The New Yorker,* he no longer cared to run from them by changing residences. Or it may simply have been a matter of indifference, since he was so little concerned with bodily comfort.

The five hundred dollars was a substantial enough sum in 1944 to have freed him from the necessity of working, at least for a time. Exactly one year before the settlement—in April 1943—he had written to Eichel, "My economic situation is probably in the worst spot it has ever been. It is beginning to look as though I will not be able to keep myself alive for much longer—barring some miracle, which I hardly expect." Since then, he had had several jobs. Even after winning the five hundred dollars he continued to work—his last position was at an actuarial research company, operating a comptometer. When the job was finished, he promptly sought another. In July 1944, he was hired for a job with a small chain of low-priced department stores, and was to begin Monday, July 17.

Early in July, he ran into Shirley Smith on the street and she asked him how he was. He answered in some detail, explaining that he felt a bit unwell; Shirley teased him, saying, "You know, William, when people ask you how you are, they don't want to hear the details." He taught his regular history group a few days later. On July 13, just after he had finished his dinner, one of the boarders in the rooming house heard a thud in the hallway. Rushing upstairs, the landlady and her son found William unconscious. Unable to revive him, they called the police, who rushed William to the Peter Bent Brigham Hospital in an ambulance.

William had suffered a stroke, the result of high blood pressure; it was a cerebral hemorrhage, the same type of stroke that had ended Boris Sidis's life. That night, the *Boston Traveler* carried a front-page story: "One-Time Child Prodigy Found Destitute Here." They reported that William was in a coma, and the hospital described him as "fairly comfortable." Because the hospital was short of rooms, William's bed was placed in a curtained-off section of hallway.

William's landlady did not know any of his friends or relatives and had no idea whom to contact. Searching William's effects, the police discovered that he had an aunt in Boston, whom they eventually notified. All his friends and his closest family members had the horrible experience of finding out what had happened by reading about it in the papers. Helena, recently returned from the hospital after a serious operation, was living in a subleased apartment in the Bronx, and Sarah had come up from Miami to be with her. The apartment had no telephone and they didn't take any newspapers, so they did not learn about William's condition until a friend of the family brought them a newspaper the next day.

Sarah and Helena rushed up to Boston. Meanwhile, a number of people had already converged on the hospital. Ann Feinzig visited William, and Rose Hirshfield, a friend and coworker, stayed at his bedside.

H. Addington Bruce, who had known William since birth, also saw the story. Bruce had written a great many articles about prodigies, and in the early forties mentioned William in one of them. William had been furious and had told him off harshly. Bruce hadn't held the incident against William, whom he regarded as practically his own son. Bruce rushed to the hospital, for some reason certain that despite the reports, William was not in a coma. At the bedside, he took William's hand and said, "Billy, this is Mr. Bruce. If you understand me, if you know me, squeeze my hand three times." William squeezed twice, and then his hand fell away, as if he hadn't the strength to press a third time. Bruce told the hospital staff to send him the bills, if they could not locate any relatives.

According to Helena, William was not actually in a coma; rather, the stroke robbed him of his power of speech, and the newspapers reported it incorrectly. Because he was not unconscious, Sarah was afraid to enter his room. She told Helena, "He may see me and have another attack." Said Helena, "It was so sad. We were very anxious to avoid any sort of excitement, so she stood outside his door. But she was afraid to go in the room, because she was afraid he was going to get excited. She still wanted to right the wrong, but she just couldn't."

While Sarah sat her lonely vigil in the hallway, Helena and Rose sat at William's bedside. By now, several newspapers had circulated the story. Between reporters and friends, the hospital was deluged with phone calls. Said Shirley Smith, "I always felt very sorry that I did not go to see him in the hospital. The news came out in the evening paper, and I thought, 'Oh, I ought to go!' And there was a tremendous thunderstorm, so I thought, 'I'll go tomorrow.' And there was no tomorrow."

William died on July 17, 1944, of a cerebral hemorrhage leading to pneumonia. Anxious to avoid the presence of the gaping press, Sarah hastily arranged the funeral, which was held at Portsmouth the following day. She allowed only a handful of friends and relatives to attend. William was buried next to his father at Harmony Grove cemetery in Portsmouth.

Sarah and Helena, joined by a few relatives, went to the Shailer Street apartment to clean up William's effects. Helena found a letter addressed to her, full of the latest batch of jokes and clippings from the *Boston Globe*. There were few possessions, but there were stacks and stacks of research materials and unpublished manuscripts and articles. There were piles of transit guides covering forty major cities, and several thousand transfers, the first one dating from 1903, when William was five years old. They found the patent for the perpetual calendar, a small book of transfer photographs, sheaves of correspondence, an assortment of maps drawn by William, the *Gregg Shorthand Dictionary,* a Russian/English dictionary, the *Pickwick Papers* and a play by Molière (both in Russian), a *Guide to American Esperanto,* a copy of the U.S. Constitution—and, curiously, William James Sidis's Harvard degree, which he had saved for thirty years.

William did not leave a will. At only forty-six years of age, he probably had little inkling that he would need one. However, he did wish Helena to be executrix of his estate, such as it was. She discovered that her brother's bankbook contained $652.81. The day of his death he was to have begun a menial job at a department store—yet the entire sum of his settlement from *The New Yorker* had been left untouched. Perhaps the money was tucked away for a rainy day. Or, more likely, William enjoyed knowing it was there, whole, the symbol of his fight and his victory.

After expenses—$211 to the funeral director, $50 to the monument company, $12 in unpaid rent, $67 in hospital bills, and $112 in legal fees—Helena was left with $200. Sarah had paid the funeral and hospital bills; but, wealthy as she was, she demanded to be repaid out of her son's account, rather than allow Helena to keep the extra $200.

This distasteful action was only the first of several that Sarah would perpetrate. Many, many times during her son's life she had been accused of exploiting him in his childhood. She made an even greater effort to exploit him in death. However, it was several years before Sarah's efforts got fully under way. The press had its day immediately.

William's obituaries were an orgy of reveling in his supposed failed life. Most of them contained a high proportion of factual errors, and all harped on the following point, as it appeared on the front page of *The New York Times*: "Acquaintances often said he never enjoyed childhood and had no conception of play or pleasure." Every obituary stated that his only published writing was *Notes on the Collection of Transfers*—not a single one referred to *The Animate and the Inanimate.* *The New Yorker* piece was the primary reference source for the obituaries and editorials that appeared in newspapers and magazines nation-wide; consequently, the story of William's childhood nervous break-down was repeated in every article. Writers theorized ineptly about the cause of William's decay. A *New York Times* editorialist wrote, "Perhaps his brain was tired and his interest dulled by long excessive stress on his intellectuals [*sic*]."

Psychiatrists were quoted. The *Boston Traveler* interviewed Pro-fessor Wayland F. Vaughan of the Boston University psychology department, who supposed that William's spectacular decline occurred because "he never had time to whittle a willow or dam up the gutter with painstakingly collected stones and twigs. He was always busy with books. . . . He was obviously a child who never had any fun." Parents who had a prodigy on their hands, advised Professor Vaughan, should seek the testing guidance given by Yale's Professor Gesell, who had developed a system for monitoring the progress of gifted children, in order to "guide parents and teachers in controlling the safe rate of progress for any young genius." Concluded the *Boston Traveler*, "How to treat a genius need worry only about 1% of the nation's parents because 90% of the population never will give evidence of sufficient brilliance to inspire anyone to push them ahead." The attitude of virtually every article can best be summed up by these words that concluded an editorial: "So I guess it doesn't pay to be too smart, either."

Both *Time* and *Newsweek* devoted several pages each to Wil-liam's obituary, and both overflowed with factual errors. *Time*'s article was titled "Prodigious Failure" and *Newsweek*'s was "Burned-Out Prodigy." Both contained every myth and bromide imaginable that pertained to William. *Newsweek* featured quotes that made William sound especially cretinous; for example, "A year ago Sidis went to work for the Financial Publishing Co. of Boston for $22 a week. 'Gee,' he exclaimed, 'that's big money for me.'" According to *Newsweek*, "The record of Sidis's later doings is sketchy. His single published work, *Notes on the Collection of Transfers,* appeared in 1926. Acquain-tances report that he discoursed occasionally on American Indian dialects. Later in life he went to the movies and liked to hang around and talk."

William's friends fought back. Shirley Smith wrote a letter to the editor of the *Boston Traveler*:

> His numerous friends do not like the false newspaper picture of him as a pauper and anti-social recluse. . . . Bill Sidis paid his way; he was not a burden on society.
>
> Sidis had plenty of loyal friends. All of them found his ideas stimulating and his personality likable. Very few people knew as much about the Indian background of our social customs as he. His manuscript study of it is worthy textbook material and very readable. He knew dozens of stories from Boston's history and told them with relish. He recently submitted a plan for post-war Boston.
>
> But William Sidis had one great cause—the right of an individual in this country to follow his chosen way of life. . . . Whenever Sidis saw interference, by individuals or governments, with anyone's "life, liberty and the pursuit of happiness," he fought it any way he could. He won a legal fight against a nationally known publication on the ground that it had invaded his privacy.
>
> Bill Sidis was a quiet man who enjoyed the normal things of life. His friends respected him and enjoyed his company. I am glad to have been one of his friends.

William Aronoff, an attorney who had represented William, wrote a particularly interesting letter, which he sent to several publications. Its curiosity lay in the fact that it contained a number of well-intentioned but utterly false statements about William's life (along with many accurate ones), which William had evidently convinced Aronoff were true. Some of them were very farfetched indeed, and William must have made them at the height of his struggle for anonymity. A portion of the letter read:

He was not a mathematical genius, nor any other type of genius or "prodigy" in spite of so many allegations to the contrary. He never lectured to any group of professors on the 4th dimension and never knew of any theory as the 4th dimension. . . . He always wanted to be a lawyer, contrary to the wishes of his parents; and in fact spent two years at Harvard Law School, during all of which time they wanted him to study medicine. His later desire to work as an office clerk rather than at any other vocation was based upon his physical inability to do any manual labor, and general inability to get and maintain any more lucrative position because of the "prodigy" publicity that hounded him for so many years.

Mr. Sidis was in my office about twenty-four hours before he was taken suddenly ill. . . . He was just as sincere, respectful, courteous and normal at that time as he had always been. He never engaged in any riot or incited others to riot. . . . It is to the shame of certain publications, which continuously published the fact that he had been sentenced, but ignorantly or conveniently neglected to mention the subsequent nol pros.

[He was] an individual who lived a decent life in a decent manner, in spite of all the handicaps that were put in his way from the time of his early childhood.

When he heard about William's death, Creighton Hill wrote to Margaret McGill: "There are real tears very close to my eyes as I write this note. . . . Bill was a gentleman and something very gracious and kind and lovely was in him. And now, we shall never see those marvelous mannerisms and gestures again. . . . I'm sure Bill doesn't like the way the government is run, wherever he may be right now. In whatever Valhalla of superior spirits he is abiding, he is unquestionably in the opposition."

Articles about William have continued to pop up in books and magazines to this day. By 1959, the facts of his life had become so distorted that in the book *Stranger Than Science* one could read about the four-year-old prodigy composing French treatises "under orders from his father," and concluding the Harvard Math Club lecture and turning from the lectern "giggling hysterically and uncontrollably." One could also learn that "he was permitted no playmates. His world was a prefabricated playhouse of the abstruse. Month by month his incredible development continued, to the amazement of his father's colleagues and to the bewilderment of his helpless mother." The article concluded, "To the bitter end, genius William Sidis refused to touch the money of the parent who had ruined his mind."

As a result of such articles, modern psychologists now refer to the Sidis fallacy—that pushing gifted youngsters may have adverse consequences. Sadly, the Sidis fallacy has given a bad name to the idea of tending to the special needs of bright children.

Sarah Sidis lived fifteen more years, dying on July 9, 1959, at the age of eighty-four. She was buried at Portsmouth beside her husband and son. Her obituary was minor national news; *The New York Times* referred to her as "a noted psychiatrist," though she had never practiced medicine or psychiatry on a single patient.

During the fifteen years that followed William's death, Sarah never gave up the ghost. In various editions she wrote and rewrote three books: her autobiography, *The Sidis Story*; and two books about raising children, *Formula for Genius* and *How to Make Your Child a Genius*. None of them was finished or published in any form. She persistently rewrote the first chapters of her life story, the ones that told the tale of her youth in Russia, her marriage to Boris, and the story of William's singular childhood. Among her effects was found the projected table of contents for the book, which was to consist of fifteen chapters. She never got past the first few pages of chapter 10, "Billy Rebels," preferring instead to repeatedly pen glowing accounts of her son's successes, dwelling on his infancy, his years in the limelight, and his startling accomplishments. Sarah's ability to avoid the bitterness of the truth is amazing. Had she completed the proposed chapter 12,

"Billy's Later Years," what would it have contained? How could she have explained for public consumption the gargantuan rift between herself and her precious wunderkind?

In the late 1940s, Sarah's personal secretary, Paula Bloom, wrote in her diary, "Dr. Sidis lives for nothing except the book. . . . She has no idea about her poor memory and everyone treats her with the greatest of respect. . . . Nephew Ben talked with Sarah about the book almost the entire day and she really kept him from his own work, interrupting him every few minutes with new ideas."

In fact, Sarah had a second obsession—the founding of a "Boris Sidis Institute," an educational institution that would teach children the "Sidis method" (nebulous as it was) and would instruct teachers in this method. Sarah wanted to found the institute at the University of Miami. She appealed to various wealthy friends and acquaintances —such as Herbert Kalmus and Howard Hughes—for donations, but she did not succeed in raising a substantial sum of money.

In 1949, Sarah received an audience with Eleanor Roosevelt, which she used to promote her plan for the institute. Mrs. Roosevelt wrote about their conversation in her syndicated column "My Day," but still nothing materialized in the way of funding. In 1952, Sarah's ideas were the subject of a lengthy article, "You Can Make Your Child a Genius," which was nationally syndicated. Quoted in the article, Sarah bragged about William's youthful accomplishments, yet said little about his adult life. She offered parents a list of eight pieces of advice about raising geniuses:

1. Avoid punishment in all ways possible—it is the first cause of fear.
2. Try not to say "Don't." Instead, explain why what you say is so.
3. Awaken curiosity—it is the key to learning.
4. Never fail to answer and never put off your child's questions.
5. Never force your child to learn nor judge his ability to learn by adult standards.

6. Implant ideas at bedtime, just before sleep. Suggestions made then will make a solid impression.
7. Never lie to your child or use evasions.
8. Refrain from showing him off.

"What happened to Billy can happen to your Johnny too," said Sarah.

When Norbert Wiener read the article, he was horrified. He wrote angrily in his autobiography:

> As a piece of reporting, it is an ordinary journalistic hack job, neither better nor worse than a thousand others that appear in the Sunday supplements and the slicks. As a human document, it scarcely merits consideration.
>
> Sidis's failure was in large measure the failure of his parents. . . . So you can make your child a genius, can you? Yes, as you can make a blank canvas into a painting by Leonardo or a ream of clean paper into a play by Shakespeare. My father could give me only what my father had: his sincerity, his brilliance, his learning, and his passion. These qualities are not to be picked up on every street corner.
>
> Galatea needs a Pygmalion. What does the sculptor do except remove the surplus marble from the block, and make the figure come to life with his own brain and out of his own love? . . . Let those who choose to carve a human soul to their own measure be sure that they have a worthy image after which to carve it, and let them know that the power of molding an emerging intellect is a power of death as well as a power of life.

Epilogue

There have always been men of intelligence who went on strike, in protest and despair, but they did not know the meaning of their action. The man who retires from public life, to think, but not to share his thoughts—the man who chooses to spend his years in the obscurity of menial employment, keeping to himself the fire of his mind . . . refusing to bring it into a world he despises—the man who is defeated by revulsion, the man who renounces before he has started, the man who gives up rather than give in, the man who functions at a fraction of his capacity, disarmed by his longing for an ideal he has not found—they are on strike, on strike against unreason . . . in the darkness of their hopeless indignation, which is righteous . . . as rebels who never learned the object of their rebellion, as lovers who never discovered their love.

—AYN RAND, *Atlas Shrugged*

What was wrong with William James Sidis? Said Ann Feinzig, "I don't know what happened to Bill. People who loved him, like my father, were always fighting someone who had no knowledge of Bill, to defend him. But it isn't quite true that nothing happened to him. If no one knew anything about Bill Sidis at all and he walked into a room he would be eccentric at least. And if he still really had all his childhood abilities, and I don't doubt that he did, then something terrible happened to him emotionally."

The answer to the question can be found by first discarding the swamp of myths and lies that surrounds the memory of America's greatest prodigy. Author Abraham Sperling, director of New York City's Aptitude Testing Institute, became deeply interested in Sidis in the period immediately following his death. Sperling had been testing intelligence quotients since the 1930s, and was startled to see the obituaries that proclaimed Sidis a burnout. Said Sperling, "My knowledge told me that this was completely erroneous. I learned, much to my satisfaction, that there's no evidence that his intellect had burned out. This business of a nervous breakdown was nonsense.

"In recent years, I have tested more than five thousand people. Of all the mentally superior individuals that I have seen, nobody begins to approach the intellect and perspicacity of William Sidis. According to my computations, he easily had an IQ between 250 and 300. [Albert Einstein's IQ was 200, and John Stuart Mill's was estimated to be 190.] I have never heard of the existence of anybody with such an IQ. I would honestly say that he was the most prodigious intellect of our entire generation. And he did not burn out."

No, the intellect did not burn out, but its owner took it underground. The double life of William James Sidis was based on a mixture of righteousness and fear. The portion of fear is highly ironic, and terribly sad, for above all else, in books, lectures, and interviews, Boris and Sarah Sidis inveighed against fear, against the tragedy of a frightened child. They failed to see that their own son was, indeed, afraid. And had the adult William been emotionally capable of applying even a portion of his intelligence to the study of his own psychology, how different his life might have been!

Where, precisely, did his parents fail him? Though the mythmakers have held Boris and Sarah's child-rearing methods at fault, there is in fact nothing to fault in them. Upon the closest inspection, they are similar to the basic, sensible techniques popularized by the brilliant educator Maria Montessori. William James Sidis was not pushed, he was taught to reason. He did not merely conquer forty languages, or one hundred—he had the mental technology to grasp any language, no matter how difficult, in a day. His was not a genius of mere retentive ability—it was that of a magnificent reasoning machine. Boris and Sarah did not create his high IQ through training—their genes provided the better part of it—but their training nurtured and encouraged in a superb manner the rare plant they had borne.

Their failure lay in the painful emotional environment created by the degeneration of their marriage, the criticizing domination Sarah Sidis exercised as William approached adolescence, and the fact that although she advised other parents against it, Sarah did show William off. The other factor that damaged William, perhaps the most important one of all, was his parents' inability to shield him from the merciless envy of the public and its vicious desire to resent and cripple greatness and reduce it to normalcy and mediocrity. While it is not easy to explain to a child, however brilliant he may be, that he will be hated for the very reason that he is brilliant—the job must be done, and it must be done well. The child must be taught, in no uncertain terms, that his own standards, carefully reasoned out, are the only standards he must live by, and that he must courageously disregard all public standards. This was not an instruction that William Sidis received clearly. Rather than teach William how and why to ignore his cruel detractors, Boris and Sarah concentrated all their attention on reforming the educators of the world. Not a poor mission, but hardly worthwhile at the expense of their son's self-confidence. Boris, blind to the urgency of this matter, made several grave mistakes. He advised William how to manipulate reporters, rather than shielding him from them as much as possible; and he permitted himself to publish a book, *Philistine and Genius,* that drew enormous attention to a child with an already insufficient coat of protective armor.

In 1957, Norbert Wiener wrote an article for *The New York Times Magazine* entitled "Analysis of the Child Prodigy." It was the era of the highly popular television stars the Quiz Kids, and the question of the proper treatment of brilliant children was strongly on the minds of millions of viewers. Wiener, speaking from the other side —as one who had been a child prodigy himself—disapproved of the television show. He urged Americans to emulate European education, where "there is much less pressure on the bright youngster to keep in lockstep with the average and below-average student, who is the darling of our American educational system." In Europe, he wrote, brilliant children were encouraged to blossom early and inconspicuously, well out of the public eye.

He continued sagely:

One thing is necessarily true of the precocious child, in so far as he is not intrinsically one-sided and a freak. He is brought up against the contradictions of the world outside him at a time when he has not begun to develop the hard shell of the adult. He finds soon enough that the copybook maxims of life are in many cases an oversimplification or a deliberate falsification of what he sees in the world about him.

This hurts him deeply at a time when his defenses are not yet developed. He thus is more bare of protection either than the average child or than the adult and can be badly hurt. Without an understanding and sympathetic environment he can easily come to grief. It is the duty of his parents and counselors, if they really wish to give him a chance to come into his own, to shelter him during this difficult stage when he is neither the one thing nor the other.

This is the time in which exploitation by the press or the radio may do him great harm, as may also the fact that he is growing up in a society which loves conformity and has little sympathy for inner achievement. It will not do merely to protect him from the realities of life nor to make believe that society really wants his sort of person, but he must be given a fair chance to develop a reasonable thick skin against the pressures which will certainly be made on him and a confidence that somewhere in the world he has his own function which he may reasonably hope to fulfill.

It has been suggested by many writers and commentators that William James Sidis, in not living up to any of the goals predicted for him in his youth, betrayed society. This is not so—Sidis owed no debt to humanity. Nor did society betray Sidis. But its many members who inspired the retreat of an intellect of Sidis's magnitude unwittingly worked against society's best interests. Sidis may have found his own path to happiness, but at what cost to the world? How many Einsteins and Galileos has the world lost by treating prodigies as unwelcome freaks in their youth? What mountains might William James Sidis have moved, had he not been stunned into hiding by the public's mockery of his eccentricities and achievements?

Let us hope that in the future all gifted, exceptional children will grow up in a world that instead of shunning them as oddities, will welcome and nurture their talents, their achievements, and their vision.

Index

Index

Harvard University (cont'd)
HCKP Club, 73
Psychological Laboratory of, 11–12
Sharfman at, 258–59
socialism at, 115–16, 125
Summer School Association, 71
William at, 48–72, 100–112
being bored, 71
boarding at dorm, 100–101
compared to other child prodigies,
56–58, 102–103
entrance requirements, 51–52
grades, 104–105
as graduate student, 112
graduation, 105, 106, 266, 275
in his own apartment, 101, 107, 125
journalists and, 51–55, 59–61, 69–70,
71–72, 102, 106–12, 174–75
in Law School, 125, 135
Mathematics Club lecture, 59–61
nervous breakdown, 69–71, 101
ostracism and humiliation at,
101–103, 112, 125
resentment in later years, 211, 229,
244
Sara on, 104
as the youngest student ever, 50
Hawthorne, Nathaniel, 208–209
Hayden, Judge Albert F., 141, 142, 144,
145
Haywood, "Big Bill," 116
Hectographing, 214, 237
Heinecken, Christian Friedrich, 63
Henderson, Kathleen Wilson, 118
Hesperia, constitution for, 73–78, 117,
204
Hill, Creighton, 221–22, 233, 278
Hill, Joe, 116
Hirshfield, Rose, 273, 274
Hitler, Adolf, 249, 262
Hoover, J. Edgar, 263
Houghton, Cedric Wing, 56
Houston Post, 124, 142
How to Make Your Child a Genius (Sidis,
S.), 19–20, 279–80
Hughes, A. L., 114
Hughes, Howard, 254, 280
Huntington, Dr. E. V., 39, 104
Hutchinson, Anne, 240
Huxley, Julian, 114, 118, 120, 123

Huxley, T. H., 114
Hypnosis, 14–15, 94, 148

Inaudi, Jacques, 62–63
Independent, The, 60
Industrial Workers of the World (IWW)
("Wobblies"), 116–17, 129
Infant of Lübeck, 63
Intercollegiate Socialist, The, 115
Intercollegiate Socialist Society, 115–16
Introduction to the Study of Stellar Structure,
An (Chandrasekhar), 157

J. P. Morgan Fund, 14
James, William, 11–18, 26, 30, 32, 50, 88,
96, 116
Wiener and, 56
William and, 19, 28, 44, 158
Janet, Pierre, 14, 31
Johansen, Bruce E., 202
Johnson, Samuel, 192, 224
Jones, Charles S., 245–47, 249–50
Jones, Frank, 83, 84
Jones, Martha, 83–84, 92
Journal of Abnormal Psychology, 50, 85, 94,
130–32

Kalmus, Dr. Herbert T., 87, 254, 280

Law of Entropy, 158–60
League for Industrial Democracy, 161
Lettish Workmen's Association, 139
Libertarian, The, 240–41
Liberty War Objectors Association
(LWOA), 238–39
Lippmann, Walter, 116, 125
Lovett, Edgar Odell, 113, 117

McClure Newspaper Syndicate, 221
McGill, Margaret, 222, 223, 233, 269,
278
Mack, Frank, 166
Magliabechi, Antonio da Marco, 63
Mahony, Dan, 157, 188–89
Mandelbaum, Bernard, 6–9
Mandelbaum, Fannie Rich, 6–7, 9, 12
Mandelbaum, Ida, 6, 7, 9, 10
Mandelbaum, Jack, 134, 135
Mandell, Joe, 89
Manley, Jared L., see Thurber, James

Index

Index

Wiener, Norbert, 228
  "Analysis of the Child Prodigy,"
    285–86
  on Billy, 58, 60, 157, 173, 281
  as child prodigy, 56–58, 96–97,
    100–101, 102–103
  compared to Billy, 173–77, 244
  at Harvard, 57, 58, 100–101, 103,
    174–75
  Jewishness of, 57, 103, 174
  marriage of, 176–77
  on *The New Yorker* article, 232–33

Wilson, Woodrow, 116, 128, 129, 141, 154
World War I, 125, 128–30, 133, 135
  aftermath of, 137–38
  Boris on, 147–48
  conscientious objectors, 129–30, 132, 263
  Espionage Act of 1917 and, 129
World War II, 237–42, 262–64; *see also*
  Conscientious objectors (COs)

Years with Ross, The (Thurber), 234
"You Can Make Your Child a Genius,"
  280–81

[297]

DATE DUE